The Complete Idiot's Comm

General Working with Program

Press	To
Alt+Print Screen	Copy the active window's image.
Ctrl+Alt+Delete	Display the Close Program dialog box.
Ctrl+C	Copy the selected data.
Ctrl+Esc	Open the Start menu.
Ctrl+V	Paste the most recently cut or copied data.
Ctrl+X	Cut the selected data.
Ctrl+Z	Undo the most recent action.
Print Screen	Copy the entire screen image.

Keyboard Shortcuts for Programs

Press	To
	Working with Program Windows
Alt+Esc	Cycle through the open program windows.
Alt+F4	Close the active program window.
Alt+Tab	Cycle through the active programs.
F1	Display context-sensitive Help.
	Working with Documents
Ctrl+F4	Close the active document window.
Ctrl+N	Create a new document.
Ctrl+O	Display the Open dialog box.
Ctrl+P	Display the Print dialog box.
Ctrl+S	Save the current file. If the file is new, display the Save As dialog box.

Keys to Hold Down While Dragging-and-Dropping

Hold Down	To
Ctrl	Copy the dragged object.
Ctrl+Shift	Display a shortcut menu after dropping a dragged object.
Esc	Cancel the current drag.
Shift	Move the dragged object.

Windows Explorer Keyboard Shortcuts

Press	To
+ (numeric keypad)	Display the next level of subfolders for the current folder.
- (numeric keypad)	Hide the current folder's subfolders.
* (numeric keypad)	Display all levels of subfolders for the current folder.
Backspace	Navigate to the parent folder of the current folder.
Ctrl+A	Select all the objects in the current folder.

Internet Explorer Keyboard Shortcuts

TPress	To
Alt+Left arrow	Navigate backward to a previously displayed Web page.
Alt+Right arrow	Navigate forward to a previously displayed Web page.
Ctrl+A	Select the entire Web page.
Ctrl+B	Display the Organize Favorites dialog box.
Esc	Stop downloading the Web page.
F4	Open the Address toolbar's drop-down list.
F5	Refresh the Web page.

Shortcuts That Use the Windows Logo (ˇ) Key

Press	To
ˇ	Open the Start menu.
ˇ+E	Open Windows Explorer.
ˇ+F	Find a file or folder.
ˇ+M	Minimize all open windows.
ˇ+Shift+M	Undo minimize all.
ˇ+R	Display the Run dialog box.

Windows Tip #1. Shutting Down Stuck Programs

If a program locks up completely, press the "three-fingered salute": **Ctrl+Alt+Delete** (also known in the trade as the "Vulcan nerve pinch"). Windows 98 should display the Close Program dialog box with a list of your open programs. xe "dialog boxes:Close Program" xe "Close Program dialog box" In particular, you should see the name of the crashed program with **Not responding** tacked on to the end. Highlight the offending application, say "Yeah, well respond to *this*," and click the **End Task** button.

Windows Tip #2. Faster Deleting

When you send a file to the Recycle Bin, Windows 98 always asks if you're sure you want to delete the file. If you're absotively, posolutely certain that a particular file can be deleted, press **Shift+Delete** to bypasses the Recycle Bin. The downside? If you nuke the wrong file by accident, it's toast, and there's zip you can do to get it back.

Windows Tip #3. Taking the "Auto" Out of AutoPlay

AutoPlay is the feature that enables Windows 98 to automatically load a CD-ROM's program when you slip the disk into the drive. If you'd prefer that Windows 98 not run AutoPlay when you insert a CD-ROM, hold down the **Shift** key while you insert the disc.

Windows Tip #4. Easier Window Maximizing

If you find that the tiny Maximize button in the upper right corner of a window is too small a target, you might prefer this: double-click the window's title bar (the blue strip that runs across the top of the window).

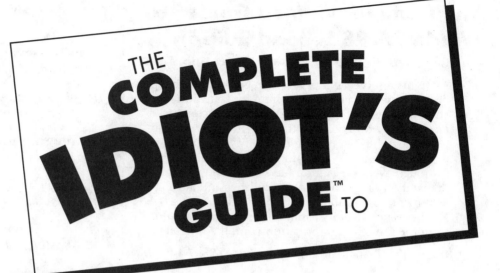

THE COMPLETE IDIOT'S GUIDE TO

Windows 98

Second Edition

by Paul McFedries

ALPHA

A Pearson Education Company

The Complete Idiot's Guide® to Windows® 98 Second Edition

International Standard Book Number: 0-7897-1493-0

Library of Congress Catalog Card Number: 97-075459

Printed in the United States of America

First Printing: September 1999

03   02   18   17

Trademarks

Warning and Disclaimer

Publisher
Greg Wiegand

Acquisitions Editor
Stephanie McComb

Development Editor
Gregory Harris

Managing Editor
Thomas F. Hayes

Copy Editor
Victoria Elzey

Indexer
Christine Nelsen

Proofreader
Ryan Walsh

Illustrator
Judd Winick

Interior Designer
Nathan Clement

Cover Designer
Michael Freeland

Copy Writer
Eric Borgert

Layout Technicians
Stacey DeRome
Ayanna Lacey
Heather Miller

Contents at a Glance

Table of Contents

25 Troubleshooting Windows Woes   335

Tell Us What You Think!

As the reader of this book, *you* are our most important critic and commentator. We value your opinion and want to know what we're doing right, what we could do better, what areas you'd like to see us publish in, and any other words of wisdom you're willing to pass our way.

I welcome your comments. You can email or write me directly to let me know what you did or didn't like about this book—as well as what we can do to make our books stronger.

Please note that I cannot help you with technical problems related to the topic of this book, and that due to the high volume of mail I receive, I might not be able to reply to every message.

When you write, please be sure to include this book's title and author as well as your name and phone or fax number. I will carefully review your comments and share them with the author and editors who worked on the book.

Email: cigfeedback@pearsoned.com

Mail: Alpha Books
          201 West 103rd Street
          Indianapolis, IN 46290 USA

Introduction

What we call progress is the exchange of one nuisance for another nuisance.

—Havelock Ellis

Do you have a love-hate relationship with your computer? That is, do you hate turning the thing on in the morning and love turning it off at night? If so, it may help to know that you're not alone. Many otherwise-brave souls are overcome by The Fear at the very prospect of sitting down in front of their cranky machines.

Why all the angst? I think there are two reasons. First, computers are nowhere near as easy to use as they should be. Seemingly simple tasks such as composing a memo or printing a file too often turn into heart-stopping, gray-hair-producing adventures.

The second reason is that the people who are charged with explaining the mysteries of computers often don't help matters much. They're usually either gee-whiz cheerleaders infatuated with the technology, or overly earnest types lacking that sixth sense: a sense of humor. (These are the people who put the "doze" in "Windows.")

In *The Complete Idiot's Guide to Windows 98, Second Edition*, my goal is to overcome both problems. I hope to show you that there *are* ways to tame the computing beast and thus mollify your machine into doing your bidding. With "just the facts ma'am" explanations, simple step-by-step instructions, and lots of useful examples, you'll see that getting your Windows work done doesn't have to cost you your sanity.

I also aim to prove that "Windows" and "fun" are not mutually exclusive concepts (as hard as that may be to believe). To that end, with most tasks I offer a casual, light-hearted approach and studiously avoid taking any of this malarkey too seriously. If you're looking for a book that enjoys having a little fun at Windows 98's expense, you've come to the right place.

Some of the Book's Fabulous Features

To make the instructions easier to read, *The Complete Idiot's Guide to Windows 98, Second Edition* uses the following conventions:

➤ Text that you type, items you select, and text that you see on your screen appear in **bold**.

➤ As you'll see, Windows 98 uses quite a few keyboard shortcuts. These shortcuts almost invariably require you to hold down one key and press another. For example, one shortcut you may use a lot requires you to hold down the **Ctrl** key, press the **Esc** key, and then release **Ctrl**. To avoid writing out a mouthful like that over and over, we needed an easier way to express these *key combinations* (a sort of "shortcut shorthand," if you will). So, key combinations appear with a plus sign (+) in the middle, as in **Ctrl+Esc**.

Also, look for the following features that point out important information:

Check This Out

You'll find these "Check This Out" sidebars scattered throughout the book. I use them to highlight important notes, tips, warnings, and other tidbits that will help further your Windows education.

Techno Talk

This book generally shuns long-winded technical explanations because they tend to be, well, *boring*. However, in cases where a bit of in-depth know-how is too interesting to pass up, I'll plop the text inside one of these "Techno Talk" boxes. This stuff won't help you get your work done any quicker, but it will arm you with a few choice geekisms that will impress the heck out of people at parties.

SEE ALSO

➤ *This "Cross-Reference" box points you to other parts of the book that contain related info. To learn more about this element, please see "Some of the Book's Fabulous Features," page 1.*

 Windows 98 isn't radically different than Windows 95, but there are still tons of shiny, new features for you to gawk at. This icon points out those new features.

 This icon points out features that are new in Windows 98 Second Edition (see "What's New in the Second Edition?," later in this introduction).

What Was New in the First Edition?

I wrote the original edition of *The Complete Idiot's Guide to Windows* way back in 1993, and the book has gone through various incarnations since then as the Windows world marched steadily on. The response from readers and reviewers alike has been nothing short of overwhelming, and the book has been an unqualified success in the market-place, too. Hundreds of thousands of regular Joes and Josephines have used this book to make the leap from complete Windows idiot to competent Windows user.

But after five years and I-don-t-know-how-many-editions, I decided to mess with suc-cess and completely rewrite the book from the ground up for Windows 98. That's right: it ain't broke, but I'm fixin' it anyway! Why? Because as an author I'm commit-ted to giving you the best possible introduction to Windows. I'm confident that this edition's fresh, new approach will make Windows even easier to learn. You'll also find that my coverage of Windows is more complete than in previous editions, so you should find answers to more of your questions. And, finally, this is the Windows 98 edition of the book, so you'll find coverage of all the new bells and whistles.

What's New in the Second Edition?

A little over a year after Windows 98 hit the shelves, Microsoft released a second edi-tion of Windows 98 called—you guessed it—Windows 98 Second Edition. It fixes a few relatively obscure problems that arose after Windows 98 shipped, and it includes some new or improved features, such as Internet Explorer 5, Outlook Express 5, and Internet Connection Sharing.

This edition of the book (coincidentally, it's also the second edition) covers the new bangles and baubles that are part of this new Windows 98 incarnation.

The Giving Credit Where Credit Is Due Department

Like Winnie-the-Pooh, "My spelling is Wobbly. It's good spelling but it Wobbles, and the letters get in the wrong places." Unlike Winnie-the-Pooh, however, I have editors to put the letters back where they belong. Near the front of the book, you'll see a page that runs through the roster of folks who had a hand in getting this book from vapor to paper. I extend my warmest thanks to all of them for a job well done.

While I'm in back-slapping mode, I'd also like to fire off a few kudos to the people I worked with directly. For the first edition, great gobs of gratefulness go to Associate Publisher—Operating Systems Dean Miller; Acquisitions Editors Jill Byus; Development Editors Melanie Palaisa and Lorna Gentry; Production Editors Karen Walsh and Susan Moore; Copy Editor Gail Burlakoff; and Technical Editor Christy Gleeson. For the second edition, more kudos go to Acquisitions Editors Angie Wethington and Angelina Ward; Development Editor Gregory Harris; Copy Editor Victoria Elzey; and again to Technical Editor Christy Gleeson.

I'd also like to thank my friends and family for being, well, friendly and familiar. And, of course, no acknowledgments section would be complete without acknowledging all the welcome feedback that I've received from my readers over the years. Keep those cards and letters coming! (If you're wired, you can send e-cards and e-letters to my email address: paul@mcfedries.com.)

Part I

The Big Windows 98 Picture

As a stranger in the strange land of Windows 98, you'll want to get your bearings before lighting out for parts unknown. Well, you've come to the right place because that's what the two chapters here in Part 1 are all about. Chapter 1 runs through all the interesting new features that come with both Windows 98 and Windows 98 Second Edition, and Chapter 2 takes you on a tour of the Windows world. So, if you're ready (a few deep breaths might help at this point), let's get under way…

What's New in Windows 98

In This Chapter

➤ What Web integration is all about

➤ Windows 98's new Internet features

➤ The new multimedia, system, and hardware tools

➤ Things to get excited about in Windows 98 Second Edition

➤ Making the move from Windows 3.1 to Windows 98

➤ A gaggle of brand-spanking new Windows 98 gadgets, gewgaws, and gismos

In this chapter, I give you a quick rundown of the new and noteworthy knickknacks that come with Windows 98 and Windows 98 Second Edition. I also give former Windows 3.1 users a few pointers to help ease their transition into Microsoft's latest and greatest operating system. Of course, this is just to give you the lay of the Windows 98 land; everything I mention here is cross-referenced to later parts of the book where I provide complete info on these features.

Some of Windows 98's Shiny New Features

If you've used Windows 95, you and Windows 98 should get along just fine, thank you. Sure, this new version is chock full of changes large and small. But you aren't likely to find anything in Windows 98 that throws you for a loop. Many of these improvements are internal tweaks that only technology jockeys find interesting, but that help your system run faster, smoother, and more efficiently. And there are plenty of new and improved goodies for average users who just want to get their work done without any extra fuss.

Windows Gets Webbed: Web Integration and the Active Desktop

Anyone who has messed around with the Internet's World Wide Web knows just how easy it can be to click links to move from page to page; it really is a quick, intuitive way to get from here to there. The Microsoft programmers have given us more of a good thing in Windows 98, with their "Web integration" design. In Windows 98, you move through the system, files, and folders just as you move through the Web—click here, jump there. Web integration alters the Windows landscape in the following ways:

➤ **One-click icon and program launching:** With Web integration, Windows 98 underlines the names of icons and files so that they resemble Web page links. Launching an icon or file now requires only a single click.

➤ **No-click icon and file selection:** Web integration also means that you can select an icon or file simply by hovering the mouse pointer over the object.

➤ **Folders are now mini Web pages:** Each folder on your system now comes with a "Web view" that makes the folder look and act like a miniature Web page. For example, check out the My Computer folder shown in the following figure. It has a Web-like look—and if you move the mouse over an icon, you get a short description of that icon (to its left).

The My Computer folder in Web view: a nicer look and "live" icons, to boot.

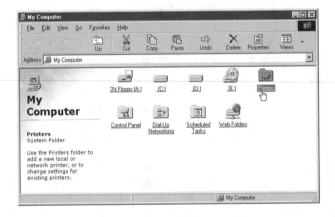

➤ **The Active Desktop:** The Windows 95 desktop was a simple all-show-and-no-go affair. That's now changed because the Windows 98 *Active Desktop* offers plenty of "go" for those who want it. The Active Desktop is capable of displaying all kinds of moveable feasts, including Web pages and miniprograms such as Java applets and ActiveX controls. The next figure shows the Active Desktop with a couple of gadgets from the Active Desktop Gallery (a satellite tracker and a stock ticker).

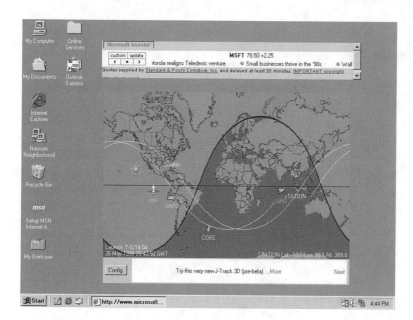

This ain't no Windows 95 wallpaper: The Active Desktop can display interactive and updateable content.

SEE ALSO

➤ *For full details on Web integration and the Active Desktop, see Chapter 3, "Making Something Happen: Launching and Switching Programs," p. 29, and Chapter 9, "Webtop Windows: Web Integration and the Active Desktop," p. 93.*

The Net and Windows 98: Internet Explorer and More

The Internet is where all the action is these days, and Windows 98 has carved out its own seat on the bandwagon. If you're itching to get online, Windows 98 has a ton of topnotch tools for getting you on the Internet and keeping you there:

➤ **Get online with a minimum of bother:** Windows 98's improved Internet Connection Wizard makes it easy to establish your Internet lifeline. There's also a new Online Services folder for quick setup of online services such as America Online and the Microsoft Network.

SEE ALSO

➤ *For more information about the Internet Connection Wizard and the Online Services folder, see Chapter 15, "How to Get Connected to the Internet," p. 162.*

➤ **Browse the Web just as you do your computer:** In Windows 98, the differences between what's on your computer and what's "out there" on the Internet are blurred. As you can see in the following figure, with the new Windows Explorer, Web pages and other Internet sites are just another resource in addition to your hard disk and CD-ROM.

SEE ALSO

➤ *For additional information, see "Leaping from Link to Link: Navigating the Web," p. 208, in Chapter 17, "Wandering the Web with Internet Explorer."*

The Internet: Think of it as a really big hard disk!

Access the Internet from Windows Explorer.

➤ **The Cadillac of browsers—Internet Explorer 4.0:** The Internet Explorer 4.0 Web browser is sewn right into the fabric of Windows 98. It's ready-to-surf, so you don't have to suffer through the whole download-and-install rigmarole. Plus you get all the nifty features found in Internet Explorer 4.0: subscriptions, channels, new and improved Search, Favorites, and History features, and much more. And if you have Windows 98 Second Edition, you get the latest and greatest: Internet Explorer 5.0, which is bursting with new features to make Web surfing easier.

SEE ALSO

➤ *For the nitty-gritty about the features in both Explorer 4.0 and 5.0, see Chapter 17, p. 205.*

➤ **Internet tools to beat the band(width):** The Windows 98 stocking is stuffed with lots of other handy Internet programs. For those who can't pass up a good conversation, there's Outlook Express for email and newsgroups, and NetMeeting for phone or video conferencing. If you feel like putting your own words on the Web, there's FrontPage Express, the Web Publishing Wizard, and Personal Web Server.

SEE ALSO

➤ *For more information about Windows 98's Internet tools, see Chapter 16, "Can We Talk? Email, Newsgroups, and Internet Phone Calls," p. 183, and Chapter 18, "Becoming a Webmaster with FrontPage Express and Other Page Publishing Tools," p. 227.*

➤ **Web-based upgrades with Windows Update:** Keeping up with the latest Windows innovations has always been a difficult task, particularly with the accelerated pace we've seen over the past few years. To help out, Microsoft now has a Windows Update Web site that checks your system and then lets you know whether new features are available. You can grab these updates from the Web, and Windows 98 will install everything for you automatically.

10

SEE ALSO
➤ *For more information, see "Getting the Latest and Greatest from the Windows Update Web Site,"*
   p. 322, in Chapter 23, "Tools for Keeping Your System in Tip-Top Shape."

New Tools for Problem-Free Computing

Computers are fairly reliable machines these days, but that doesn't mean that trouble
never rears its ugly head. You can help lessen the chances of a problem arising by performing regular system maintenance chores. That's not as much of a burden as it
might seem because Windows 98 has some excellent tools for the job:

➤ **A better Backup:** Doing the backup thing has never been easier, thanks to
   Windows 98's revamped and "wizardized" Backup utility.

SEE ALSO
➤ *To learn how Windows 98 makes backing up a breeze, head for Chapter 24, "Keeping Your Data Safe*
   and Sound with Backup," p. 325.

➤ **The Maintenance Wizard:** This new member of the wizard family (shown in
   the next figure) takes you step-by-step through the process of setting up and
   scheduling automatic system maintenance.

SEE ALSO
➤ *To learn all about this wizard, see the "Using the Maintenance Wizard to Get Your System Firing on*
   All Cylinders" section, p. 319, in Chapter 23.

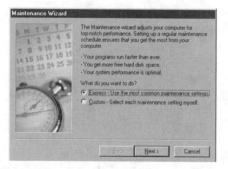

The new Maintenance
Wizard.

➤ **Scheduled Tasks folder:** The easiest way to make sure that regular maintenance chores stay regular is to use the new Scheduled Tasks folder to force
   Windows to perform those chores at scheduled intervals.

➤ **More space on your drive with DriveSpace:** Windows 98's version of the
   DriveSpace disk-compression program is much better at squeezing data down to
   size. It can also do much of the work behind the scenes so that you'll rarely
   have to worry about it.

SEE ALSO
➤ For the full scoop, see Chapter 23's "Doubling Your Disk Space Pleasure with DriveSpace" section, p. 315.

Sights for Sore Eyes and Ears: Windows 98 Multimedia

If the right side of your brain is wondering, "Hey, what's in this for me?" tell it not to worry—Windows 98 has no shortage of multimedia marvels:

➤ **Watch TV on your PC:** Windows 98 comes wired for cable! With the right equipment in your PC, you can use WebTV for Windows to find and watch TV broadcasts.

SEE ALSO
➤ *For more information, flip to Chapter 21, "Bells and Whistles: Multimedia and Windows 98," and read the "Small-Screen Windows: Watching TV" section, p. 277.*

➤ **"What's on the Web tonight?"—The NetShow Player:** The Web gets more TV-like each day, and Windows 98's built-in NetShow Player hastens that transition. NetShow enables you to view videos and other "live" Web-based multimedia content without having to wait for a huge file to download (see the following figure).

SEE ALSO
➤ *To learn how NetShow works, check out Chapter 17's "The Internet Show Must Go On: Using the NetShow Player" section, p. 220.*

The NetShow player lets you eyeball videos and live feeds from the Web in real time.

➤ **Pentium MMX support:** If you purchased your computer recently, there's a good chance it's an MMX (MultiMedia eXtensions) machine. This means it's capable of displaying fancy graphics images, such as the ones found in the latest games. Because Windows 98 has built-in support for MMX, you'll be able to get the most out of your graphics hardware.

➤ **Digital Versatile Disc (DVD) support:** DVD is the would-be successor to both videotape and CD-ROMs. It hasn't taken off yet, but it probably will soon. When it does, you'll be ready because Windows 98 and DVD are fast friends.

➤ **Image and video capture:** Windows 98 supports a number of devices that capture still images (scanners and digital cameras) and video streams (conferencing cameras and desktop video camcorders).

SEE ALSO

➤ *To learn more, scan Chapter 20, "Image is Everything: Windows 98's Graphics Tools," p. 263.*

Support for the Latest Hardware Toys

One of Windows' goals is to make it easy for you to interact with the devices attached to your computer. The hardware manufacturers have been busy over the past couple of years, and Windows 98 has been beefed up to handle a wide variety of recent hardware innovations. You probably don't want to know much about things like the Universal Serial Bus and FireWire, and thanks to Windows 98's support for these initiatives, you won't have to. Here's a list of a few of the hardware-related features that Windows 98 is friendly with:

➤ **Real wheel mouse support:** Windows 98 has built-in support for the extra wheel "button" found on the Microsoft Intellimouse (and a few other mice). In most Windows 98 windows, you can scroll up or down by rotating the wheel.

SEE ALSO

➤ *For more information, see the "Manipulating the Mouse" section, p. 22 in Chapter 2, "Windows 98: The 50¢ Tour."*

➤ **Niceties for notebooks:** If you use a notebook computer, Windows 98 has plenty of fun things in store for you. For example, you can manage the notebook's power consumption to save battery life. Windows 98 also has new tools for working with PC Cards (the credit card-size modems and things that slip into your machine—especially into notebook computers; they're also know as PCMCIA cards), infrared ports, and docking stations.

SEE ALSO

➤ *To learn more about all of this, see Chapter 22, "Windows 98's Notebook Knickknacks," p. 293.*

➤ **More storage options:** Windows 98 has increased support for storage devices outside the standard floppy disk/hard disk/CD-ROM realm. In addition to working with DVD drives, as mentioned earlier, Windows 98 can also deal with Zip drives and Jaz drives.

SEE ALSO

➤ *For more information, read the "Zip and Jaz: Floppy Disks on Steroids" section in Chapter 14, "Storage Solutions: Working with Folders and Floppy Disks," p. 162.*

A Few More New Features to Get Excited About

To finish our look at what's new in the Windows 98 world, here's a list of a few miscellaneous improvements:

➤ **Faster start up and shut down:** The Microsoft engineers have streamlined some of the startup and shut down chores, and now Windows 98 loads and quits faster than before.

➤ **It's easier to find the things you need:** Windows 98 comes with a folder called My Documents that you can use as a central storage area for the files you create. Also, you can use the Favorites folder to store locations you visit often, whether on the Internet, your network, or your hard disk. And because the Favorites folder is now accessible from the Start menu, dialing up your fave spots is more convenient than ever.

SEE ALSO

➤ *For more information, see the "Taking Advantage of the My Documents Folder" section, p. 68, in Chapter 6, "A Few Workaday Document Chores."*

➤ **Easier Start menu customization:** Windows 98 enables you to reposition Start menu items by dragging them up or down in a menu.

SEE ALSO

➤ *For a more detailed explanation of this technique, see the "Reconstructing the Start Menu" section, p. 113, in Chapter 10, "Customizing the Desktop and Taskbar."*

➤ **Improved Accessibility options:** Windows 98 continues the excellent support for the needs of disabled users that was pioneered in Windows 95. To make these Accessibility options even easier to use, Windows 98 comes with a new Accessibility Wizard (see the following figure). Windows 98 also includes a new utility, called the Microsoft Magnifier, that enables you to zoom in on the screen and view the contents at increased magnifications.

The Accessibility Wizard makes it easier than ever to customize Windows for users with special needs.

The Sequel: What's New in Windows 98 Second Edition

Remember the Windows Update Web site that I prattled on about earlier? As I write this new edition about a year after Windows 98 first shipped, I can tell you that Microsoft certainly made good use of that site. In fact, they used Windows Update to offer folks dozens of new and improved features. Indeed, there were so many enhancements that Microsoft decided to package everything into a CD-ROM and call it Windows 98 Second Edition.

What's new? Well, there are lots of fixes to the inevitable problems that cropped up during Windows 98's first year (most of these were insignificant; unless, of course, you were one of the ones affected). Microsoft also discovered lots of security breaches in programs such as Internet Explorer and Outlook Express, and these holes have now been plugged.

Besides these tweaks, Windows 98 Second Edition also comes with a few new features. Here are the ones you're most likely to give a darn about:

➤ **Internet Explorer 5.0:** This new version of Windows 98's Web browser contains only small improvements over its version 4.0 predecessor. For example, searching is a bit easier, and it's easier to retrieve previously typed Web addresses. My personal favorite is a new Radio toolbar that lets you listen to tunes while surfing.

➤ **Outlook Express 5:** This is an improved version of the email program that originally shipped with Windows 98. Again, there's nothing earth-shattering, but there are lots of little improvements that will make your email life a bit easier.

➤ **Internet Connection Sharing:** This may be the one feature that really makes Windows 98 Second Edition worthwhile. Put simply, Internet Connection Sharing enables you to share a single Internet connection among multiple networked computers.

SEE ALSO

➤ *Get more information on Internet Connection Sharing in the section titled "Sharing an Internet Connection" on p. 358 in Chapter 26, "Working with Network Connections and Email."*

➤ **Windows Media Player:** This program is now Windows 98's jack-of-all-media-trades, which means you use it to play everything from sounds to animations to movies.

SEE ALSO

➤ *See "A Better Way to Play: Windows Media Player" p. 279 in Chapter 21.*

The Transition from Windows 3.1 to Windows 98

Lots of people will be heading into Windows 98 having already struggled with the intricacies of Windows 3.1. That's a good start, but Windows 98 is different enough that you'll face a bit of a learning curve.

The overall design of Windows 98 is simpler and cleaner than that of Windows 3.1. Launching programs is more straightforward and the things you need are much easier to find. For my money, though, Windows 98's Most Valuable Feature award definitely goes to its support for longer file names. That's right—no more trying to shoehorn a meaningful name into a measly eight-plus-three characters. Now you can go crazy because the limit has been bumped up to a positively verbose 255 characters! (One word of warning, though: only programs designed for Windows 95 or Windows 98 can understand these long-winded names.)

Directories? Nope—Folders

You may as well remove the word "directory" from your Windows vocabulary. Directories are called "folders" in Windows 98.

By far the most annoying thing about Windows 3.1 was its perverse tendency to go up in flames whenever an important deadline or meeting loomed large. Windows 98 was designed from the ground up to be more stable and not give up the ghost as easily as Windows 3.1 did. (Again, however, you'll need to use programs created specifically for Windows 95 or Windows 98 to get semi-bullet-proof operations.)

To give you an idea of what to expect from your new operating system, the following table names a few common Windows 3.1 tasks (and some DOS 6 ones, too), tells you the Windows 98 equivalents, and points you to the relevant chapters in the book.

Windows 3.1 tasks and their Windows 98 counterparts.

Task	Windows 3.1/DOS 6	Windows 98	Chapter(s)
Launch a program	Program Manager	Start menu	3
Switch programs	Alt+Tab	Taskbar or Alt+Tab	3
Word processing	Write	WordPad	19
Create pictures	Paintbrush	Paint	20
Work with files	File Manager	Windows Explorer	12–14
Find files	File, Search in File Manager	Start | Find	13
Undelete a file	UNDELETE (DOS)	Recycle Bin	13
Repair a disk	SCANDISK (DOS)	ScanDisk	23
Defragment files	DEFRAG (DOS)	Disk Defragmenter	23
Compress files	DRVSPACE (DOS)	DriveSpace	23
Back up files	BACKUP (DOS)	Backup	24
Control print jobs	Print Manager	Printers folder	7
Customize Windows	Control Panel group	Control Panel folder	9–11
Connect computers	INTERLNK (DOS)	Direct Cable Connection	22
Use accessories	Accessories group	Start, Programs, Accessories	3
Get help	Help menu in Program Manager	Start, Help	8
Exit Windows	File, Exit in Program Manager	Start, Shut Down	2

AND IF YOU'LL STEP TO YOUR LEFT YOU'LL SEE OUR DESKTOP...

Windows 98: The 50¢ Tour

In This Chapter

➤ A look around the Windows 98 screen

➤ Useful mouse and keyboard techniques

➤ Crucial info about shutting down Windows

➤ A leisurely amble through the Windows landscape

After all that Windows theory in Chapter 1, "What's New in Windows 98," things take a turn for the practical here in Chapter 2. I'll walk you through the Windows 98 startup process, and then when Windows 98 is up and running I'll give you a tour of the screen. If you've never used Windows before, you'll appreciate the mouse and keyboarding lessons that come next. I'll close by showing you how to shut down Windows 98 for the night.

Please bear in mind that this chapter assumes you already have Windows 98 on your system. That is, I assume your computer came with Windows 98 already installed, or else you have (or a nearby computer guru has) performed the upgrade to Windows 98.

Starting Windows 98

As you'll see throughout this book, the vast majority of Windows tasks are quite straightforward, *provided* that you follow a few simple instructions. There's nothing even remotely complicated about starting Windows 98, however, because it requires only a single step: Turn on your computer. Yup, that's all there is to it. After you throw the switch, your computer contemplates its digital navel for a while, and then the Windows 98 logo appears.

At this point, Windows 98 may display a box like the one shown here, which pesters you to supply a password (especially if you're using Windows 98 at work). If so, and assuming that you know your password (the person at work who administers your computer system should have told you what it is), go ahead and type your password in the **Password** box. (The letters you type will appear as asterisks [*], but that's okay. It's a security feature that prevents some snoop from eyeballing your password.) Then press **Enter** to continue loading Windows 98.

You may see this box while Windows 98 is loading.

A few seconds later, the dust clears and—voilà!—Windows 98 is ready for action. If this is the first time you've started Windows 98, chances are you'll hear the strains of some modern-sounding music. No, your machine isn't going through some sort of second childhood. This is just Windows 98's way of welcoming you to its world. When the show's over, you'll end up with the Welcome to Windows 98 screen shown in the following figure. (If you don't see this screen, I'll show you a bit later on how to get there.) We don't need to worry about any of this stuff right now, so you can get rid of this screen by using your mouse to click the X in the upper-right corner.

The Windows 98 welcome mat.

A Tour of the Screen

The screen shown next is typical of the face that Windows 98 presents to the world. (Note, however, that your screen may appear slightly different.) All that eye candy sure looks intriguing, doesn't it? If you're used to Windows 95's rather bland exterior, this new world of Windows wonders will be a welcome change. If you're new to Windows 98, however, you need to get comfortable with the lay of the Windows land. To that end, let's examine the vista you now see before you, which I'll divide into two sections: the desktop and the taskbar:

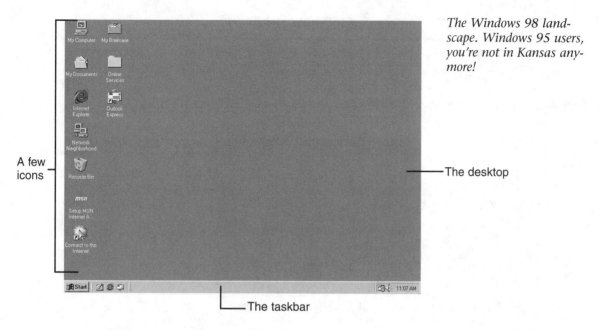

The Windows 98 landscape. Windows 95 users, you're not in Kansas anymore!

A few icons

The desktop

The taskbar

First Stop, the Desktop

The desktop is the vast teal expanse that takes up the bulk of the screen. Why is it called a *desktop*? Well, it's a metaphor, you see. In the same way that you pull out files and documents and work with them on the top of a real desk, so too do you place your computer's electronic files and documents on the Windows desktop.

Although the desktop is mostly empty right now, it's not entirely barren. The left side of the screen boasts a few little pictures, called *icons* in Windowspeak. These icons represent various features of Windows 98. In most cases, you open these icons by using your mouse to double-click the icon. I'll discuss each of these icons as we progress through the book—you don't need to worry about them much now. For the curious, however, here's a quick synopsis of what each one represents (these are just the default icons in Windows 98; your mileage may vary):

Default Windows 98 Icons

Start menu item	What it does	More info
My Computer	Opens the My Computer window.	Chapter 12
My Documents	Represents a storage area (called a *folder*) that Windows 98 sets up on your computer's hard disk. You use the My Documents area to store the various documents and files you create while working with Windows applications.	Chapter 6

continues

Continued

Start menu item	What it does	More info
Internet Explorer	Launches the Internet Explorer Web browser.	Chapter 17
Network Neighborhood	Gives you access to resources on your local area network. This friendly-sounding icon appears only if your computer is part of a larger network of computers.	Chapter 26
Recycle Bin	This represents, literally, the Windows 98 garbage can. When you delete files from your computer, Windows 98 tosses them inside this Recycle Bin.	Chapter 9
Set Up The Microsoft Network	Gets you set up with Microsoft's online service: In Windows 98 Second Edition, this icon is called Setup MSN Internet Access.	Chapter 15
Connect to the Internet	You use this icon to run a wizard that helps you set up an Internet connection.	Chapter 15
My Briefcase	This is a special storage area that makes it easy to move files between a desktop computer and a notebook computer.	Chapter 22
Online Services	Takes you to a collection of programs that you can use to set up accounts with some of the major online service providers.	Chapter 17
Outlook Express	Launches Outlook Express so that you can send and read email messages.	Chapter 18

A Few Words About Web Integration

The big story with Windows 98 is this Web integration business that makes it possible for you to "browse" your computer just like World Wide Web pages. Whether the Web integration feature is on or off when you first start Windows 98 depends on various factors (who set up your computer, whether you had the Internet Explorer browser installed, and so on). To be consistent, I'll assume throughout this book that you have Web integration turned on. For now, here are the steps to follow to switch between Web integration (what Microsoft calls *Web style*) and the regular desktop (*Classic style* in Microsoftspeak):

1. Click **Start**, then click **Settings**, and then click **Folder Option**s. Windows 98 displays the Folder Options dialog box.

2. Activate one of the following options:

   Web style: Activate this option to use Web integration.

   Classic style: Activate this option to use the regular Windows way of doing things.

3. Click **OK**. If you chose Web style, Windows then asks whether you want to use the single-click method for opening icons.

4. If you want to use the single-click method (which I recommend), make sure that the **Yes** option is activated, and then click **OK**.

SEE ALSO

> ➤ *I'll discuss Web integration in gory detail in Chapter 9, "Webtop Windows: Web Integration and the Active Desktop," p. 93.*

Next Up, the Taskbar

The gray strip along the bottom of the Windows 98 screen is called the *taskbar*. In its basic guise, the taskbar sports four distinct features (pointed out in the following figure):

➤ **Start button:** Believe it or not, this tiny chunk of screen real estate is one of the most important features of Windows 98. As its name implies, the Start button is your starting point for most of the Windows 98 features and goodies.

SEE ALSO

> ➤ *The Start button is discussed in depth in Chapter 3, "Making Something Happen: Launching and Switching Programs," p. 29.*

➤ **Quick Launch:** This area boasts a few more of those icon things. As with the desktop icons, these Quick Launch icons give you easy access to common features. I'll discuss these icons individually as you progress through the book.

➤ **Notification area:** Unlike early versions of Windows, Windows 98 likes to keep you abreast of what's going on. One of the ways it does that is to display little indicators in the taskbar's *notification area* (sometimes called the *system tray* by those in-the-know). Depending on what's happening in your system, you may see four or five icons in this area or none at all. Again, I'll discuss what the various indicators mean as you work through the book.

➤ **Clock:** The clock's purpose is obvious enough: it just tells you the current time. To set the time or the date, you can use the Date/Time feature. To get there, double-click the clock.

The rest of the taskbar is empty right now, but that will change soon enough. As you'll see in the next chapter when I show you how to start programs, Windows 98 uses the taskbar to keep track of all your running programs. You can use the taskbar to switch between the programs, shut them down, and do other handy things.

The features of the taskbar.

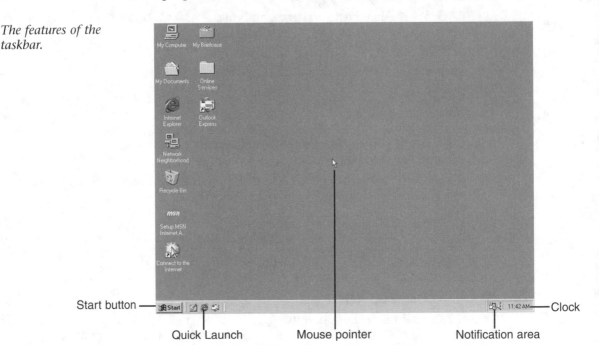

Point, Click, Type: Using Your Mouse and Keyboard

Okay, so Windows 98 has icons up the wazoo. How do I get at 'em?

Ah, that's where your mouse and keyboard come in. You use them as "input devices" to give Windows 98 its marching orders. The next few sections show you the basic mouse and keyboard techniques you need to do just that.

Manipulating the Mouse

You'll be happy to know that manipulating the mouse doesn't take some superhuman level of hand-eye coordination. In fact, if you're coordinated enough to feed yourself more or less successfully, you'll be able to master the basic mouse moves in no time flat.

All that's required is that you move the mouse slowly on its pad or on your desk. As you move the mouse, keep an eye on the mouse pointer on the screen (it's the little white arrow you can see in the preceding figure). Notice that the pointer moves in the same direction as the mouse itself. For example, if you move the mouse a bit to the left, the pointer also moves to the left. Using slow, gentle movements, practice moving the mouse up, down, and all around until you're comfortable with this basic technique.

As you wend your way through this book, you'll find me constantly telling you to use your mouse to "point" at this, "click" that, or "drag" something else. These are all run-of-the-mill mouse actions that will soon become second nature to you. If you're a new mouse user, however, they're probably not even third or fourth nature (or even in the top 10, for that matter), so let's see what they're all about:

➤ **Point:** When I tell you to point at something, move the mouse until the pointer sits on the specified part of the screen. For example, if I say "point at the **Start** button," you should move the mouse until the pointer rests over the Start button in the lower-left corner of the screen.

➤ **Click:** To "click" means to press and release the left mouse button. Note that you always have to point at something before you can click it. For example, point the mouse at the **Start** button and then click. See how Windows 98 displays a menu? (This is called the Start menu. Because you don't need it right now, click an empty part of the desktop to get rid of it.)

➤ **Double-click:** As you might expect, "double-click" means to press and release the left mouse button twice quickly. This can be a bit tricky until you get the rhythm of it, so don't worry if Windows seems to be ignoring you. Again, you'll always point at something before you double-click it.

➤ **Right-click:** This is similar to a regular click, except you quickly press and release the *right* mouse button. (If your mouse has three buttons, use the one on the far right.) When you right-click most things in Windows 98, a *shortcut menu* appears, giving you quick access to common commands.

SEE ALSO

➤ *For more information on shortcut menus, see Chapter 5, "Your Click Is My Command: Using Menus, Toolbars, and Dialog Boxes," p. 51.*

➤ **Drag:** This means that you point the mouse at a particular object, press and *hold down* the left mouse button, and then move the mouse. In most cases, the object you point at moves right along with the mouse pointer, so you'll generally use dragging to shift things from one spot and drop them on another.

➤ **Scroll:** Microsoft's latest mouse product—the IntelliMouse—shoehorns a little wheel between the two mouse buttons. In programs that know about this wheel (most of Windows 98 does, as do the Office 97 and Office 2000 program suites), you can scroll up and down within a document by rotating the wheel forward and back.

Ctrl, Alt, and Other Keyboard Conundrums

I mentioned earlier that getting comfy with your mouse is crucial if you want to make your Windows 98 life as easy as possible. That's not to say, however, that the keyboard never comes in handy as a timesaver. On the contrary, Windows 98 is chock-full of keyboard shortcuts that are sometimes quicker than the standard mouse techniques. I'll tell you about these shortcuts as we go along. For now, let's run through some of the standard keyboard parts and see how they fit into the Windows way of doing things.

➤ **The Ctrl and Alt keys:** If you press **Ctrl** (it's pronounced "control") or **Alt**, nothing much happens, but that's okay because nothing much is supposed to happen. You don't use these keys by themselves, but as part of *key combinations*. (The Shift key often gets into the act as well.) For example, hold down the **Ctrl** key with one hand, use your other hand to tap the **Esc** key, and then release **Ctrl**. Like magic, you'll see a menu of options sprout from the Start button. (To hide this menu again, press **Esc** by itself.)

A Shortcut Shorthand

This method of holding down one key while pressing another is called a *key combination* or a *keyboard shortcut*. As I said, Windows 98 has all kinds of them, so they'll pop up regularly throughout the book. Because I'm *way* too lazy to write out something like "Hold down the **Ctrl** key with one hand, use your other hand to tap the **Esc** key, and then release **Ctrl**" each time, however, I'll use the following shorthand notation instead: "Press *key1+key2*," where *key1* is the key you hold down and *key2* is the key you tap. In other words, instead of the previous long-winded sentence, I'll say this: "Press **Ctrl+Esc**."

➤ **The Esc Key:** Your keyboard's Esc (or Escape) key is your all-purpose get-me-the-heck-out-of-here key. For example, you just saw that you can get rid of the Start menu by pressing Esc. In many cases, if you do something in Windows 98 that you didn't want to do, you can reverse your tracks with a quick tap (or maybe two or three) on Esc.

➤ **The Numeric Keypad:** On a standard keyboard layout, the numeric keypad is the separate collection of numbered keys on the right. The numeric keypad usually serves two functions, and you toggle between these functions by pressing the **Num Lock** key. (Most keyboards have a Num Lock indicator light that tells you when Num Lock is on.)

When Num Lock is on, you can use the numeric keypad to type numbers.

When Num Lock is off, the other symbols on the keys become active. For example, the 8 key's upward-pointing arrow becomes active, which means you can use it to move up within a program. Some keyboards (called *extended keyboards*) have a separate keypad for the insertion point movement keys, and you can keep Num Lock on all the time.

SEE ALSO
➤ *For more information about using the numeric keypad keys to move the cursor, see Chapter 6, "A Few Workaday Document Chores," p. 63.*

Shutting Down Windows for the Night

When you've stood just about all you can stand of your computer for one day, it's time to close up shop. Please tape the following to your cat's forehead so that you'll never forget it: *Never, I repeat, never, turn off your computer's power while Windows 98 is still running.* Doing so can lead to data loss, a trashed configuration, and accelerated hair loss. Now that I've scared the daylights out of you, here are the steps to follow to properly shut down your computer:

1. Click the **Start** button to pop up the Windows 98 Start menu.
2. Click the **Shut Down** option. Windows 98 then displays a little box, as shown in the following figure. (This is an example of a *dialog box*.)

SEE ALSO
➤ *I'll tell you all about dialog boxes in Chapter 5, p. 56.*

When you shut down Windows 98, this dialog box shows up to ask whether you're sure you want to.

3. You have several choices at this point (click the one you want):
    ➤ **Stand by:** This command appears only on computers that have "power management" features that enable then to turn off things like the monitor and hard drive without shutting everything down. This is a good choice (if you have it) because it means you can wake up your system later by simply jiggling the mouse.
    ➤ **Shut down:** Use this option if you want to turn off your entire system.
    ➤ **Restart:** Use this option to start all over again. You'll use this option only if a program has told you that you have to restart your system.

➤ **Restart in MS-DOS mode:** Use this option if you want to restart your system and display only DOS, not Windows. This option is useful if you have an older DOS game or program that refuses to run under Windows 98.

4. Click the **OK** button, or press **Enter**. If you chose Shut down, Windows 98 takes a few seconds to prepare itself for bed, and then it displays a screen telling you it's okay to shut off your computer.

5. Turn off the computer and monitor. (Again, you need to do this only if you chose the Shut down option.)

Part II

Basic Windows 98 Survival Skills

Survival in the wild requires a few basic survival skills: building a fire, pitching a tent, opening beer bottles with your teeth, and so on. Surviving the wilds of Windows 98 also requires mastering a few fundamental skills. (Not the same skills, mind you; rest assured you'll rarely need to build a fire or open anything with your teeth when working with Windows.) The chapters here in Part 2 take you through these skills, from starting programs to printing documents.

WE'RE LAUNCHED!
CONFIDENCE IS HIGH!
CONFIDENCE IS HIGH!

Chapter 3

Making Something Happen: Launching and Switching Programs

In This Chapter

➤ A couple of ways to get a program off the ground

➤ Getting the hang of the taskbar

➤ Techniques for switching between programs

➤ Shutting down a program

➤ Lots of useful tidbits for dealing with programs within Windows 98

When Windows 98 shows up for work, it presents a rather placid exterior. The desktop is mostly empty, the icons just sit there, and the taskbar merely updates the clock with each passing minute. It's a nice pastoral scene, but it's probably not why you forked over the big bucks for your computer. Instead, you want to get your money's worth by making the unruly beast do something useful. That's just what you learn how to do in this chapter as I show you a few techniques for cranking up programs and the Windows 98 components.

Let's Do Launch: The Start Menu

The Start button is the most obvious point of attack and it is, in fact, your royal road to most of the Windows 98 world. So, without further ado, let's head down that road. Use your mouse to point at the Start button and then click. As you can see in the following figure, Windows 98 responds by shooting a list of options—called the Start menu—up the screen. (Note that the specific items displayed on the Start menu depend on how Windows 98 is set up. Therefore, the items you see on your Start menu may be a bit different from the ones you see here.)

The Start menu: your Windows 98 launch pad.

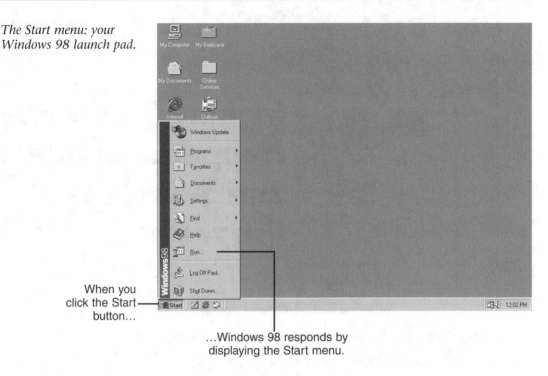

When you click the Start button...

...Windows 98 responds by displaying the Start menu.

To select one of the items shown on the Start menu, click it with your mouse. What happens next depends on which item you clicked:

➤ If the item represents a built-in Windows command or a program, Windows 98 will launch the command or program.

➤ On the other hand, some of the Start menu items represent *submenus*. Specifically, these are the five items (such as Programs and Favorites) with the little arrow on the right. Here's a bonus: You don't even need to click these items. When you move your pointer over the arrow, a new menu slides out to the right of the Start menu automatically (see the following figure).

Don't be surprised if you find yourself wading through two or three of these submenus to get the program you want. For example, here are the steps you'd follow to fire up WordPad, the Windows 98 word processor:

1. Click the **Start** button to display the Start menu.

2. Select **Programs** to open the submenu.

3. Select **Accessories** to open another submenu.

4. Click **WordPad**. Windows 98 launches the WordPad program.

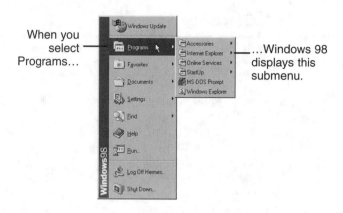

When you select Programs...

...Windows 98 displays this submenu.

The Start menu is loaded with all kinds of sub-menus.

SEE ALSO

➤ *For more information about WordPad, see the "Full Fledged Word Processing with WordPad" section, p. 252, in Chapter 19, "The Write Stuff: Windows 98's Writing Tools."*

In the future, I'll abbreviate these tedious Start menu procedures by using a comma (,) to separate each item you click, like so: "Select **Start**, **Programs**, **Accessories**, **WordPad**".

The following table provides a summary of each item on the main Start menu.

Let's Get Started

Start menu item	What it does	More info
Windows Update	Launches Internet Explorer and takes you to the Windows Update Web page.	Chapter 25
Programs	Displays a submenu that takes you to a collection of programs and Windows 98 components. People upgrading from Windows 3.1 should note that their old Program Manager program groups appear on this submenu.	Throughout book
Favorites	Displays a submenu with a list of frequently accessed locations, which can be sites on the World Wide Web or folders on your hard drive.	Chapters 13, 17

continues

31

Continued

Start menu item	What it does	More info
Documents	Opens a list of the last 15 documents you worked with in any of your applications. When you select a document from this folder, Windows automatically launches the appropriate program and loads the document.	Chapter 6
Settings	Displays a submenu with several options. For example, you use Control Panel to play around with various Windows 98 settings; you use Printers to set up and work with a printer; and you use Taskbar & Start Menu to customize—you guessed it—the taskbar and Start menu.	Chapters 7, 9–11
Find	Contains tools that help you find things on your computer, the Internet, and the Windows Address Book.	Chapters 13, 16, 17
Help	Starts up the Windows 98 Help system.	Chapter 8
Run	Enables you to run a program by typing its name and location.	Chapter 3
Log Off	Logs the current user off Windows or the network.	Chapter 26
Shut Down	Tells Windows 98 that you've had enough for one day and want to return to the real world.	Chapter 2

SEE ALSO

➤ *For more information about Run, see "Launching a Program with the Run Command," later in this chapter, p. 33.*

Other Ways to Unfurl the Start Menu

Clicking the Start button is probably the most common way to get at the Start menu, but Windows 98 also offers a couple of keyboard methods that you should have in your arsenal:

➤ Press **Ctrl+Esc**.

➤ If you have the Microsoft Natural Keyboard—the one with the alphanumeric keys split down the middle and the curvaceous, left-the-darn-thing-too-long-in-the-microwave-again look—press the key with the Windows logo on it (⊞). Note, as well, that most recent keyboards sport the Windows logo key.

Launching a Program with the Run Command

In rare cases, the program you want to run might not appear on any of the Start menus. This is particularly true of older DOS programs that don't do Windows. For the time being, you can use the Run command to get these old geezer programs under way.

SEE ALSO

➤ *In Chapter 10, "Customizing the Desktop and Taskbar," p.103, I show you how to add your own Start menu commands for launching such programs.*

This process isn't for the faint of heart, however, because it requires a bit more work, as the following steps show:

1. Select **Start**, **Run**. Windows 98 displays the Run dialog box shown in the following figure.

SEE ALSO

➤ *To learn how to use dialog boxes, see Chapter 5, "Your Click is My Command: Using Menus, Toolbars, and Dialog Boxes," p. 51.*

You can use the Run dialog box to launch programs by hand.

2. In the **Open** text box, type the name of the disk drive where the program resides (for example, **c:**), its folder (such as **\wp51**), and then the name of the file that starts the program (for example, **wp51.exe**).

3. Click **OK** to run the program.

Whew! Compared to the Start menu, that's true, calluses-on-the-fingertips manual labor. Here are a few points to bear in mind when you're working with the Run dialog box:

➤ Instead of typing the command, you can click the **Browse** button and choose the program from the Browse dialog box that appears.

➤ If any part of the filename or folder name contains spaces or is longer than eight characters, you have to surround the whole thing with quotation marks (as shown in the figure). If you're not sure about this, go ahead and add the quotation marks anyway.

➤ Although you'll normally use Run to enter program files, you can also use Run to enter the name and location of documents, folders, and even World Wide Web addresses. In each case, Windows 98 launches the appropriate program and loads the item you specified.

➤ Windows 98 "remembers" the last few commands you entered in the Run dialog box. If you need to repeat a recent command, drop down the **Open** list and select the command.

➤ If you have a keyboard with the Windows logo key on it, press ⊞ **+R** to display the Run dialog box.

Belly Up to the Bar: How the Taskbar Works

When you fire up a program, Windows 98 marks the occasion by adding a button to the taskbar. If you then coax another program or two onto the screen (remember, Windows 98 is capable of *multitasking*—running multiple programs simultaneously), each one gets its own taskbar button.

Multitasking Is Slick, But...

Although it's true that Windows 98 is happy to deal with multiple running programs—think of it as the electronic equivalent of walking and chewing gum at the same time—that doesn't mean you can just kickstart every program you have and leave them running all day. The problem is that because each open program usurps a chunk of Windows' resources, the more programs you run, the slower each program performs, including Windows itself. The number of applications you can fire up at any one time depends on how much horsepower your computer has and how resource-hungry the program is. You'll probably need to play around a bit to see just how many applications you can launch before things get too slow.

For example, the following figure shows Windows 98 with two programs up and running: WordPad and Paint. (To run the latter, select **Start**, **Programs, Accessories, Paint**.) It looks as though Paint has lopped off a good portion of the WordPad window, but in reality Windows 98 is just displaying Paint "on top" of WordPad. In addition, the taskbar has changed in two ways:

➤ There are now buttons for both WordPad and Paint.

➤ In the taskbar, the *active* program's button (the Paint button in this figure) looks as though it's been pressed. (The active program is the one you're currently slaving away in.)

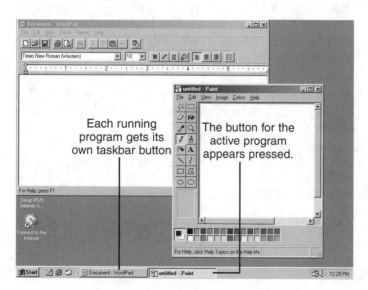

Each running program gets its own taskbar button

The button for the active program appears pressed.

Windows 98 with two programs on the go.

The taskbar has another trick up its digital sleeve. Specifically, you can switch from one running program to another by clicking the appropriate taskbar button. For example, when I click the WordPad button, the WordPad window comes to the fore, as shown in the following figure.

You can use the taskbar buttons to switch from one program to another.

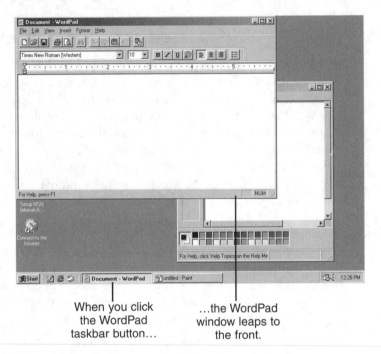

When you click
the WordPad
taskbar button...

...the WordPad
window leaps to
the front.

A Few More Ways to Switch Programs

One of the confusing things about Windows 98 is that it often gives you two or three ways to accomplish the same task. It may seem as though Windows 98 is being redundant, but one method usually is better than another in a particular set of circumstances. In addition to clicking the taskbar buttons, Windows 98 gives you three other ways to get from here to there:

➤ **Click the program's window:** This is perhaps the simplest and most obvious method. All you do is point the mouse inside the program's window and then click. This method is most useful if your hand is already on the mouse and you can see at least part of the window you want to activate.

➤ **Hold down Alt and tap Tab:** When you do this, Windows 98 displays the box shown in the next figure. This box lists all the running programs and highlights each one in turn as you tap the Tab key. When you get to the one you want, release the Alt key—Windows 98 then switches to the program. This technique is useful if your hands are on the keyboard and you have only a few programs running.

Hold down Alt and tap Tab repeatedly to cycle through the names of your running programs.

➤ **Hold down Alt and tap Esc:** This method is similar to the Alt+Tab method, in that Windows 98 cycles through the open programs. The difference is that with each tap of the Esc key, Windows 98 brings each program window to the fore. Use this method when you want to check out the contents of each window before you decide which program you want to work with.

Quitting a Program

When you're finished with a particular program, you should close it to keep your screen uncluttered and to reduce the load on Windows' resources. The easiest way to do this is to click the Close button (the X in the upper-right corner of the program's window.

You can also use a few other methods, which you may find faster under certain circumstances:

➤ Press **Alt+F4**.

➤ Pull down the program's **File** menu and select the **Exit** command (or, more rarely, the **Close** command).

SEE ALSO

➤ *For more information about working with pull-down menus, see Chapter 5, p. 51.*

➤ Right-click the program's taskbar button and then click Close in the little menu that appears.

Depending on the program you're closing and the work you were doing with it, you might be asked whether you want to "save" some files.

Chapter 4

Working with Windows 98's Windows

In This Chapter

➤ Window parts and pieces

➤ Moving, sizing, maximizing, and minimizing Windows Explorer

➤ Working with scrollbars

➤ Your field guide to window flora and fauna

As you saw in the last chapter, when you launch any kind of program, it shows up inside a box on your screen. That box is called a *window*, and it's these windows that give Windows 98 its name. Because you'll be playing around in one window or another throughout your Windows 98 career, it pays to become familiar with a few basic techniques for controlling the darn things before they start getting out of hand. This chapter gives you all the window know-how you'll need to get by.

The Parts Department: Window Gadgets and Doodads

Let's begin with a bit of an anatomy lesson, using the WordPad window shown in the following figure. (Select **Start**, **Programs**, **Accessories**, **WordPad** to get this window onscreen.)

The WordPad window and some of its nuts and bolts.

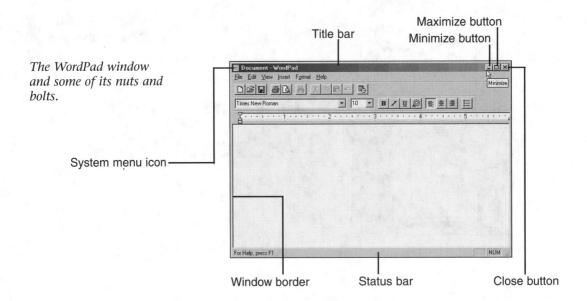

All kinds of trinkets are on display in this window, but just the ones pointed out in the figure are of interest to us here. The following list gives you a brief description of some of these features (I'll discuss the others as you work through this chapter):

➤ **Title bar**: This is the blue strip across the top of the window. The title bar usually shows two things: the name of the current document ("Document" in the WordPad window shown in the previous figure) and the name of the program, separated by a dash.

➤ **Border**: Most windows are surrounded by a thin border that you can manipulate, with your mouse, to change the size of a window.

➤ **System menu icon**: The system menu sports several commands that enable keyboard users to perform routine window maintenance.

➤ **Status bar:** This is the gray strip that runs along the bottom of the window. Most programs use the status bar to provide helpful hints and to let you know what the heck the program is doing at a given moment.

SEE ALSO

➤ *To learn the ins and outs of the WordPad program, check out the "Full-Fledged Word Processing with WordPad" section, p. 252, in Chapter 19, "The Write Stuff: Windows 98's Writing Tools."*

Button Confusion? The ToolTips Will Tell You

With all those buttons crowded into the upper-right corner of a window, it's tough keeping them straight. To help us out, Windows 98 has a feature that tells the name of each button. Just move your mouse pointer over a button—a second or two later you'll see a little banner with the button's name. (The preceding figure shows an example of this feature.)

Working with Windows

With the various window parts stored safely in your memory banks, you can now use them to manipulate any window that comes your way. Why bother with any of this, you ask? Why not just deal with the window as is and get on with your work? You could do that, I suppose, but manhandling a window does have its advantages. Let's see how the four main window techniques—minimizing, maximizing, moving, and sizing—can help you work better in Windows 98:

➤ You'll often find that you have an open window you know you won't need right away. If you want to reduce the clutter on your desktop, you can close the window, but then you may have to open it again in a little while. *Minimizing* the window is a better alternative because it removes the window from the desktop *without* closing it. A simple click of the mouse is all it takes to get the window back in view.

➤ Most people prefer to use the largest possible work area in their windows. You could resize a window to make it larger, but it's easier to just *maximize* it: the window expands to fill the entire desktop area.

➤ One of the problems with having several windows open at once is that they have a nasty habit of overlapping each other. And what's covered up in a window is usually the information you want to see. (Chalk up another one for Murphy's Law, I guess.) Instead of cursing Windows 98's ancestry, you can try moving your windows around so that they don't overlap (or so that they overlap less). Note, however, that you can only move a window when it's not maximized.

➤ Another way to reduce window clutter is to change the size of the open windows. For example, you can reduce the size of less important windows and increase the size of windows in which you do the most work. Again, you can only size a window that's not maximized.

The next few sections discuss these techniques and a few more, for good measure.

Extreme Windows: Minimizing and Maximizing

When you click a window's Minimize button, the window disappears from view. The window isn't closed, however, because its taskbar button remains in place, as you can see in the next figure. When you need the window again, a quick click on the taskbar button restores the window to its rightful place on the desktop.

When you minimize a window, all that remains is the window's taskbar button.

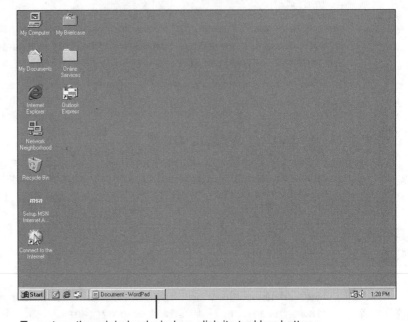

To restore the minimized window, click its taskbar button.

Clicking a window's Maximize button is a whole different kettle of window fish. In this case, the window grows until it fills the entire desktop, as you can see in the following figure.

To return the window to its normal size, click the Restore button.

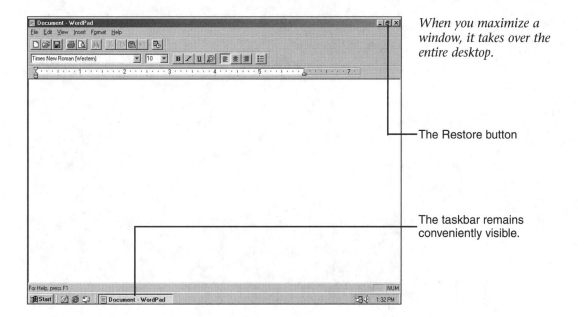

When you maximize a window, it takes over the entire desktop.

The Restore button

The taskbar remains conveniently visible.

Organizing Your Windows: Moving and Sizing

Moving a window from one part of the desktop to another takes a simple mouse maneuver. Here are the steps to follow:

1. Make sure the window isn't maximized (or that it's not, duh, minimized).
2. Position the mouse pointer inside the window's title bar (but not over the system menu icon or any of the buttons on the right).
3. Drag the title bar. As you drag, the window moves along with your mouse.
4. When the window is in the position you want, release the mouse button.

If you want to change the size of a window, instead, you need to plow through these steps:

1. Make sure the window isn't maximized or minimized.
2. Point the mouse at the window border you want to adjust. For example, if you want to expand the window toward the bottom of the screen, point the mouse at the bottom border. When you've positioned the pointer correctly, it becomes a two-headed arrow, as shown in the next figure.
3. Drag the border to the position you want.
4. Release the mouse button to set the new border position.
5. Repeat steps 2–4 for any other borders you want to size.

You resize a window by dragging the window borders hither and thither.

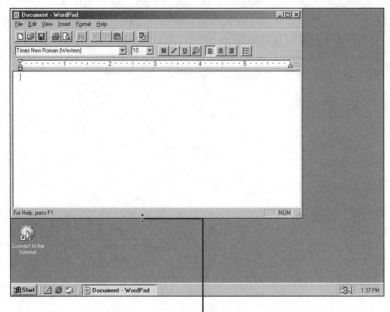

At a window border, the mouse pointer changes to a two-headed arrow.

Two-Sided Sizing

If you want to change both the height and width of a window, you can save yourself a bit of effort by sizing two sides in one fell swoop. To do this, move the mouse pointer over a window corner. (The pointer will change to a diagonal two-sided arrow.) When you drag the mouse, Windows 98 sizes the two sides that create the corner.

Letting Windows Do the Work: Cascading and Tiling

These techniques for minimizing, maximizing, moving, and sizing aren't hard and it won't take you long to master them. They can get a bit tedious, however, if you have a lot of windows on your desktop. For these situations, Windows 98 has a few features that take much of the drudgery out of working with windows.

To get at these features, right-click an empty section of the taskbar. The shortcut menu that shows up contains (among others) the following commands:

➤ **Cascade Windows:** This command automatically arranges all your nonminimized windows in a diagonal pattern that lets you see the title bar of each window. The following figure shows three cascaded windows.

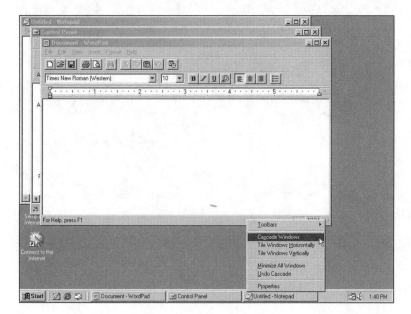

The Cascade Windows command arranges your windows neatly in a diagonal pattern.

➤ **Tile Windows Horizontally:** This feature automatically arranges all your nonminimized windows into horizontal strips so that each of them gets an equal amount of desktop real estate without overlapping each other. The next figure shows the same three windows arranged horizontally.

➤ **Tile Windows Vertically:** This command is similar to the Tile Windows Horizontally command, except that it arranges the windows into vertical strips.

➤ **Minimize All Windows:** This feature minimizes every open window in one shot. This is handy whenever you need to see what's on your desktop.

With Windows 98's new Active Desktop, you'll probably want to visit your desktop constantly. The Minimize All Windows command is a handy way to clear the deck, but Windows 98 offers an even easier way: Just click the Show Desktop button in the Quick Launch toolbar.

The Tile Windows Horizontally command carves out equal-size horizontal desktop chunks for your windows.

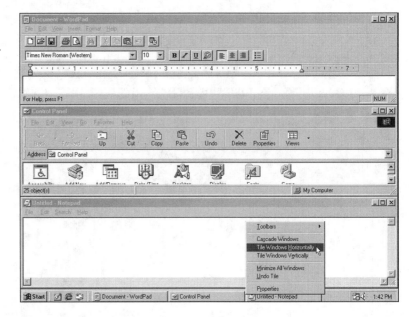

The easiest way to clean your desktop's slate is to click the Show Desktop icon in the Quick Launch toolbar.

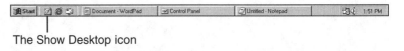

The Show Desktop icon

What About the System Menu?

Earlier I showed you the system menu icon in the upper-left corner of the window. What's that all about? Well, if you click this icon, you see the *system menu* shown in the next figure. As you can see, this menu's commands correspond to the four basic window actions: Move, Size, Minimize, and Maximize. There's also a Restore command for restoring a minimized or maximized window, and a Close command for closing the window. (Note that you can also close a window by double-clicking the system menu icon.)

When you click this icon...

The system menu gives you another way to get at the basic window commands.

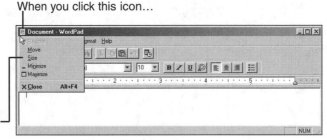

...Windows 98 displays the system menu.

46

Mouse users will certainly find themselves using the system menu from time to time. For example, you might move a window to the right so that its Minimize, Maximize, and Close buttons are no longer visible. In this case, you can still use the system menu to work with the window.

The system menu is most often used from the keyboard, however. You press **Alt+Spacebar** to display the menu, use the **up** and **down** arrow keys to highlight the command you want to run, and then press **Enter**. Most of the system menu commands are straightforward when they're launched from the keyboard, but Move and Size require a bit more explanation.

Follow these steps to move a window, using the keyboard:

1. Press **Alt+Spacebar** to display the system menu.
2. Select the **Move** command. A four-headed arrow appears inside the window's title bar. (Can't select the Move command? This will happen if the window is maximized. The Move command is available only in windows that aren't maximized.)
3. Use the arrow keys to move the window.
4. When the window is in the location you want, press **Enter**. If you decide that you don't want to move the window after all, you can press the **Esc** key at any time to bail out of the move.

You need to run through these steps to size a window from the keyboard:

1. Press **Alt+Spacebar** to display the system menu.
2. Select the **Size** command. A four-headed arrow appears inside the window. (Again, you won't be able to select the Size command if the window is maximized.)
3. To select a border to size, press the corresponding arrow key. For example, to size the right border, press the right arrow key. The mouse pointer changes to a two-headed arrow and moves to the selected border.
4. Use the arrow keys to adjust the border.
5. When the window is the size you want, press **Enter**.

Another System Menu

Keep in mind that another version of the system menu is also available on the taskbar. To access it, right-click a window's taskbar button.

Using Scrollbars to Navigate Inside a Window

Depending on the program you're using, you'll often find that the document you're dealing with won't fit entirely inside the window's boundaries, even when you maximize the window. When this happens, you need some way to move to the parts of the document you can't see.

From the keyboard, you can use the basic navigation keys (the arrow keys, Page Up, and Page Down). Mouse users, as usual, have all the fun. To navigate through a document, they get to learn a new skill: how to use scrollbars. The *scrollbar* is the narrow strip that runs along the right side of most windows. Using the WordPad window shown in the following figure, I've pointed out the major features of the average scrollbar. Here's how to use these features to get around inside a document:

➤ The position of the scroll box gives you an idea of where you are in the document. For example, if the scroll box is about halfway down, you know you're somewhere near the middle of the document.

➤ To scroll up through the document one line at a time, click the up scroll arrow. To scroll continuously, press and hold down the left mouse button on the up scroll arrow.

➤ To scroll down through the document one line at a time, click the down scroll arrow. To scroll continuously, press and hold down the left mouse button on the down scroll arrow.

➤ To leap through the document one screen at a time, click inside the scrollbar between the scroll box and the scroll arrows. For example, to move down one screen, click inside the scrollbar between the scroll box and the down scroll arrow.

➤ To move to a specific part of the document, drag the scroll box up or down.

Note, as well, that many of the windows you work in will also sport a second scrollbar that runs horizontally along the bottom of the window. Horizontal scrollbars work the same as their vertical cousins, except that they let you move left and right in wide documents.

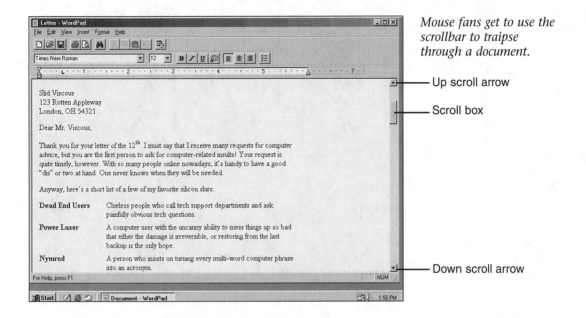

Mouse fans get to use the scrollbar to traipse through a document.

— Up scroll arrow

— Scroll box

— Down scroll arrow

Scrolling with the IntelliMouse

In early 1997, Microsoft introduced a radical new mouse design that incorporates a little wheel between the two buttons. If you're lucky enough to have one of these rotary rodents (or one of the knock-offs that some other mouse makers have put out), you can scroll up and down through a document by rotating the wheel forward or backward.

Some applications (such as Microsoft's Internet Explorer and the Office 97/Office 2000 programs) also support a feature called *panning* that lets you scroll automatically through a document and control the speed. To enable panning, click the wheel button. The application will then display an *origin mark* (the position of this mark varies from application to application). Drag the pointer above the origin mark to scroll up; drag the pointer below the origin mark to scroll down. Note also that the farther the pointer is from the origin mark, the faster you scroll. To turn off panning, click the wheel again.

Chapter 5

Your Click Is My Command: Using Menus, Toolbars, and Dialog Boxes

In This Chapter

➤ Learning about pull-down menus

➤ Using toolbars to make your life easier

➤ Dealing with Windows 98's ubiquitous dialog boxes

➤ Handy techniques that let you show Windows 98 who's boss

Well, your Windows 98 education is off to a fine start. You know how to launch programs, how to switch from one to another, and how to manipulate the windows that each program serves up. So what's next? Ah, now you get to go on a little personal power trip because this chapter shows you how to boss around your programs. Specifically, you'll learn how to work with pull-down menus, toolbars, and dialog boxes.

A Pull-Down Menu Primer

Remember in the last chapter when I showed you how to use a window's system menu? You saw that this menu gave you access to all the basic commands for manipulating that window. Pull-down menus offer a similar service for your programs. That is, they hold various commands that you use to work with the program. In fact, every feature in every Windows program you'll ever use is available to you via the program's pull-down menu system. Sure, there are easier ways to tell a program what to do (I'll talk about some of them later in this chapter), but pull-down menus offer a complete road map for any program. This section gets you up to speed on this crucial Windows topic.

The first thing you need to know is that a program's pull-down menus are housed in the *menu bar*, the horizontal strip that runs just beneath the title bar. The following figure shows the menu bar in Windows Explorer. (You can open this window yourself by selecting **Start**, **Programs**, **Windows Explorer**.)

The pull-down menus are lurking inside each program's menu bar.

The menu bar

The various items that run across the menu bar (such as File, Edit, and View in Windows Explorer) are the names of the menus. To see (that is, *pull down*) one of these menus, use either of the following techniques:

➤ Use your mouse to click the menu name. For example, click **View** to pull down the View menu.

➤ Hold down the **Alt** key and press the underlined letter in the menu name. In Windows Explorer, for example, the "V" in View is underlined, so you pull down this menu by pressing **Alt+V**.

As you can see in the next figure, the menu you select opens up below the menu bar. (This is why they're called "pull-down" menus.)

Windows Explorer's View menu.

When you click View in the menu bar…

…Windows 98 pulls down the View menu.

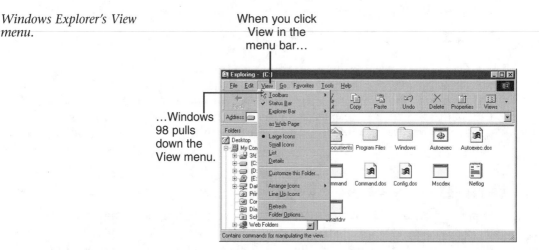

The various items you see in the menu are called *commands*. From here, you use any of the following techniques to select a command:

➤ Use your mouse to click the command you want.

➤ Use the up- and down-arrow keys to highlight the command, and then press **Enter**.

➤ Press the underlined letter in the command. For example, the "R" in the View menu's Refresh command is underlined, and you can select this command by pressing **R**.

Throughout this book, I'll tell you to select a pull-down menu command by separating the menu name and command name with a comma, like this: "Select the View, Refresh command."

Bailing Out of a Menu

What do you do if you pull down a menu and then discover that you don't want to select any of its commands? You can remove the menu by clicking any empty part of the program's window, or you can pull down a different menu by clicking the appropriate menu bar option.

From the keyboard, you have two choices:

➤ To get rid of the menu, press **Alt** by itself.

➤ To pull down a different menu, press **Alt** plus the underlined letter of the new menu.

What happens next really depends on which command you picked. Here's a summary of the various possibilities:

➤ **The command runs without further ado.** This is the simplest scenario, and it just means that the program carries out the command, no questions asked. For example, clicking the Refresh command updates Explorer's display automatically.

➤ **Another menu appears.** For example, if you click the View menu's Arrange Icons command, a new menu—called a *submenu*—appears on the right, as shown in the following figure. You then click the command you want to execute from the new menu.

➤ **The command is toggled on or off.** Some commands operate like light switches: they toggle certain features of a program on and off. When the feature is on, a small check mark appears to the left of the command to let you know (see the Status Bar command in the following figure). Selecting the command turns off the feature and removes the check mark. If you select the command again, the feature turns back on and the check mark reappears.

➤ **An option is activated:** Besides having features that you can toggle on and off, some programs have features that can assume three or four different states. (I call them the "Three or Four Faces of Eve" features.) Explorer, for example, gives you four ways to display the contents of your computer, according to your choice of one of the following View menu commands: Large Icons, Small Icons, List, and Details. Because these states are mutually exclusive (you can select only one at a time), you need some way of knowing which of the four commands is currently active. That's the job of the *option mark*: a small dot that appears to the left of the active command (see the Large Icons command in the following figure).

➤ **A dialog box appears:** Dialog boxes are mini windows that show up whenever the program needs to ask you for more information. You'll learn more about them in the "Talking Back to Windows: How Dialog Box Controls Work" section, later in this chapter.

A check mark tells
you that a feature
is activated.

*A few pull-down menu
features.*

The option
mark tells
you which
command in
this group is
currently
activated.

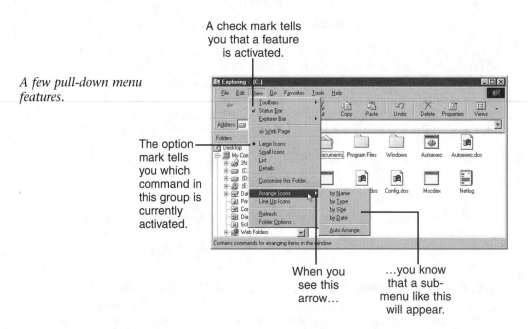

When you
see this
arrow...

...you know
that a sub-
menu like this
will appear.

Shortcut Menus

Many Windows programs (and Windows 98 itself), use *shortcut menus* to give you quick access to oft-used commands. The idea is that you right-click something and the program pops up a small menu of commands, each of which is somehow related to whatever it is you right-clicked. If you see the command you want, great: just click it (the left button this time). If you don't want to select a command from the menu, either left-click an empty part of the window or press **Esc**.

The Quick Click: Toolbar Techniques

Pull-down menus are a handy way to access a program's commands and features. A click, click here, a click, click there, and you're off to the digital races. It probably won't take very long, however, before you start resenting the few clicks you need to get at the menu commands you use most often. This has certainly happened to the world's programmers, because they keep inventing easier ways to make things happen in a program.

One of their most useful inventions has to be the *toolbar*. This is a collection of icons designed to give you push-button access to common commands and features. No unsightly key combinations to remember; no pull-down menu forests to get lost in.

Toolbars play a big role in Windows 98, and you'll reap some big dividends if you get to know how they work. Although most Windows 98 components have a toolbar or two as standard equipment, let's stick with Windows Explorer. As you can see in the following figure, the toolbar is the horizontal strip that runs just south of the menu bar.

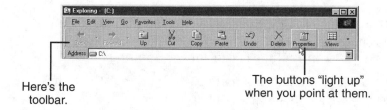

Like most Windows 98 components, Windows Explorer comes with a toolbar.

Here's the toolbar.

The buttons "light up" when you point at them.

Most toolbar icons are buttons that represent commands you'd normally access by using the pull-down menus. All you have to do is click a button, and the program runs the command, no questions asked.

Here's a summary of a few other toolbar-related techniques you ought to know:

➤ Most toolbars come in two flavors: text and nontext. In Explorer's toolbar, for example, each button has a text label beneath the icon (Back, Forward, Up, and so on). You can eke out a bit more window real estate by telling Windows 98 not to display those text labels. To do so, right-click the toolbar and then click the Text Labels command to deactivate it.

➤ If you decide to do without the text labels, you may forget what a particular button does. Instead of turning the text labels back on, just point the mouse at the button you're furrowing your brow over and wait a second or two. Eventually, you'll see a little yellow banner below the button that tells you the button's name.

➤ Many Windows 98 components ship with multiple toolbars. To turn these toolbars on and off, select the View, Toolbars command to display a list of the available toolbars. Then activate or deactivate the toolbar commands.

➤ Some toolbar buttons act like pull-down menus. For example, click the downward-pointing arrow beside Explorer's Views toolbar button. You'll see a menu of commands, as shown in the following figure.

Some toolbar buttons have a menu of commands lurking inside them.

Click the arrow to display the menu.

Talking Back to Windows: How Dialog Box Controls Work

I mentioned earlier that after you select some menu commands, the program might require more info from you. For example, if you run a Print command, the program might want to know how many copies of the document you want to print.

In these situations, the program sends an emissary to parlay with you. These emissaries, called *dialog boxes*, are one of the most ubiquitous features in the Windows world. This section preps you for your dialog box conversations by showing you how to work with every type of dialog box control you're likely to encounter. (They're called *controls* because you use them to manipulate the different dialog box settings.) Before starting, it's important to keep in mind that most dialog boxes like to monopolize your attention. When one is on the screen, you usually can't do anything else in the program (such as select a pull-down menu). Deal with the dialog box first, and then you can move on to other things.

Most of the dialog boxes you'll encounter in the rest of this chapter are part of the WordPad program; you might want to crank it up so that you can play along. Without further ado, here's a list of the various control species that inhabit the dialog box world, along with a brief explanation of how you work each control:

➤ **Command buttons:** All dialog boxes have at least one command button. They're called command buttons because when you click one, you're telling the program to execute the command written on the face of the button. In the Options dialog box shown in the next figure (select **View**, **Options** in WordPad), there are three command buttons: OK, Cancel, and Help. These are by far the most common command buttons, and you'll see them on most of the dialog boxes you deal with. Here's when to use them:

➤ Select **OK** when you finish with the dialog box and want to put all your selections into effect.

➤ Select **Cancel** to bail out of the dialog box without putting your selections into effect.

➤ Select **Help** to fire up the program's Help system and get more information about something in the dialog box.

Another Way to Get Help

Most dialog boxes have a **?** button in the upper-right corner. You can use this button to get a description of any dialog box control. To try it out, first click the **?** button. Your mouse pointer sprouts a question mark. Now click the control you're wondering about. In a few seconds, a brief description of the control appears onscreen. Press **Esc** to remove this message.

➤ **Check boxes:** Windows uses this type of control to handle yes-or-no, on-or-off decisions. The check box enables you to control whether a particular program setting is activated (checked) or deactivated (not checked). A check box setting is currently active when a check mark appears inside the box. The control is deactivated when there's no check mark. To toggle a check box on and off, click the box or its name.

WordPad's Options dialog box is loaded with controls.

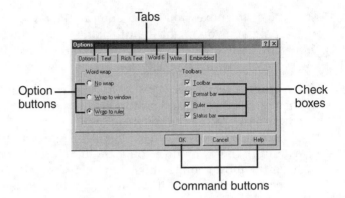

➤ **Option buttons:** You'll see this type of control when you deal with the Windows equivalent of the multiple-choice question. That is, when you're faced with two or more mutually exclusive choices, and you can pick only one. To activate a particular option button, click the button or its name. A black dot appears inside the circle when you select an option.

➤ **Tabs:** Many dialog boxes have a series of tabs running across the top. Each of these tabs represents a different set of controls. When you click a tab, a new bunch of controls appears, as shown in the following figure.

This is an example of a tabbed dialog box.

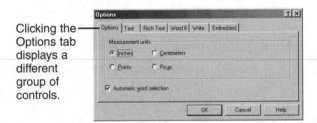

➤ **Text boxes:** This is a control in which you type text information such as a description or a filename. A text box is active when the text appears highlighted or when a blinking vertical bar appears inside the box. This blinking vertical bar is the *insertion point cursor* (or just *cursor*, for short) and it tells you where the next character you type will appear. The next figure includes several examples (select **Format**, **Paragraph** in WordPad).

This highlight tells
you that the text box
is the active control.

*You use text boxes to type
text info.*

These
are text
boxes.

Watch Out for Highlighted Text Box Text!

When the text in a text box appears highlighted, the next letter or number you
press replaces the contents of the text box! If you don't want to replace all the
text, first press the left- or right-arrow key to remove the highlight, position the
cursor appropriately, and then start typing.

➤ **List boxes:** This type of control presents you with a list of items. (To get the
dialog box shown in the following figure, select **Insert**, **Object** in WordPad.)
Your job is to select one of the items by clicking it. (A highlight bar shows you
the currently selected item.) In some cases, you may need to select several items
from the same list box. To do that, hold down the **Ctrl** key and click each item
you need.

List box

*You use list boxes to select
an item from a list of
choices.*

The currently
selected item
is highlighted.

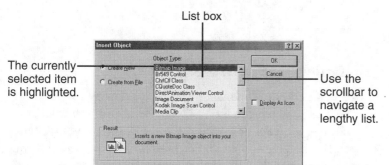

Use the
scrollbar to
navigate a
lengthy list.

59

➤ **Combo boxes:** This is a variation on the list box theme. It's actually a hybrid control that combines a list box and a text box (hence the name). The idea is that you can select the item you want from the list box, or you can type what you want in the text box. The following figure shows several examples. (Select **Format**, **Font** in WordPad.)

The Font dialog box contains several combo boxes and drop-down list boxes.

These are the combo boxes.

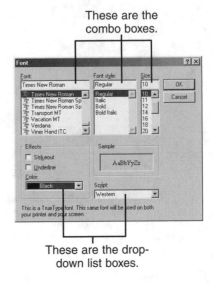

These are the drop-down list boxes.

➤ **Drop-down list boxes:** This is yet another variety of list box. This type of control normally shows only the currently selected item (see the examples in the preceding figure). To choose a different item, you "drop down" the list and then select the item you want, just as you would in a regular list box. Dropping down a drop-down list box is easy: click the downward-pointing arrow on the right side of the box.

Check This Out

Easier List Box Navigation

Here's a tip that can save you oodles of time when you muck about with both regular and drop-down list boxes. When the list box is active, press the first letter of the item you want. Windows 98 leaps down the list and highlights the first item in the list that begins with the letter you pressed. For example, if you drop down the **Color** list and press **G**, the highlight immediately moves to the **Green** item. If you press **G** again, the highlight moves to the **Gray** item.

➤ **Spin boxes:** You use this type of control to cycle up or down through a series of numbers. WordPad has no spin boxes, unfortunately. To get a specimen onscreen, select **Start**, **Settings**, **Control Panel**, and then open the **Date/Time** icon. The Date/Time Properties dialog box comes your way (see the following figure). Each spin box has two parts:

Spinner Ranges

Most spinners have a maximum and minimum value, and you can select any number within that range.

➤ The box on the left is a text box in which you can type the number you want (which is the boring way to do it).

➤ The right side of the spin box contains an upward-pointing arrow and a downward-pointing arrow. You click the upward-pointing arrow to increase the number that appears in the text box. To decrease the number, click the downward-pointing arrow. For some real fun, press and hold down the mouse button on one of the arrows and watch the numbers fly!

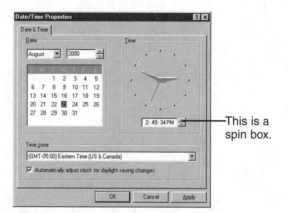

You use spin boxes to cycle through a range of numbers.

This is a spin box.

➤ **Sliders:** This kind of control helps you enter values that have no intrinsic numeric meaning (at least to non-nerds and other mere mortals). To see one, open Control Panel's **Keyboard** icon to display the dialog box shown in the following figure. The slider is a ruler-like line with opposite values on either end. The idea is that you enter a "value" by dragging the pointer (called the *slider bar*) either left or right.

The Keyboard Properties dialog box uses sliders to let you enter "values" without numbers.

This is a slider bar.

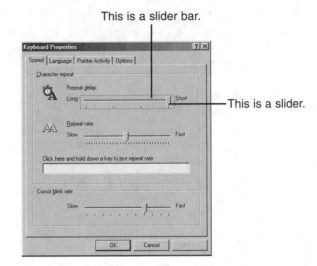

This is a slider.

Chapter 6

A Few Workaday Document Chores

In This Chapter

➤ Creating a new document

➤ Saving a document

➤ Opening and closing a document

➤ All kinds of ways to reduce document drudgery

Now that you know how to crack the electronic whip and make your programs hop to it, it's time to harness that power and put it to good use. Most programs have a few menu commands that deal with basic document tasks such as opening, saving, and closing. This chapter provides you with a compendium of these commonplace, nose-to-the-grindstone Windows 98 chores. I'll show you the appropriate menu commands to select (and, in some cases, the corresponding toolbar buttons and shortcut keys) and I'll tell you how to deal with any dialog boxes that come your way.

Before the fur starts flying, however, let's just be clear on exactly what I mean by a *document.* It's no big whoop: A document is anything you create by using a program or one of the Windows 98 accessories. This could be a letter or memo you cobble together in WordPad, a drawing or logo you create in Paint, or a Web page you construct in FrontPage Express.

Cranking Out a Fresh Document

Most Windows programs are kind enough to present you with a new, ready-to-use document when you launch the program. If you were looking to conjure up a new document for yourself, then great: just start typing or drawing or whatever.

Later on, however, you may need to start another new document. To do so, use one of the following techniques:

➤ Select the **File, New** command.

➤ Click the **New** button in the program's toolbar.

➤ In many Windows programs, you can spit out a new document by pressing **Ctrl+N**. or right-clicking the desktop and selecting New.

In most cases, the program will then toss a fresh document onscreen. Some programs (WordPad is one) display a dialog box that asks you what kind of new document you want.

Windows 98 also enables you to create a new, empty document without even opening the appropriate program. Here's how to accomplish this seemingly miraculous feat:

1. Open My Computer, Windows Explorer, or the My Documents folder. (For the latter, see "Taking Advantage of the My Documents Folder," later in this chapter.)

2. If you're working in My Computer or Windows Explorer, open the folder in which you want to store the new document.

3. Right-click an empty part of the folder. A shortcut menu will appear.

4. Click **New** to open the submenu shown in the following figure. (Note that some programs add their own document types to this menu, so you may see a different collection of items.)

5. Click the type of document you want.

6. Type a name for the new document, and then press **Enter**. (Windows 98 lets you enter long file names, but it does have a few restrictions you'll need to honor. I tell you about them in the "Saving a New Document" section, later in this chapter.)

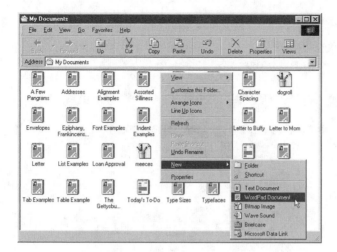

Right-click and then click **New** *to see a list of document types you can create.*

At this point, the document you created is just an empty shell. To add stuff to the document, launch the new icon you just created. (See "Together Again: Opening an Existing Document," later in this chapter to learn more about opening documents.)

Saving Your Work for Posterity

Working with a new document is a lot like working with an Etch-A-Sketch. That is, one false move and everything can get wiped out in the blink of an eye. Why is that? Well, when you work with a new document (or with an existing document), you're actually making all your changes in the volatile confines of your computer's memory. When you shut off your computer (or if a power failure forces it off), everything in memory is wiped out. If you haven't saved your document to your hard disk (which maintains its contents even when your computer is turned off), you lose all the changes you've made and it's impossible to get them back.

With that caveat out of the way, this section shows you how to avoid trouble by saving your documents.

Saving a New Document

As soon as you start a new document, you should save it immediately. Saving a new document takes a bit of extra work, but once that's out of the way, subsequent saves require only a mouse click or two. (I should mention here that you don't have to bother with any of this if you used the New command technique illustrated in the previous figure. If you used that technique to create your document, skip to the "Saving an Existing Document" section.)

To save a new document, use either of the following techniques:

➤ Select the **File, Save** command.

➤ Click the **Save** button in the program's toolbar.

Most programs will display a Save As dialog box like the one shown in the next figure.

The Save As dialog box appears when you're saving a new document.

Here are the steps you need to walk through to get your document safely stowed on your hard disk:

1. The **Save in** drop-down list tells you the name of the current folder. (Remember: A folder is a storage location on your hard disk.) If this is the folder you want, skip to Step 3. To choose a different folder, first drop down the list and choose the disk drive that contains the folder you want to use to store the file (see the following figure).

Use the Save in list to choose the disk drive that contains the folder you'll be using to save the document.

2. The Save As dialog box then shows you a list of the folders on the selected disk drive. Click the folder you want to open (see the next figure). You may need to repeat this several times to get to the folder you want.

Open the folder you want to use to store your document.

3. Use the **Filename** text box to enter a name for your document. In Windows 98, you can use file names that are up to 255 characters long. Your names can include spaces, commas, and apostrophes, but not the following characters: \ | ? : * " < >

4. Now use the **Save as type** drop-down list to choose the type of document you want to create (see the next figure). In the vast majority of cases you won't have to bother with this because you'll want to use the default type. Many programs can create different document types, however, and this capability often comes in handy.

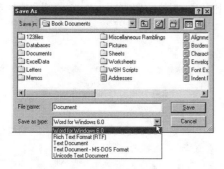

You won't need it all that often, but the Save as type list enables you create different kinds of documents.

5. Select the **Save** button. The program makes a permanent copy of the document on your hard disk.

Here are some notes about saving new documents:

➤ Happily, you won't have to go through the rigmarole of choosing a folder every time you save a new file. Most programs are smart enough to "remember" the most recent folder you worked with and will select it for you automatically the next time you're in the Save As dialog box. (Unfortunately, this memory only applies to the current session with the program. If you exit the program and then restart it, you have to reselect the folder.)

➤ If you want your new document to replace an existing file, open the folder that contains the file and then click the filename. The program will ask whether you want to replace the file, and you then click **Yes**.

➤ The rub with long filenames is that only programs written specifically for Windows 95 or Windows 98 can take advantage of them. DOS programs and those meant to work with Windows 3.1 will scoff at your attempts to break through the old "8.3" filename barrier (8 characters for the filename and a 3-character extension). What happens if you create a document with a long name, using a Windows 98 program, and then try to open that document in an older program? Well, the document will probably open just fine, but you'll notice that the filename has been knocked down to size. You see, Windows 98 actually keeps track of *two* names for each document: the long name and a shorter DOS-compatible name. The latter is just the first six characters of the long name (sans spaces), followed by a tilde (~), followed by a number. For example, a file named Fiscal 1997—First Quarter Budget Spreadsheet would also use the DOS alias FIS-CAL~1.

Saving an Existing Document

After all that hard work saving a new document, you'll be happy to know that subsequent saves are much easier. That's because when you select the **File**, **Save** command (or click the **Save** toolbar button), the program simply updates the existing hard disk copy of the document. This takes just a second or two (usually) and no dialog box shows up to pester you for information. Because this is so easy, there's no excuse not to save your work regularly.

Simpler Saves

If you're a fan of keyboard shortcuts, here's one you'll use all the time: Press **Ctrl+S** to save your document. (This shortcut works in the vast majority of Windows programs.)

Taking Advantage of the My Documents Folder

 One of the new features you get with Windows 98 is the special My Documents folder. This folder is designed to be a central storage area for all your documents. Using this folder is a good idea for three reasons:

➤ It makes your documents easy to find because they're all stored in one place.

➤ When you want to back up your documents, you need only select a single folder (rather than hunting around your hard disk for all your documents).

SEE ALSO

➤ *For more information about how to back up your documents, see Chapter 24, "Keeping Your Data Safe and Sound with Backup," p. xx.*

➤ It's easy to get to: Just open the My Documents icon on the desktop, as shown in the following figure. (You can also get there by selecting the My Documents folder within My Computer or Windows Explorer.)

When you open
this icon...

...Windows 98
displays this folder.

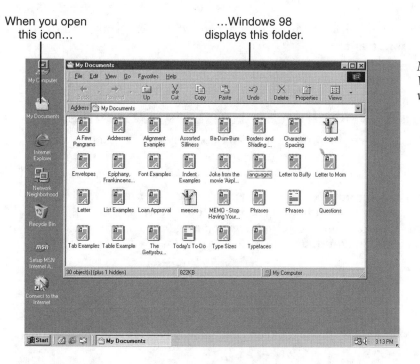

My Documents: Your Windows 98 document warehouse.

Using the Save As Command to Avoid Reinventing the Wheel

As you slave away in Windows 98, you'll sometimes find that you need to create a second, slightly different, copy of a document. For example, you might create a letter and then decide that you need a second copy to send to someone else. Rather than create the entire letter from scratch, it''s much easier to make a copy of the existing document and then change just the address and salutation.

The easiest way to go about this is to use the Save As command. This command is a lot like Save, except that it enables you to save the document with a new name or to a new location. (Think of it as the don't-reinvent-the-wheel command.) To use Save As to create a new document, follow these steps:

1. Open the original document. (If you're not sure how to go about this, skip ahead to the next section, "Together Again: Opening an Existing Document," to find out.)

2. Select the **File**, **Save As** command. The program displays the same Save As dialog box that you saw earlier.

3. Either select a different storage location for the new document or enter a different name (or both).

4. Select Save. The program closes the original document, makes a copy, and then opens the new document.

5. Make your changes to the new document.

Together Again: Opening an Existing Document

After you've saved a document or two, you'll often need to get one of them back onscreen to make changes or review your handiwork. To do that, you need to *open* the document by using any of the following techniques:

➤ **Use the Open dialog box:** Select the program's **File**, **Open** command, or click the Open toolbar button. As you can see in the following figure, the Open dialog box that appears is similar to the Save As dialog box. Find the document you want to open, highlight it, and then click **Open**.

Check This Out

Faster Opening

Pressing **Ctrl+O** in most Window 98 programs also invokes the Open command.

➤ **Use the My Documents folder:** If you're using the My Documents folder to store your stuff, you can open a document by displaying My Documents and then launching the document's icon. (What do I mean by "launching" the icon? If Web integration is on, then click the icon; if Web integration is off, double-click the icon.) You can also highlight the document and then select **File**, **Open**. If the appropriate application isn't running, Windows 98 will start it for you and load the document automatically.

➤ **Use My Computer or Windows Explorer:** Along similar lines, you can also use My Computer or Windows Explorer to open a document. Again, find the document you want and launch its icon.

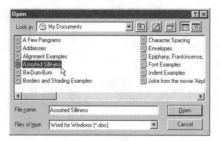

Use the Open dialog box to pick out the document you want to work with.

➤ **Use the Documents menu:** This menu maintains a list of the last 15 documents you opened, as shown in the following figure. To open one of these documents (and, of course, launch the program you used to create the document), select **Start**, **Documents**, and then click the document you want.

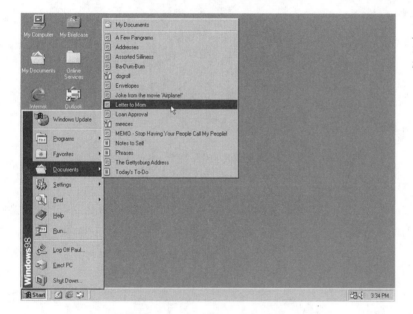

The Start menu's Documents folder keeps track of the last few documents you opened.

Closing a Document

Some weakling Windows 98 programs (such as WordPad and Paint) allow you to open only one document at a time. In such programs, you can close the document you're currently working on by starting a new document, by opening another document, or by quitting the program altogether.

Most full-featured Windows 98 programs let you open as many documents as you want, however. Because things can get crowded pretty fast, though, you'll probably want to close any documents you don't need at the moment. To do this, activate the document you want to close and select the **File**, **Close** command. If you made changes to the document, a dialog box appears asking whether you want to save those changes. Click **Yes** to save, **No** to discard the changes, or **Cancel** to leave the document open.

Chapter 7

Getting Hard Copy: Windows 98 Printing

In This Chapter

➤ Installing a printer in Windows 98

➤ Basic printing steps

➤ Controlling your print jobs

➤ Tips and techniques for perfect printing

What the heck ever happened to the "paperless office" concept? For years, technology pundits assured us that "real soon now" paper documents would be a thing of the past and electronic files would rule the office roost. Geez, if anything, the amount of paper we consume each year has actually *increased*. It seems that people are still fond of hard copies. Part of the reason may be that Windows makes it so darned easy to get your documents from vapor to paper, as you'll see in this chapter. I'll show you how to set up a printer in Windows 98, how to crank out print jobs, and how to control those jobs when they're under way.

Letting Windows Know You've Got a Printer

In the pre-Windows days (the Dark Ages of computing, when a DOS plague infested the land), every program had its own unique way of installing and using a printer. That's all changed because now Windows itself handles all the printing particulars behind the scenes. The main advantage of this for the likes of you and me is that we need only tell Windows about what kind of printer we have. After that, printing from any program is simple because the program just passes the buck to Windows and says, "Here, you do it!"

Even better, there's a special Add Printer Wizard that takes you step-by-step through the entire process of setting up your computer in Windows 98. (In case you don't know, a *wizard* is a special program that displays a series of dialog boxes asking you for information.) Let's run through those steps now:

1. To get the printer installation show on the road, select **Start, Settings, Printers**. Windows 98 opens the Printers folder.

2. Launch the **Add Printer** icon. Windows 98 brings the Add Printer Wizard on stage.

3. The first dialog box just displays some introductory text; click **Next** to move on.

4. If your computer is attached to a network, the next wizard dialog box presents you with two options: Local printer and Network printer (see the following figure). Because this section assumes that you're setting up a printer attached to your computer, make sure that **Local printer** is activated, and then click **Next**.

SEE ALSO

➤ To learn how to set up a network printer, see "Using a Network Printer" in Chapter 26, "Working with Network Connections and Email, " p. 354.

You only see this dialog box if your computer is part of a network.

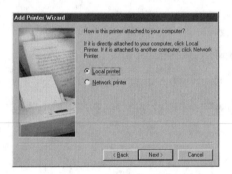

5. The next wizard dialog box, shown in the following figure, lists the hundreds of printers that Windows 98 is on friendly terms with. In the **Manufacturers** list, select the manufacturer of your printer, and in the **Printers** list, select your printer model. Click **Next** to proceed.

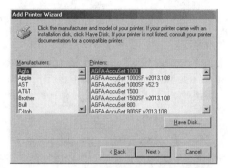

Use this wizard dialog box to select the printer you have.

Can't Find Your Printer?

What do you do if your printer isn't on the wizard's list of printers? You have three choices:

➤ If your printer came with an installation disk, insert the disk, click the **Have Disk** button, and follow the wizard's instructions.

➤ Check your printer manual to see whether the printer works like (or emulates, as the manuals often say) another printer. If it does, see whether you can find the emulated printer in the list. For example, many dot-matrix printer models emulate printers from Epson and IBM. Similarly, many laser printer models emulate the HP LaserJet printer.

➤ If your printer is a dot-matrix, select **Generic** for the manufacturer and **Generic/Text Only** for the printer. For a laser printer, select **HP** for the manufacturer and try the **HP LaserJet** printer.

6. If the printer driver file is already on your hard disk, the wizard gives you two choices (click **Next** when you've made your decision):

Keep existing driver (recommended): This option is activated by default, which is fine because it's the one you'll choose 99 per cent of the time.

Replace existing driver: If you're having trouble printing, one of the solutions you can try is to reinstall your printer in Windows 98. In this case, you need to select the **Replace existing driver** option. If you're not having trouble printing, however, don't select this option because it may affect how your existing programs print.

75

SEE ALSO

➤ *To learn about reinstalling you printer, see the "Repairing Printing Perplexities" section, p. 347, in Chapter 25, "Troubleshooting Windows Woes."*

7. Now the next Add Printer Wizard dialog box, shown in the following figure, asks you to specify which *port* to use with the printer (see the following sidebar for a short port report). Highlight the port to which your printer is attached and click **Next**.

This wizard dialog box wants to know where your printer is attached.

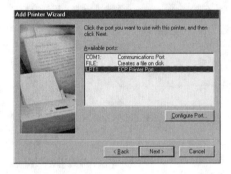

The Printer Port Puzzle

A port is the connection where you plug in the cable for a mouse, printer, or some other computer-related toy. If you're not sure which port is the correct one, check the printer cable connection at the back of your computer. Some thoughtful computer companies actually label their ports—look for something like LPT1 (which is the port used by the vast majority of printers) or COM2. If there are no labels, your computer manual should tell you (provided, that is, you can make heads or tails out of all that geek-speak). If you're still not sure, just choose LPT1 and cross your fingers.

8. The wizard prompts you to enter a name for the printer, as shown in the following figure. You can either leave the suggested name as is, or you can enter a creative 32-characters-or-less name of your own.

Use the Printer name text box to enter a clever name for your printer.

9. The wizard might also ask whether you want the printer to be the *default* for Windows-based programs. (This doesn't happen when you install your first printer.) The default printer is the one that Windows programs use automatically when you run the Print command. If this is the printer you use most of the time, make sure that the **Yes** option is activated. Click **Next** once again. (Don't worry; you're almost out of the wizard woods.)

10. The final wizard dialog box wonders whether you want to print a test page. It can't hurt; make sure that your printer is connected to your computer and that it's fired up. Make sure that the **Yes** option is activated, and then click **Finish**.

11. Now Windows 98 will ask you to insert your Windows 98 CD-ROM. Place the disk in the drive and then click **OK**. Windows 98 copies the files it needs and then cranks out the test page.

12. Another dialog box appears asking you whether the test page printed correctly. If it did (it may take a minute or so for the page to appear), click **Yes**. If it didn't, click **No** to invoke the Help system's Print Troubleshooter.

SEE ALSO

➤ *I discuss Windows 98's Help Troubleshooters in Chapter 25's "Rescue 911: Using Windows 98's Troubleshooters" section, p. 336.*

When the smoke clears, the wizard drops you off at the Printers folder where you'll see a new icon for your printer, as shown in the following figure. That's all she wrote; your printer is now ready for action.

The Printers folder displays icons for all your installed printers.

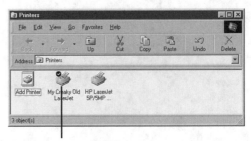

This symbol marks the default Windows printer.

Changing the Default Printer

As pointed out in the previous figure, Windows 98 displays a check mark on the icon of the default Windows printer. If you have multiple printers installed, you can change which one is the default by using either of the following methods:

➤ Highlight the printer you want to be the default and then select the **File, Set as Default** command.

➤ Right-click the would-be default printer and then click the **Set as Default** command in the shortcut menu.

Printing: The Basic Steps

The nice thing about printing in Windows 98 is that the basic steps you follow are more or less identical in each and every Windows program. After you learn the fundamentals, you can apply them to all your Windows applications. Okay, enough jawing. Here are the steps you need to follow:

1. Make sure that your printer is powered up, has plenty of paper, and is online. (*Online* means that your printer is ready, willing, and able to handle the blizzard of characters your program will be throwing at it. Most printers have some kind of Online button that you can press, just to make sure.)

2. In your program, open the document you want to print.

3. Select the **File, Print** command. You'll see a Print dialog box similar to the one shown here for the WordPad word processor.

Putting the Pedal to the Printing Metal

If your fingers are poised over your keyboard, you may find that in most applications pressing **Ctrl+P** is a faster way to get to the Print dialog box.

If you just want a single copy of the document, click the Print toolbar button to bypass the Print dialog box and print the document directly.

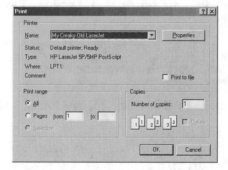

WordPad's Print dialog box is a typical example of the species.

4. The options in the Print dialog box vary slightly from application to application, but you'll almost always see three things:

➤ A drop-down list for selecting the printer to use. In WordPad's Print dialog box, for example, use the **b** drop-down list to select the printer.

➤ A text box or spin box to enter the number of copies you want. In the WordPad Print dialog box, use the **Number of copies** text box.

➤ Some controls for selecting how much of the file to print. You normally have the option of printing the entire document or a specific range of pages. (WordPad's Print dialog box also includes a **Selection** option button that you can activate to print only the currently highlighted text.)

5. When you've chosen your options, click the **OK** button to start printing (some Print dialog boxes have a **Print** button, instead).

Keep watching the information area of the taskbar (the area to the left of the clock). After a few seconds (depending on the size of the document), a printer icon appears, as shown in the following figure. This tells you that Windows 98 is hard at work farming out the document to your printer.

The printer icon tells you that Windows 98 is printing.

Here's the printer icon.

Taking Control of Your Print Jobs

After you send a job to the printer, you normally don't have to bother with it again. Windows 98 just goes about its business behind the scenes—and it's usually best to leave it that way. There may be times when you want to cancel a print job or change the order in which the documents will print, however, and you need to stick your finger in the printing pie to do that.

You can see the list of pending print jobs by using either of the following techniques:

➤ Double-click the taskbar's printer icon. This is your best bet because print jobs can get processed quickly, and speed is of the essence.

➤ Select **Start, Settings, Printers** to display the Printers folder, and then launch the printer you're using.

As shown in the next figure, Windows 98 lists the print jobs in the order they were sent to the printer and displays the following information:

Document Name: The name of the document (duh).

Status: The current status of the print job. You'll usually see either Spooling (which means that Windows 98 is still preparing to print the document) or Printing.

Owner: The username of the person who sent the document to the printer. The username matters only if you set up Windows 98 for multiple users or on a network.

SEE ALSO

➤ *For more information about setting up Windows 98 for multiple users or on a network, see Chapter 26, p. 351.*

Progress: The size of the document and how much of it has been printed.

Started At: The time and date the document was sent to the printer.

"Opening" your printer displays all the pending print jobs.

Here's a review of the tasks you can perform when you have the list of print jobs on-screen:

Pause all the print jobs: If you need to add paper to your printer or change the toner cartridge, you can tell Windows 98 to hold its printing horses. To do this, activate the **Printer, Pause Printing** command. This prevents Windows 98 from sending any more data to the printer. When you're ready to roll again, deactivate the **Printer, Pause Printing** command.

Pause one of the print jobs: If you just want to pause a particular document, click it and then activate the **Document, Pause Printing** command. To resume printing, click the document and deactivate the **Document, Pause Printing** command.

Change the order of the print jobs: If you send more than one document to the printer in a short span of time, Windows 98 starts printing the first document and tells the others to get in line—it's literally called the *print queue*—and wait their turn. If you want to change the order in which these waiting documents will print, all you have to do is use your mouse to drag any document up or down in the list. (Note, however, that you can't supplant the document that's printing—you either have to let it run its course or else cancel it, as explained next.)

Cancel a print job: If you accidentally print the wrong document, or if you simply change your mind about printing it, deleting a print job from the queue is no problem. To do so, highlight the document and select the **Document, Cancel Printing** command.

Canceling all the print jobs: If the whole printing process is a complete fiasco, you can cancel every print job by selecting the **Printer, Purge Print Documents** command.

Chapter 8

Calling Up the Windows 98 Help Desk

In This Chapter

➤ Cranking up the Help system

➤ Searching the Help topics

➤ Getting Web-based Help

➤ A helpful guide to the Help system

This book tells you the easiest and fastest ways to accomplish the most common Windows 98 tasks. I can't cover everything, however, and you may occasionally stumble upon Windows 98 features that leave you scratching your head. To save some wear and tear on your scalp, Windows 98 provides a comprehensive Help system that you can turn to for explanations and instructions. It's not the greatest way to learn new Windows techniques—the Help text is quite sparse and not particularly friendly—but it will do in a pinch. This chapter shows you how the Help system works.

Hungry for More? Here's How to Get It

If you're looking for more Windows 98 know-how, you may be interested in my book *The Complete Idiot's Guide to MORE Windows 98*. That book picks up where this one leaves off, and gives you lots of techniques for getting the most out of Windows 98.

Getting Online Help Onscreen

To get online with the Windows 98 Online Help system, all you have to do is select the **Start**, **Help** command. In a flash, you see the Windows Help window shown in the following figure. The left side of the window holds the list of Help topics, and contains the following three tabs:

Contents: This is the table of contents for the Online Help system. It's discussed in the next section: "Topic Traveling I: Using the Contents."

Index: This is an alphabetical list of topics. See "Topic Traveling II: Using the Index to Find a Topic," later in this chapter.

Search: This tab lets you specify your search text (a word or phrase) and then display a list of all the topics that contain the search text. Check out "Topic Traveling III: Searching for Help Topics," later in this chapter.

The right side of the window is where each Help topic will appear.

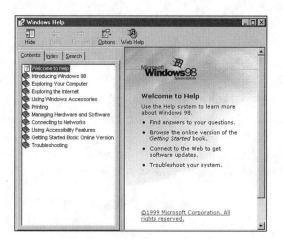

*Select **Start**, **Help** to toss this window onto the screen.*

Topic Traveling I: Using the Contents

The Contents tab sports a list of "books" that contain Help info on a particular subject. You open one of these books by clicking it (or by double-clicking it if you have Web integration turned off). When the book opens, you may see more books. Keep opening these books until you see items with a question mark icon. These are the Help topics. Click a Help topic and the text will appear on the right side of the window.

The next figure shows the screen after I opened the **Explore Your Computer** book, then the **Work with Programs** book, and then clicked the **Start a program** topic.

Click the books to open them.   ...the topic text appears here.

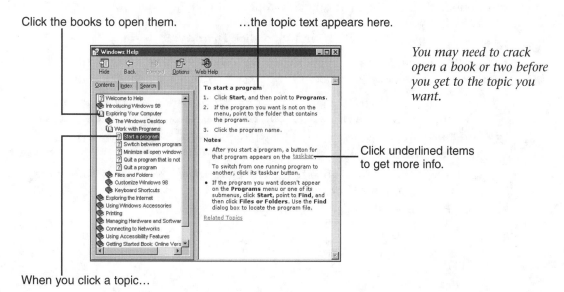

You may need to crack open a book or two before you get to the topic you want.

Click underlined items to get more info.

When you click a topic...

85

Besides reading the topic text, you can also perform any of the following actions:

➤ Click underlined text to jump to more information related to that text.

➤ Click **Related Topics** at the bottom of the window to see a menu of topics related to the current topic.

➤ Click the **Back** button to see the previous Help topic.

➤ If you went back to a topic, click the **Forward** button to return to the topic you just left.

➤ To print the current topic, click **Options** and then click **Print**. The Print dialog box that appears (see the following figure) asks you to choose what to print.

Use the Print dialog box to tell Windows 98 exactly what you want printed.

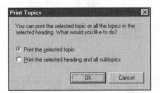

Topic Traveling II: Using the Index to Find a Topic

Getting Online Help up and at 'em is easy enough, but the Contents tab may not be the best way to negotiate the topics. After all, if you find yourself in some strange neck of the Windows woods, you want help fast before panic sets in. If you find yourself constantly opening and closing books in the Contents tab to find the info you need, your clicking finger may wear out before you get there.

A better way is to use the Index tab to type a key word or phrase for the topic you want to find. Help will highlight the first topic that matches what you typed. If that's not quite what you want, scroll up or down the list until the topic is displayed. Then you click the topic to highlight it, and then click **Display**.

Let's run through an example. Suppose you want to find out more about the Notepad accessory. Here's one way to go about it:

1. Display the Index tab. (The first time you do this, Windows 98 displays a windows that says **Preparing index for first use**. This will take a few seconds.)

2. In the text box at the top of the Index tab, type **note**. Help displays the **notebook computers** topic.

3. Scroll down the list until you see the **Notepad** topic. (You could also edit the text box so that it reads **notepad**.)

4. Click the **Notepad** topic.

5. Click **Display**. (At this point, depending on the current topic, Help may display a dialog box that lists a few related topics. If so, use the dialog box to click the topic you want and then click Display.) Help then displays the topic, as shown in the following figure.

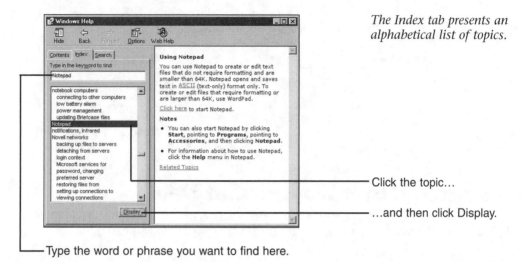

The Index tab presents an alphabetical list of topics.

Click the topic…

…and then click Display.

Type the word or phrase you want to find here.

Topic Traveling III: Searching for Help Topics

The Index tab is well constructed and should suffice for finding most topics. But what if the word you type doesn't correspond to an appropriate topic? Or what if you want to see a list of all the Help topics that contain a particular word?

For these situations, you'll want to give the Search tab a whirl. This tab is a bit like the Index tab because you also have to type a word. In this case, however, Help checks its records and displays a list of every Help topic that contains the word. If you enter multiple words, Help finds all the topics that contain every word you entered.

To try this, select the Search tab, type a word or two, and then click **List Topics**. Help then displays a list of all the topics that contain the word or words you typed. The next figure shows the results when I entered **active desktop** as the search words. Again, you display a topic by clicking it and then clicking **Display**. (Note, too, that Help usually highlights the search words when it displays the topic.)

The Search tab displays a list of Help topics that contain the word or words you type.

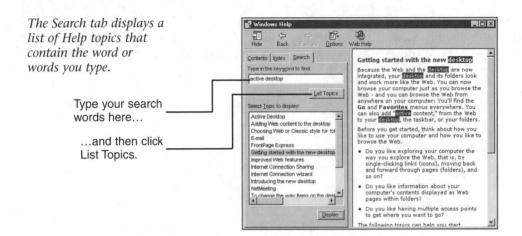

Type your search words here...

...and then click List Topics.

Assorted Other Ways to Get Help

Windows 98 has more ways than ever to access the Help system. In addition to the **Start, Help** command, there are three other methods you can use:

➤ In any program, press F1 to get help that's *context sensitive*. This means that the Help screen that appears is related to the Windows area you're in when you press F1. For example, when you're in WordPad, pressing F1 displays the WordPad Help dialog box with WordPad-specific Help topics.

➤ Most Windows applications have a Help menu that has one or more commands for accessing different parts of the program's own Help system.

➤ Some dialog boxes have a question mark (?) button in the upper-right corner. If you click this button and then click a dialog box control, a pop-up box appears that tells you a bit about the control. This is called, appropriately enough, *What's This?* Help.

Getting Help on the World Wide Web

If you have access to the World Wide Web, Microsoft has a Web site you can turn to for extra technical support. To get there, connect to the Internet and then select **Start, Windows Update**. After you've registered (see Chapter 23's "Getting the Latest and Greatest from the Windows Update Web Site" section) click the **Support Information** link. This displays a page that lists the various support options.

Part III

Customizing Windows 98 to Suit Your Style

Although Windows 98 looks a bit different than it's Windows 95 predecessor, Microsoft still set things up for the "typical" computer user, whoever the heck she is. There are plenty of folks who will enjoy this plain vanilla approach, but the rest of us prefer something with a little more flavor (make mine a mango!). If you'd like to liven up your Windows taste buds, the three chapters here in Part 3 offer some tasty customization treats that should satisfy your sweet tooth. Among other things, I'll show you how to customize the new Web integration and Active Desktop features, how to redo the Start menu and taskbar,, and how to install new software and hardware.

Chapter 9

Webtop Windows: Web Integration and the Active Desktop

In This Chapter

➤ Turning Web integration on and off

➤ Switching folders between Web view and Classic view

➤ Customizing folders

➤ Working with the newfangled Active Desktop

➤ Your welcome to the wonderful world of Web integration

As you saw in Chapter 1, "What's New in Windows 98," Windows 98 is a veritable department store filled with new electronic baubles, beads, and bangles. But of all these newfangled trinkets, perhaps the brightest and shiniest are Web integration and its kissin' cousin, the Active Desktop.

Although I talked a bit about Web integration back in Chapter 2, "Windows 98: The 50¢ Tour," this chapter gives you the full scoop. I'll show you how to turn Web integration on and off, how to view folders and Web pages, how to customize your folders, and how to work with the Active Desktop.

Your Computer as a Web Site: Controlling Web Integration

 When Web integration is turned on, it radically changes the way you operate Windows 98. Here's a summary:

The hyperlink makeover: Windows 98 revamps its icons to make them look like Web page hyperlinks. That is, icon titles get underlined, and when you hover your mouse pointer over an icon, Windows 98 turns the title text blue.

One-click launching: You can launch everything in Windows 98 with a single click. There are now very few areas where you'll still need to double-click anything.

No-click selecting: You select an icon by hovering your mouse pointer over it. After a second or two, Windows 98 will highlight the icon to indicate that it's selected. You can also select multiple icons without having to click a thing, as follows:

➤ To select several icons in a row, move the mouse pointer over the first icon until it's selected. Then hold down Shift and move the mouse pointer over the last icon. Windows 98 will then select all the icons between and including the first and last icons.

➤ To select random icons, hold down Ctrl and move the mouse pointer over each icon in turn. Remember to pause briefly over each icon to give Windows 98 time to select it.

Folders become Web pages: Web integration means that you can view any folder as though it was a Web page.

Turning Web Integration On and Off

Microsoft made it easy to turn Web integration off and on at will. To do so, select the **Start, Settings, Folders Options** command. You'll see the Folder Options dialog box, shown in the following figure. Two of the options in the **General** tab toggle Windows 98 between Web integration and the old Windows 95 interface:

Web style: This is the Web integration option. When you activate this option, Windows 98 asks if you want to use the single-click method for opening icons. Make sure the **Yes** option is activated and then click **OK**.

Classic style: This is the style you may be familiar with from Windows 95. Selecting this option means that you return to double-clicking to launch icons, and single-clicking to select icons.

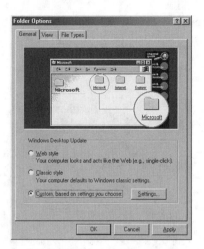

Use the Folder Options dialog box to toggle Web integration on and off.

The General tab also sports a third option: **Custom, based on settings you choose.** This option enables you to create a custom configuration somewhere between Web integration and the classic style. If you activate this option and then click the Settings button that becomes activated, you'll see the Custom Settings dialog box shown on the next page. Here's a rundown of the controls in this dialog box:

Active Desktop: These options enable you to turn the Active Desktop on and off. See the "Desktop Dynamism: Working with the Active Desktop" section, later in this chapter.

Open each folder in the same window: Activate this option if you prefer to navigate folders by using a single window that changes with each opened folder.

Open each folder in its own window: If you prefer to leave the windows open for all the previous folders you display, activate this option instead.

For all folders with HTML content: If you activate this option, Windows 98 displays every folder window as a Web page. (Folders are not shown as Web pages in Windows Explorer.)

Only for folders where I select "as Web Page" (View menu): Activating this setting means that you have to display each folder as a Web page by manually selecting each one. (See "Web View versus Classic View," later in this section.)

Single-click to open an item (point to select): Activating this option turns on the one-click launching and no-click selecting features. Windows 98 also enables the following option buttons:

➤ **Underline icon titles consistent with my browser settings:** If you turn on this option, Windows 98 underlines all the icon titles.

➤ **Underline icon titles only when I point at them:** In this case, Windows 98 applies the text underlining only when you point at an icon.

Double-click to open an item (single-click to select): Activate this option to use the "classic" mouse techniques for launching and selecting icons.

Use this dialog box to set up a custom folder configuration somewhere in between Web style and Classic style.

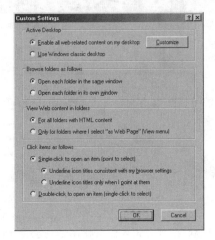

Web View versus Classic View

With Web integration on, the default settings for folders are as follows:

➤ All folder windows appear in Web page view.

➤ Folders displayed in Explorer show only the folder contents.

Either way, you can easily toggle the Web page view on or off for any folder by toggling the **View**, **as Web Page** command on or off. The following figure shows the My Computer folder displayed as a Web page. Note, too, that when you place the mouse pointer over an icon, Windows 98 displays a description of the icon on the left side of the page.

*Use the **View, as Web Page** command to toggle the Web page view on and off.*

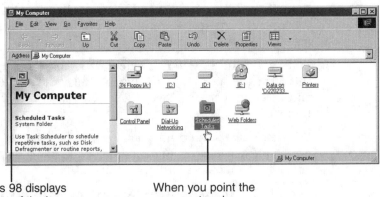

...Windows 98 displays a description of the icon.

When you point the mouse at an icon...

Creating Custom Web Views for Your Folders

The Web view is pretty slick but, surprisingly, the layout isn't fixed. In fact, Windows 98 gives you not one but two ways to customize the Web view for any folder:

➤ You can add a custom background image.

➤ You can tweak the Web page code that displays the Web view.

Note, however, that you can't customize Windows 98's built-in folders, such as My Computer and Control Panel.

The simplest way to give a folder a new look is to specify a custom background image. Here are the steps to follow:

1. Open the folder you want to customize.

2. Select **View**, **Customize this Folder**. Windows 98 loads the Customize this Folder wizard.

3. Activate **Choose a background picture** and click **Next**.

4. In the next wizard dialog box (shown in the following figure), use the list box to choose a background image. If the image you want resides outside the main Windows 98 folder, click **Browse** and select the image you want from the Open dialog box that appears.

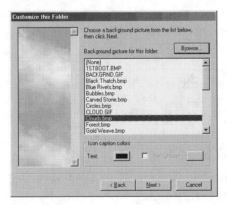

Use this dialog box to choose the background picture and text colors.

5. Use the controls in the **Icon caption colors** group to set the text color of the folder's icon titles.

6. Click **Next**.

7. Click **Finish**. Windows 98 applies the custom background to the folder. The following figure shows an example.

A folder with a back-ground image.

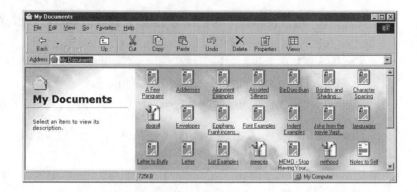

Getting Rid of the Background

Some of the available background images are real eyesores. If you choose an image that you don't like, run the Customize this Folder command again. When the wizard appears, you can choose a different image, or you can remove all folder formatting by activating the Remove customization option.

Modifying the folder background certainly adds a bit of pizzazz to a folder, but there's a lot more you can do. Specifically, if you know how to work with Hypertext Markup Language (HTML), you can use this knowledge to add your own images and text to the Web page view. Here are the steps to follow:

1. Open the folder you want to customize.

2. Select **View**, **Customize this Folder** to launch the Customize this Folder wizard.

3. Activate **Create or edit an HTML document** and click **Next**. The wizard displays a description of what to do.

4. Click **Next**. Windows 98 loads the folder template into Notepad for editing.

5. Modify the template to suit your style.

6. Save your work and then exit Notepad. Windows 98 returns you to the Customize this Folder wizard.

7. Click **Finish**.

Don't Know HTML? No Problem!

If you're not sure about this HTML stuff, may I not-so-humbly recommend my book, The Complete Idiot's Guide to Creating an HTML 4 Web Page. It takes you through everything from the most basic HTML tags to fancy-schmancy things like tables, forms, and style sheets.

Desktop Dynamism: Working with the Active Desktop

A big part of this Web-integration technology is, of course, the Active Desktop, which enables you to do two things:

➤ **Set a background Web page:** Rather than the static backgrounds used in Windows 95, the Active Desktop's background can be a full-fledged Web page, complete with all the images, text, and components that come with the territory.

➤ **Add "Desktop items":** You can also add things called *desktop items,* which sit on top of the desktop background. These items include other Web pages, Java applets, ActiveX controls, and images. Because these items aren't embedded in a Web page, they can be sized and moved on the desktop to achieve the look you want.

Active Desktop Options

As with the other interface changes wrought by Web integration, you can turn the Active Desktop on or off at will. To do so, first select **Start, Settings, Active Desktop**. In the submenu that appears, toggling the **View As Web Page** command on and off will turn the Active Desktop on and off.

With the Active Desktop cranked up, you can now set the background Web page:

1. Select **Start**, **Settings**, **Active Desktop**, **Customize my Desktop**. Windows 98 opens the Display Properties dialog box.

2. Select the **Background** tab.

3. You have two choices at this point:

   ➤ In the **Wallpaper** list, highlight **Windows98** (This is the default Active Desktop background).

➤ Click **Browse** and then use the Browse dialog box to choose a Web page from your computer (or on your network).

4. Click **OK**.

Adding Stuff to the Active Desktop

As I mentioned earlier, you can also plop desktop items on top of your background Web page. To add items to the desktop, follow these steps:

1. Select **Start**, **Settings**, **Active Desktop**, **Customize my Desktop**. Windows 98 opens the Display Properties dialog box and selects the **Web** tab, as shown in the following figure.

Use the Web tab to add desktop items.

2. Click the **New** button. Windows 98 asks whether you want to connect to Microsoft's Active Desktop Gallery Web site. This page contains various items you can place on your desktop, including a stock ticker, a weather map, and more.

3. If you want to see what's on the Active Desktop Gallery site, click **Yes** and you'll be whisked to a page similar to the one shown here.

The Active Desktop Gallery Web site contains all kinds of knickknacks that you can add to your desktop.

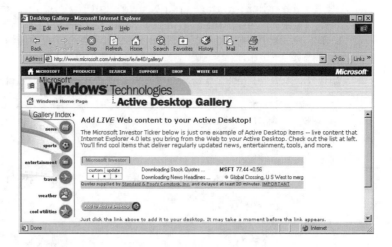

4. In the Gallery index, click a category and then click the link that corresponds to the desktop item you want. Internet Explorer displays a description of the desktop item.

5. Below this description you'll likely see some kind of **Add to Active Desktop** button. Click that button and Internet Explorer will ask whether you want to add a desktop item.

6. Click **Yes**. Now you'll see the Add item to Active Desktop dialog box, shown in the next figure.

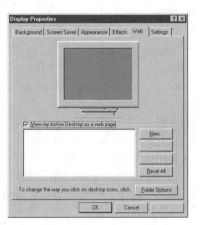

You'll see this dialog box when you add an item to your desktop.

7. What's happening here is that you're "subscribing" to the item, which means it will update on a regular schedule. Click OK to download the item.

SEE ALSO

➤ *I describe subscriptions in detail in the "Hands-Free Surfing: Setting Up Subscriptions" section of Chapter 17, "Wandering the Web with Internet Explorer," p. 216.*

The following figure shows a desktop.

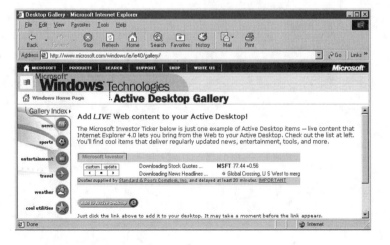

A desktop with a couple of items.

Notice that when you pass the mouse over an item, the item sprouts a border. You can use the following techniques to work with the item:

➤ Drag a border to resize the item.

➤ Drag the top border to move the item.

➤ Click the arrow in the upper-left corner to display the system menu.

➤ Click the **Close** button in the upper-right corner to remove the item from the desktop.

You can also work with your items from the Web tab in the Display Properties dialog box. As you can see in the next figure, Windows 98 displays each installed item in the **Items on the Active Desktop** list. Here's a rundown of the techniques you can use to work with the items from this tab:

➤ To modify an item's properties (such as the subscription schedule), highlight the item and then click **Properties**.

➤ To disable an item, deactivate its check box.

➤ To remove an item from the list, highlight it and click **Delete**. When Windows 98 asks whether you're sure, click **Yes**.

➤ To disable all the desktop items (as well as the underlying desktop Web page), deactivate the **View my Active Desktop as a web page** check box. When you click **OK**, Windows 98 may warn you that the current wallpaper can only be shown if the Active Desktop is enabled. Click **No** to disable the wallpaper.

The Web tab lists all the installed desktop items.

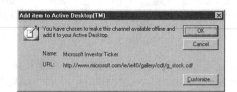

Chapter 10

Customizing the Desktop and Taskbar

In This Chapter

➤ Changing the desktop's colors and background

➤ Customizing the taskbar

➤ Creating Start menu shortcuts for your programs and documents

➤ Remaking the desktop and taskbar in your own image

The previous chapter showed you a few useful techniques for customizing Windows 98's new Active Desktop. If you don't use the desktop's background Web page, however, you're stuck with that vast and wholly uninspiring expanse of teal, right? Not so. The Windows 98 desktop is a flexible piece of digital real estate that gives you a seemingly endless supply of customization options. But that's not all. Windows 98 also offers a fistful of features for giving the taskbar and Start menu a makeover. This chapter gives you the goods on all these customization options.

A Desktop to Call Your Own

If you regularly work with large or maximized windows, you may rarely see your desktop. That doesn't mean, however, that the desktop's umpteen customization options can be dismissed out of hand. Many of these options apply not to the desktop directly, but to objects that appear on the desktop. For example, changing the color of the window title bar affects *all* the windows you work with. This section looks at the various methods you can employ to remake the desktop in your own image.

Renovating the Desktop: Working with the Display Properties

To get started, get the Display Properties dialog box onscreen by using either of the following methods:

➤ **The easy way:** Right-click an empty area of the desktop and click **Properties** in the shortcut menu.

➤ **The hard way:** Select **Start, Settings, Control Panel**. In the Control Panel window, launch the **Display** icon.

Whichever method you choose, the Display Properties dialog box appears, as shown in the following figure.

Use the Display Properties dialog box to customize the look and feel of the desktop.

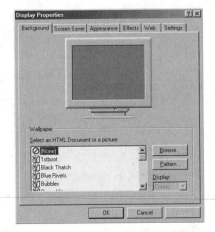

Let's start with the **Background** tab. If you read the previous chapter, you'll recall that you used this tab to select the background Web page for the Active Desktop. If you're just using the basic desktop, however, you can use this tab to spruce up the background with either a wallpaper design or a pattern, as follows:

➤ **Setting the wallpaper:** Use the **Wallpaper** list to browse through the selection of wallpapers. When you see one that sounds like fun, highlight it and check out the sample computer screen. (Note that most of the wallpapers are just tiny squares; to get the full effect, you need to select the **Tile** option in the **Display** list.)

➤ **Setting a pattern:** Windows 98 also comes with a selection of desktop patterns. To pick out one of these patterns, make sure that (None) is selected in the Wallpaper list, and then click the **Pattern** button. Use the Pattern dialog box, shown next, to pick out a pattern you like, and then click **OK**.

104

Use this dialog box to choose a pattern for the desktop background.

Now let's turn to doing Windows colors. For this use the **Appearance** tab, shown in the following figure. The easiest way to change Windows 98's colors is to select one of the predefined color schemes from the **Scheme** list. Here are some notes to bear in mind:

➤ These schemes control the colors of just about everything you see in Windows, including the desktop background, the pull-down menus, and all the window nuts and bolts (the title bars, borders, scroll bars, and so on).

➤ The box above the **Scheme** list contains a couple of phony windows—one active and one inactive—and a pretend dialog box. By looking at the way your color choices affect these objects, you can see what havoc each scheme will wreak on your desktop, without actually changing anything.

➤ If your eyesight isn't what it used to be, Windows 98's title bar and dialog box text may be a strain on your peepers. If so, try out any of the Scheme items that have (large) or (extra large) in their names—such as Rose (large) or Windows Standard (extra large).

These fake windows show what effect the selected scheme will have.

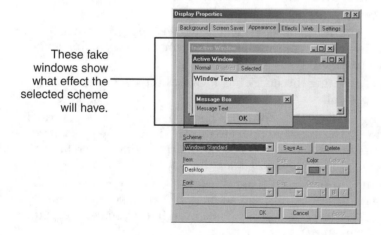

Use the Appearance tab to select a different Windows 98 color scheme.

105

Custom Color Schemes

If you feel really brave, you can create your own color scheme. To do this, use the **Item** drop-down list to select the element you want to work with (such as Desktop or Active Title Bar), and then use the **Color** list to change its color. (In some cases, you can also change the element's Size and Font.) When you're finished, click **Save As**, enter a name for the new scheme in the dialog box that appears, and then select **OK**.

 The controls in the **Effects** tab (see the next figure) deal with settings related to the desktop icons. Here's a rundown of the goodies you get on this tab:

➤ **Desktop icons:** This group lets you modify the icon for the three basic desktop folders: My Computer, Network Neighborhood, and Recycle Bin (both the full and the empty icons). Highlight the icon you want to change, click the **Change Icon** button, choose the new icon from the Change Icon dialog box, and click **OK**. To change an icon back to its original form, highlight it and click the **Default Icon** button.

➤ **Hide icons when the desktop is viewed as a Web page:** If you activate this check box, Windows 98 removes the desktop icons whenever you clothe the desktop in its Web page garb.

➤ **Use large icons:** Activating this check box increases the size of the desktop icons by about 50 percent.

➤ **Show icons using all possible colors:** When activated, this check box tells Windows 98 to use all the available colors to display the desktop icons. If you have a slower computer or video card and you find that Windows 98 takes a long time to refresh your desktop, deactivate this option.

➤ **Animate windows, menus and lists:** When this option is activated, Windows 98 displays menus by using an animation that makes the menus appear to "scroll" onto the screen. That's kinda neat, but if you deactivate this feature, the menus will appear a bit faster.

➤ **Smooth edges of screen fonts:** If you activate this check box, Windows 98 smoothes the jagged edges of large fonts, which makes them more readable.

➤ **Show window contents while dragging:** This check box toggles a feature called *full-window drag* on and off. When it's deactivated, Windows 98 shows only the outline of any window you drag with the mouse (by dragging the title bar); if you activate full-window drag, however, Windows 98 displays the window's contents while you're dragging.

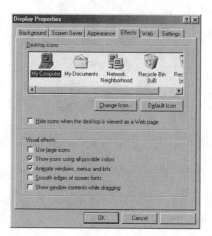

The Effects tab controls the look of the desktop icons.

Screen Saver Silliness

A screen saver is a moving pattern that displays after you haven't used your computer for a while. To set up a screen saver in Windows 98, click the **Screen Saver** tab in the Display Properties dialog box, and then choose the one you want from the **Screen Saver** list. Use the **Wait** spin box to set the amount of time your computer must be inactive before the screen saver starts doing its thing. You can enter a number between 1 and 60 minutes.

The **Settings** tab of the Display Properties dialog box, shown in the following figure, controls various properties of your video display. Here's a summary:

➤ **Screen area**: This slider controls the screen resolution, which measures the number of dots (pixels) Windows 98 uses to display screen images. For example, a resolution of 800 by 600 means that your screen uses 800 columns of dots and 600 rows of dots. Move the slider to the left to get a lower resolution; move the slider to the right to get a higher resolution.

➤ **Colors:** The values in this list determine the number of colors Windows 98 uses to display screen images. (High Color gets you about 65,000 colors, and True Color gets you about 16 million colors). The more colors you use, the better your screen images will appear, although using lots of colors may slow down machines that don't have a lot of horsepower. Changing these setting may also affect programs that are optimized to use a different number of colors.

107

Use the Settings tab to customize your video display.

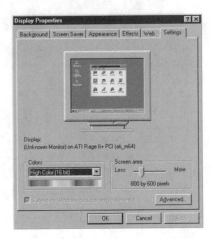

If you change the resolution or the number of colors, Windows 98 may display the Compatibility Warning dialog box shown here. In most cases, you can get away with activating the **Apply the settings without restarting?** option and clicking **OK**.

Windows 98 enables you to make changes to the display settings without having to restart your computer.

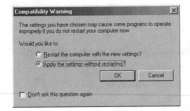

If you click the **Advanced** button and choose the **General** tab in the dialog box that comes your way, you'll be faced with the following video nuggets:

➤ **Font Size:** This list contains settings that control the size of the Windows 98 system font (the font Windows 98 uses for objects such as desktop icons, taskbar text, dialog boxes, menus, and windows).

➤ **Show settings icon on task bar:** When this check box is activated, Windows 98 adds a display settings icon to the system tray. Clicking this icon produces a list of all the resolutions and color depths your video card supports. Click one of these values to change your display settings.

➤ **Compatibility:** These options determine what Windows 98 does when you change the number of colors. The default is **Ask me before applying the new color settings**, which tells Windows 98 to display the dialog box shown in the previous figure. You can use the other options to tell Windows 98 to either restart the computer or apply the new setting automatically.

Creating Shortcuts on the Desktop

For our next desktop customization trick, I'll show you some methods for creating shortcuts directly on the Windows 98 desktop. Why would you want to do that? Well, because anything on the desktop is accessible with a simple click (assuming that Web integration is turned on), there are lots of good reasons for such convenience:

➤ If you have a favorite program buried under interminable Start menu folders, placing a shortcut for it on the desktop lets you crank it up lickety-split.

➤ If you have a document you use regularly (such as a to-do list or, like me, a never-put-off-until-tomorrow-what-you-can-put-off-until-the-day-after-tomorrow list), you can create a shortcut for the document to keep it within easy reach.

➤ If you do a lot of work in a particular folder, you can create a shortcut for the folder. Clicking the folder's shortcut icon opens the folder right away. (No more wading through windows in My Computer, or tracking down the folder in Windows Explorer.)

➤ You can also create shortcuts for disk drives. For example, you might want to add a shortcut for your CD-ROM drive or for a floppy disk drive.

➤ The Start menu's Favorites folder stores your most-surfed Web sites. For even easier access to a fave site, however, you can add a shortcut for a Web site to the desktop.

➤ Printers are shortcut candidates, too. If you create a printer shortcut, you have quick access to your printer's folder so that you can watch the progress of your print jobs. You can also drag a document from Explorer or My Computer, drop it on the printer shortcut, and Windows 98 will print it for you, no questions asked!

A Desktop Shortcut Bonus

As an added bonus, if you have a folder or disk drive shortcut on the desktop, you can move or copy files by dragging them from Windows Explorer or My Computer and dropping them on the shortcut.

To create a shortcut, first rearrange your windows so that you can see an empty chunk of the desktop. Now right-drag the program, document, folder, drive, Control Panel item, printer, or whatever from Explorer (or My Computer) and drop it on the desktop. In the shortcut menu that appears, click **Create Shortcut(s) Here**, as shown in the following figure.

Desktop shortcuts give you easy access to programs, files, folders, drives, printers, and more.

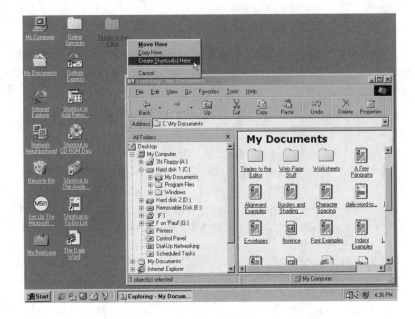

This figure also shows my desktop with a random sampling of shortcuts. Notice that each shortcut icon has a small arrow in its lower-left corner; this is Windows 98's way of telling you that an icon is a shortcut.

Arranging Desktop Icons

Are you wondering how I got my shortcuts to line up in apple-pie order in the previous figure? It's easy: Just right-click an empty part of the desktop, click **Arrange Icons** in the shortcut menu, and then click **by Name**, **by Type**, **by Size**, or **by Date**, by Jove. Neat freaks can also activate the **Auto Arrange** command to tell Windows 98 to keep the desktop spic-and-span all the time.

To delete a shortcut, either right-click it and select **Delete** from the menu, or drag the shortcut and drop it on the **Recycle Bin**. (If you use the right-click method, a dialog box appears asking whether you're sure you want to delete the shortcut. In this case, select **Yes**.) Note, however, that deleting a shortcut does *not* delete the program, file, folder, or whatever—only the shortcut icon.

Touching Up the Taskbar

As you've seen throughout most of this book, the taskbar and the Start menu are two of Windows 98's truly indispensable features. It's nice to know that, handy as they are, there are ways to make both the taskbar and the Start menu even handier. It's all done through the Taskbar Properties dialog box, which you can plop onto the desktop by using either of the following methods:

➤ Select **Start, Settings, Taskbar & Start Menu**.

➤ Right-click an empty part of the taskbar and click **Properties** in the shortcut menu.

Windows 98 displays the Taskbar Properties dialog box, shown next. The rest of this section gives you the scoop on the options available in the Taskbar Options tab. I'll turn to the Start Menu Programs tab a bit later. When you complete your labors in this dialog box, select **OK** to put your changes into effect.

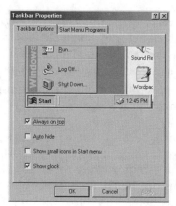

Use the Taskbar Properties dialog box to renovate the taskbar and Start menu.

Watch the Sample Taskbar

The Taskbar Options tab displays a sample taskbar and Start menu in a box above the check boxes. As you play with the various settings, keep an eye on this area to see what effect each option has on the taskbar.

The **Taskbar Options** tab presents several check boxes that control the behavior of the taskbar. Here's a rundown:

➤ **Always on top:** As you saw back in Chapter 4, "Working with Windows 98's Windows," when you maximize a program's window, it enlarges to consume all the screen *except* the taskbar. If you want to eke out a little bit of extra screen acreage for your programs, deactivate the **Always on top** check box. Then, when you maximize a program, its window takes up the entire screen, taskbar and all. To see the taskbar again, press **Ctrl+Esc** to display the Start menu, and then press **Esc**.

➤ **Auto hide:** This check box gives you a better way to create more room for your programs. When you activate **Auto hide**, Windows 98 reduces the taskbar to a thin, gray line at the bottom of the screen whenever you work in a program's window. This gives you, effectively, the entire screen to work with. The trick, though, is that you can redisplay the full taskbar simply by moving your mouse pointer to the bottom of the screen. Move the mouse back up again, and the taskbar retreats to its gray line.

➤ **Show small icons in Start menu:** Activating this check box reduces the icons used for each item in the Start menu to smaller, cuter, versions of themselves. Although this makes each icon a little harder to see, it reduces the overall size of the Start menus, which makes them a bit easier to navigate.

➤ **Show clock:** This check box toggles the clock in the bottom-right corner on and off. If you're not into time, man, deactivate this check box.

Although you'll probably only work with, at most, a few programs at once, Windows 98's multitasking capabilities sure make it tempting to open a boatload of applications. The problem, though, is that it doesn't take long for the taskbar to become seriously overpopulated. With 10 programs on the go, the taskbar buttons become all but indecipherable. ("Hey, Vern! What's this here 'Ph...' program supposed to do?") If you can't figure out what a particular taskbar button represents, point your mouse at the button that puzzles you, and after a couple of seconds a banner appears telling you the full name of the program.

If you'd prefer to take in everything at a glance and you don't mind giving up a little more screen area, you can expand the taskbar to show two or more rows of buttons. To give 'er a go, follow these steps:

1. Point your mouse at the top edge of the taskbar. When it's positioned properly, the pointer changes to a two-headed arrow.

2. Drag the edge of the taskbar up until you see a second row appear in the taskbar area. You should now see the taskbar buttons on the bottom row and the Quick Launch icons on the top row.

3. Point your mouse at the left edge of the taskbar buttons. Again, the pointer will change to a two-headed arrow.

4. Drag the taskbar buttons up into the second row and drop them to the right of the Quick Launch icons.

Reconstructing the Start Menu

When you install a program, it's usually decent enough to add an icon for itself to your Start menu. Most DOS-based programs wouldn't know the Start menu from a Denny's menu, however, and they won't create Start menu icons for themselves. DOS programs, Windows-ignorant savages that they are, have an excuse, but you may come across a few ornery Windows-based programs that won't do it, either. That means you have to add these programs to the Start menu manually (ugh). To try it, follow these steps:

1. Select the **Start Menu Programs** tab in the Taskbar Properties dialog box.

2. Click the **Add** button to display the Create Shortcut dialog box, shown in the next figure.

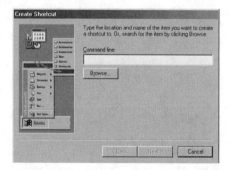

Use the Create Shortcut dialog box to fire a program onto the Start menu.

3. If you happen to know the name of the file that starts the program, and if you know the drive and folder where it resides, type all that in the **Command line** text box. For example, suppose that the file that starts your program is WP51.EXE, and it's on drive C in the WP51 folder. You would enter the following in the **Command line** box: **c:\wp51\wp51.exe**.

If you're not sure about any of this, select the **Browse** button to display the Browse dialog box, hunt down the file that starts the program, highlight it, and then click **Open**.

4. Click **Next**. Windows 98 displays the Select Program Folder dialog box, shown here.

*Use the Select Program
Folder dialog box to pick
out a Start menu home
for your program.*

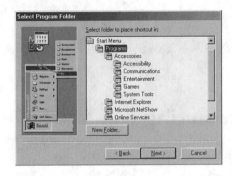

5. Highlight the folder where you want the program's icon to appear. Note that if you highlight Start Menu, the icon appears on the main Start menu (the one that appears when you click the Start button). If you highlight Desktop, the program's icon appears right on the Windows 98 desktop.

6. Click **Next**. The Select a Title for the Program dialog box appears.

7. Use the **Select a name for the shortcut** text box to enter the name you want to appear on the Start menu, and then click Next. The Select an Icon dialog box appears.

8. Highlight the icon you want to use for the shortcut.

9. Click **Finish** to, well, finish.

Starting Programs Automatically When You Start Windows 98

Windows 98 has a slick feature that makes starting programs a breeze: the Startup folder. The icons you stuff into this folder load automatically each time you start Windows 98. This is great for applications, such as WordPad or Explorer, that you use constantly or for documents (such as a to-do list) that you start up first thing every day.

Use the same technique I outlined in this section to create a Start menu icon for the program or document. When you get to step 5, highlight the **Startup** folder. When you finish, you can see what's in your Startup folder by selecting **Start**, **Programs**, **Startup**.

As you'll see in Chapter 11, "Installing and Removing Software and Hardware," Windows 98 has a feature that enables you to "uninstall" some programs.

SEE ALSO

➤ *"Kicking a Program Off Your Computer" in Chapter 11, p. 122.*

One of the chores this feature takes care of for you is to expunge any traces of the program from the Start menu. If it misses something, however, or if you need to get rid of a Start menu shortcut that you added manually, you need to clean up the Start menu yourself.

To try it, select the **Start Menu Programs** tab in the Taskbar Properties dialog box, and then click the **Remove** button to display the Remove Shortcuts/Folders dialog box. Open the folder containing the shortcut, highlight the shortcut, and then click **Remove**. Select **Close** to head back to the Taskbar Properties dialog box.

If that sounds like too much work, you're right, it is. An easier way is to open the Start menu folder that contains the shortcut you want to delete, right-click the shortcut, and then click **Delete** in the menu that appears. Click **Yes** when Windows 98 asks if you're sure.

Chapter 11

Installing and Removing Software and Hardware

In This Chapter

➤ Installing chunks of Windows 98

➤ Installing new programs and hardware

➤ Saying sayonara to Windows 98 components

➤ Saying adios to programs and devices you no longer need

➤ A treasure trove of techniques for renovating your Windows 98 house

One of the major problems with computers is that installing new hardware and software gizmos isn't as easy as it should be. I'm convinced that Murphy must have just finished setting up some kind of computer doohickey when he formulated his famous Law—If anything can go wrong, it will.

I suppose that the makers of Windows 98 must have become fed up dealing with installation irritations, because they built several features into Windows 98 that make setting up and removing both hardware and software practically painless. This chapter checks out these features and shows how they can make your life easier.

The Ins and Outs of Software Installation and Removal

Most new PCs come stocked with a few programs, but it's a rare computer owner who's satisfied with just these freebies (or even wants them in the first place). Most of us want something better, faster, *cooler*. If you decide to take the plunge on a new program, this section shows you how to install it in Windows 98. To get you started, however, I'll show you how to install new Windows 98 components.

Adding and Removing Windows 98 Components

Like a hostess who refuses to put out the good china for just anybody, Windows 98 doesn't install all its components automatically when you run the Windows Setup program. Don't feel insulted; Windows is just trying to go easy on your hard disk. The problem, you see, is that some of the components that come with Windows 98 are software behemoths that will happily usurp acres of your precious hard disk land. In a rare act of digital politeness, Windows bypasses these programs (as well as a few other nonessential tidbits) during a typical installation. If you want any of these knick-knacks on your system, you have to grab Windows 98 by the scruff of its electronic neck and say "Yo, bozo! Install this for me, will ya!"

Now, you're probably saying:

That's all well and good, Author Boy, but this is the first I've heard about Windows 98 having a neck. Don't I just rerun the installation program?

Nope. The good news about all of this is that Windows 98 comes with a handy "Windows Setup" feature that enables you to add any of Windows 98's missing pieces to your system without having to trudge through the entire Windows installation routine. Here are the steps to follow:

1. Select **Start, Settings, Control Panel** to display the Control Panel window.
2. Open the **Add/Remove Programs** icon. Windows 98 tosses the Add/Remove Programs Properties dialog box onto your screen.
3. Select the **Windows Setup** tab, shown here. (Windows 98 takes inventory of the currently installed components, so this tab takes a few seconds to appear.)

The Windows Setup tab lets you add the bits and pieces that come with Windows 98.

4. The **Components** box lists the various chunks of Windows 98 that are already installed as well as those you can add. You have two ways to proceed:

> ➤ To add an entire component, activate its check box.

> ➤ To add only part of a component (assuming that it has multiple parts), click **Details**, use the new dialog box to activate the check boxes for the subcomponents you want to install, and click **OK**.

5. Click **OK**. Windows 98 will likely ask you to insert your Windows CD-ROM.

6. Insert the disc and click **OK** to continue.

7. Depending on the components you add, Windows 98 may ask you to restart your computer. If it does, click **Yes** to let Windows 98 handle this for you. When the restart is complete, the new components are ready to roll.

Welcoming a New Program onto Your Computer

Before Windows 98 came along, you were on your own when it came time to install a program on your system. Now, however, that's all changed. In your program's journey from floppy disk to hard disk, you can bring along Windows 98's Add/Remove Programs Wizard, which will walk you through a series of dialog boxes to get the program's installation show on the road.

Before I show you the "prestidigital" tricks the Add/Remove Programs Wizard has up its sleeve, there's a chance you might not have to bother with any of that hocus-pocus. Why? Well, when you read Chapter 21, "Bells and Whistles: Multimedia and Windows 98," you'll see Windows 98 has an *AutoPlay* feature. If a CD-ROM disc supports AutoPlay, it means that the disc runs its application automatically as soon as you plop the disc in the CD-ROM drive.

Interpreting the Check Boxes

Here's a translation of what the various check box states mean in the Windows Setup tab:

Unchecked: The component is not installed. If the component comes in several pieces, none of those pieces is installed.

Checked with a gray background: The component is partially installed. That is, the component has multiple chunks, but only some of those chunks reside on your system.

Checked with a white background: The component is installed. If the component comes in several pieces, all of those pieces are installed.

To find out how many of the component's pieces are installed, check out the **Description** box; below the component description, you'll see something like **15 of 20 components selected**. This tells you that the component consists of 20 programs and only 15 of them are installed on your system.

But what if you have to install the application first? Ah, in this case, most AutoPlay CDs will crank up their installation programs automatically after you insert the disc. For example, a few seconds after I insert my Microsoft Bookshelf 1998 CD, I see the following dialog box. All I have to do is click **Continue** and the installation proceeds without further ado.

If your program comes on CD-ROM, your first task is to insert the disc and see whether anything happens. If not, don't sweat it because you can always fall back on the Add/Remove Programs Wizard. Here are the steps to plow through:

1. Select **Start, Settings, Control Panel** to get to the Control Panel window.

2. Open the **Add/Remove Programs** icon.

3. Make sure that the **Install/Uninstall** tab is visible.

4. Click the **Install** button. The dialog box that appears asks you to insert the first installation disk or the program's CD-ROM.

5. Insert the appropriate disk and click **Next.** The wizard checks all your floppy and CD-ROM drives, searching desperately for any installation program it can find:

➤ If it locates a likely candidate, it displays it in the **Command line for installation program** text box, as you can see in the following figure.

➤ If it doesn't find an installation program, the wizard asks you to enter the appropriate command in the **Command line for installation program** text box. If you know where the installation program is located, type the drive, folder, and filename. You can also click **Browse** to use a dialog box to pick out the program.

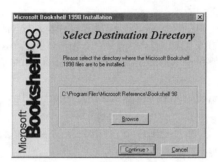

CD-ROMs that support AutoPlay are often kind enough to launch their installation programs automatically when you insert the disc.

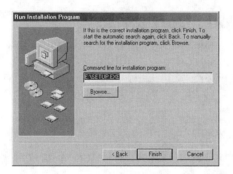

The Add/Remove Programs Wizard can hunt down your software's installation program automatically.

6. Click **Finish**. Windows 98 launches the installation program.

7. Follow the instructions that appear.

Removing a Windows 98 Component

You've seen how the Windows Setup feature makes it easy to bring Windows 98 components in from the cold of the CD-ROM to the warmth of your hard drive. What happens, though, if you grow tired of a particular component's company? For example, the artistically challenged may want to get rid of that Paint program they never use, or the hopelessly unwired may be itching to expunge HyperTerminal from their systems.

Happily, with Windows Setup, giving these and other Windows 98 components the bum's rush is even easier than installing them. And as an added bonus, lopping off some of Windows' limbs serves to free up precious hard disk space, giving you more room for *really* important games—uh, I mean, applications. As you might expect, removing Windows 98 components is the opposite of adding them:

1. Select **Start, Settings, Control Panel** to display the Control Panel window.

2. Open the **Add/Remove Programs** icon.

3. Display the **Windows Setup** tab.

4. Deactivate the check boxes for the components you want to blow away. For multiprogram components, click **Details** to see the individual programs, deactivate the check boxes for those you want to nuke, and then click **OK** to return the Windows Setup tab.

5. Click **OK**. Windows 98 removes the components you specified without further delay.

6. Depending on the components you removed, Windows 98 may ask to restart your computer. If so, click **Yes** to make it happen.

Kicking a Program off Your Computer

If you have a Windows application that has worn out its welcome, this section shows you a couple of methods for uninstalling the darn thing so that it's out of your life forever. The good news is that Windows 98 has a feature that enables you to vaporize any application with a simple click of the mouse. The bad news is that this feature is only available for some programs.

To check whether it's available for your program, follow these steps:

1. Display the Control Panel by selecting **Start, Settings, Control Panel**.

2. Open the **Add/Remove Programs** icon.

3. Make sure that the **Install/Uninstall** tab is visible.

4. As shown in the following figure, the bottom half of the Install/Uninstall tab displays a list of the programs that Windows 98 knows how to remove automatically. If the program you want to blow to kingdom come is on this list, highlight it and then click the **Add/Remove** button.

5. What happens next depends on the program. You may see a dialog box asking you to confirm the uninstall, or you may be asked whether you want to run an "Automatic" or "Custom" uninstall. For the latter, be sure to select the **Automatic** option. Whatever happens, follow the instructions on the screen until you return to the Install/Uninstall tab.

6. Click **OK** to wrap things up.

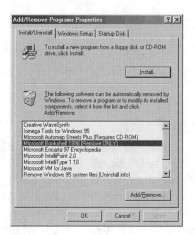

The Install/Uninstall tab maintains a list of programs that you can annihilate automatically.

For those applications that can't be uninstalled automatically, you need to roll up your sleeves and do the whole thing by hand. Here's what to do:

1. Use Windows Explorer or My Computer to display the program's folder.

2. Check to see whether the folder contains any data files you want to preserve. If you spent any time at all creating documents (or whatever) in the application, it's a wise precaution to save them for posterity. For one thing, you may want to use them in another application; for another, you may change your mind six months from now and decide to reinstall the application. If you want to save your data, highlight the files and then *move* (not copy) them to another folder, or to a floppy disk.

3. With that step out of the way, go ahead and delete the application's folder.

SEE ALSO

➤ *Not sure how to delete a folder? See the "Deleting Your Folders" section in Chapter 14, "Storage Solutions: Working with Folders and Floppy Disks," p. 151.*

4. Erase any traces of the program from your Start menu.

SEE ALSO

➤ *To learn how to do this, refer to the "Reconstructing the Start Menu" section in Chapter 10, "Customizing the Desktop and Taskbar," p. 113.*

5. If the program added any shortcuts to the desktop, delete them, too.

6. To be safe, exit and then restart Windows 98.

Handling Hardware Installation and Removal

Playing around with your computer's hardware is usually a job best left to serious geeks. This is especially true if the hardware is part of your computer's delicate and not-to-be-messed-with-lightly innards. Having said that, however, there are a few external hardware upgrades that are well within the abilities of all but the most dedicated technophobes. For example, you can install most external devices—such as a mouse, modem, CD-ROM drive, printer, and scanner—simply by connecting a cable to the appropriate port in the back of the computer. This section assumes that you have a piece of hardware that's easy to add and remove, and shows you how to use Windows 98 to work with that hardware.

Adding a New Hunk of Hardware

In the prehistoric age of computing (before Windows 95), getting a lump of hardware attached to your computer was the easy part. The real challenge occurred afterward when you had to configure the hardware to ensure that it wouldn't conflict with any of the other devices in your system. This was rarely a simple task. In most cases, it required settings to be tweaked, switches to be flipped, hair to be pulled, moons to be howled at, and hardware deities to be placated with the appropriate sacrifices.

Thankfully, you can now move beyond these arcane rites into an era of easy and painless hardware installation. The reason is that Windows 98 now supports a wonderful initiative called *Plug and Play*. This means that, in most cases, when you add a new device to your system, turn it on (if necessary), and then restart the computer, Windows 98 recognizes the device automatically and makes the appropriate adjustments. (The latter process may require you to insert your Windows 98 CD-ROM or one of the floppy disks.)

Happy Hardware Trails

For best results, make sure that you buy hardware that's Plug and Play-compatible. This should be mentioned somewhere on the box. If you don't see anything about Plug and Play (or PnP, as Plug and Play is usually abbreviated), chances are the device doesn't support it. (You may want to ask the salesperson, just to be safe.) Getting a Plug and Play device ensures that Windows 98 will "communicate" with the device and grill it for the info that Windows 98 needs for proper setup.

Part IV

Windows 98 "F" Words: Files, Folders, and Floppy Disks

You'll spend the bulk of your Windows 98 life involved in creative pursuits such as writing letters and memos, building spreadsheets, and drawing icons and logos. At some point, however, these relatively glamorous activities will have to give way to the grunt work of dealing with files and folders and such. If that kind of stuff ranks right up (or down, as the case may be) there with things like root canal and paying taxes, I have some good news. Windows 98 comes with a couple of useful tools—called My Computer and Windows Explorer—that reduce the effort required for dealing with files, folders, and floppy disks, too. (Gruntless grunt work!) The three chapters here in Part 4 show you how to wield these tools.

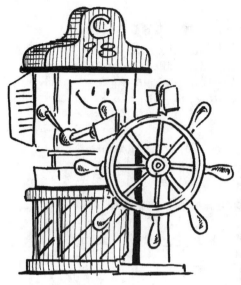

Chapter 12

Navigating Your Computer with My Computer and Windows Explorer

---

In This Chapter

➤ Getting to know the My Computer window

➤ Checking out Windows Explorer

➤ Customizing My Computer and Windows Explorer

➤ Navigation techniques using the Windows equivalent of maps and compasses

---

Using the Start menu to launch programs or open documents is analogous to traveling by airplane, because you don't need to know how you get from here to there. You just pick your destination (program or document) and leave the navigating up to the flight crew (Windows 98).

What if you have to perform a chore such as renaming or deleting a file or folder? In this case, you need to traverse the highways and byways of your system to find the thing you want to work with. You have to navigate your system yourself, which means that you're going on more of a road trip than a plane trip. Happily, you don't need an armful of maps and compasses to get around your system because Windows 98's My Computer and Windows Explorer tools offer everything you need. This chapter shows you the basics of navigating your system using these tools.

Using My Computer to Tour Your Machine

Because My Computer is a bit simpler than its Windows Explorer cousin, I'll use it to begin our journey. To get My Computer on the road, double-click the **My Computer** icon on the desktop. (Remember: If you have Web integration turned on, you'll only need to click My Computer.) You should now see a window that looks something like the one shown here.

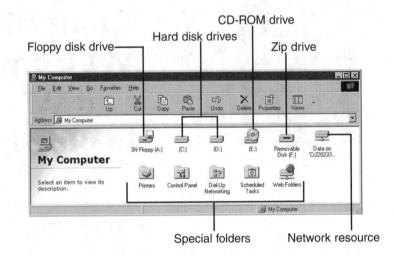

My Computer's icons represents the various components attached to your computer.

The My Computer window is like a map that lays out all of your computer's landmarks. With the exception of a few special folders, each of the icons you see represents a computer component, such as a floppy drive, hard disk drive, or CD-ROM drive.

With this map in hand, you continue on your journey by clicking the icon you want to work with. For example, the following figure shows the window that appears when I open a hard disk drive (drive C). As you can see, Windows 98 again represents everything with an icon. In my case, I have three folders on this hard disk—My Documents, Program Files, and Windows—as well as a few files.

The contents of my hard disk drive (drive C).

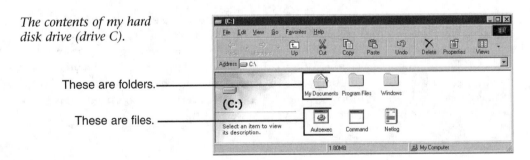

Files, Folders, and Disks Made Easy

If you're a little shaky when it comes to files and folders, it might help to think of your computer as a filing cabinet. In particular, imagine a filing cabinet where each drawer represents a disk drive on your computer. What do you find when you open a drawer in a typical filing cabinet? Folders, of course, lots of folders. Disk drives, too, can have lots of folders. In this case, you can think of a folder as just a chunk of disk real estate set aside for storage. As with filing cabinet folders, computer folders usually contain only related items.

What kinds of "related items" am I talking about? Most filing cabinet folders contain memos, invoices, letters, lists, contracts, artwork, and whatever else relates to the subject of the folder. The computer equivalents of these items are *files*.

And just as a filing cabinet folder may contain other folders, so too can a hard disk folder contain other folders. These are called *subfolders*.

To see the contents of a folder, give it a double-click. For example, try opening your Windows folder. (At this point, you'll see a warning about viewing the contents of the Windows folder. Say "Tough beans!" and click the **Show Files** link to see the contents.) A new window appears, similar to the one shown here.

As you can see, the Windows folder contains all kinds of interesting looking file icons. The icons indicate the type of files they represent. For example, the icon shown with the files named Black Thatch and Carved Stone is the icon for the Paint program, so these are files you could work with in Paint.

Note, too, that the Windows folder contains even more folders, which are known as *subfolders*. You can continue opening these subfolders to march ever deeper into the folder forest. How do you get back out, though? First you need some lingo: The folder-subfolder connection is often regarded as a sort of parent-child relationship because a subfolder is, in a sense, the "offspring" of the main folder. (I know, I know: The geeks who make up this stuff *really* need to get out more.) Anyway, given this parent-child malarkey, here's a summary of the techniques you use to navigate folders in My Computer:

➤ To display the parent folder, either click the **Up** button in the toolbar or select **Go, Up One Level**.

The contents of my Windows folder.

These are subfolders.

These are files.

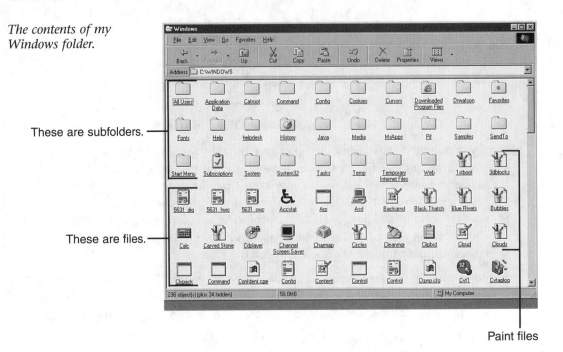

Paint files

➤ To return to the previous folder you viewed, either click the **Back** button or select **Go, Back**.

➤ To return to any previously viewed folder, click the Back button's arrow to drop down a list of the folders you've visited, as shown in the following figure. Then click the one you want to display.

Click this arrow to drop down the list.

Drop down the Back button to return to a previously viewed folder.

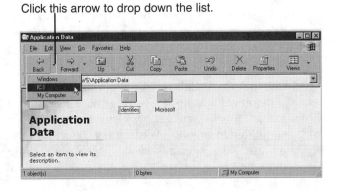

➤ After you've gone back to a folder, you can use the Forward button to head in the opposite direction. To move ahead to the next folder, either click the **Forward** button or select **Go, Forward.** You can also click the Forward button's arrow to see a list of folders.

Folder Navigation Shortcuts

Here are a few keyboard shortcuts you might want to use while navigating folders:

➤ Press **Backspace** instead of clicking the Up button.

➤ Press **Alt+Left arrow** instead of clicking the Back button.

➤ Press **Alt+Right arrow** instead of clicking the Forward button.

➤ The File menu also keeps track of the last few folders you visited. To head for a recent folder, pull down the **File** menu and select one of the folder names that appears near the bottom of the menu.

➤ Use the **Address** list to jump anywhere on your system. As you can see in the next figure, this list contains not only the various My Computer icons, but also the icons that appear on your desktop.

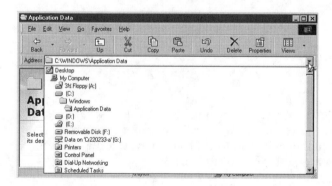

Use the Address list to leap anywhere on your system in a single bound.

Customizing the My Computer Window

My Computer is stocked with a few options and settings that can help make things a bit easier to manage. This section shows you how to customize these settings to suit the way you work.

By default, My Computer shows you just the name and icon for each folder or file. You can adjust this display to show more items or to show more detail about each item. Both the **View** menu and the **Views** toolbar button offer the following choices:

➤ **Large Icons:** This is the default view in My Computer.

➤ **Small Icons:** This view switches to smaller icons so that you can see more items within the window. As you can see in the following figure, the icons are displayed in rows (that is, left to right and down the window).

My Computer, using the
Small Icons view.

➤ **List:** This view also uses smaller icons, but it displays them in vertical columns.

➤ **Details:** This view shows you not only the name and icon, but also the size of the file, the type of file, and the date and time it was last modified. The next figure shows the Windows folder in Details view.

My Computer, using the
Details view.

Click here to see
the Views list.

My Computer normally shows your files in alphabetical order by name, which makes it easy to find the file you want. The **View, Arrange Icons** command, however, displays a cascade menu that enables you to choose how you want the icons arranged. You have five commands at your disposal:

➤ **by Name:** This is the default sort order.

➤ **by Type:** Sorts the files in alphabetical order by file type.

➤ **by Size:** Sorts the files in ascending order by file size.

➤ **by Date:** Sorts the files in ascending order by the last modified date.

➤ **Auto Arrange:** When this command is activated, Windows 98 rearranges the icons automatically whenever you change the size of the window. (Note that this command doesn't work in Details view.)

When working in Details view, mouse users get a couple of bonus customization techniques, as seen in the next figure:

➤ You can sort the contents of a My Computer window by clicking the buttons that sit at the top of each column. For example, click the **Size** button to sort the contents by size. (To reverse the sort order, click the column button again.)

➤ To adjust the width of a column, point the mouse at the right edge of the column's button. The pointer will change to a two-headed arrow, as shown in the figure. Now drag the pointer left (to get a narrower column) or right (to get a wider column).

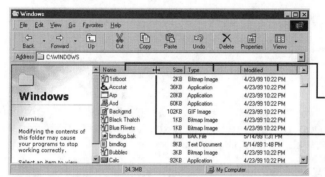

In Details view, you can use the column buttons to sort the contents and adjust the column width.

Click these buttons to sort the folder contents.

Drag the right edge of a column button to change the column's width.

Another Route: Using Windows Explorer

My Computer is simple to use, but many folks have trouble with it because they get lost after opening a subfolder or two. Those people often prefer the bird's-eye view of the system that they get with Windows Explorer. This section shows you how to use Windows Explorer for all your file and folder fun and games.

To get Windows Explorer's motor running, select **Start, Programs, Windows Explorer**. You'll see a window like the one shown in the following figure.

As you can see, Windows Explorer looks a lot like My Computer. The big difference is that the window is split into two lists:

Folders: This list gives you access to everything on your system. It remains onscreen at all times, so that you can easily choose a different folder and you always know where you are within the folder levels.

Contents: This is the right side of the Windows Explorer window and, like My Computer, it displays icons for what's in the current folder. In this case, though, the current folder is the one that's selected in the Folders list.

Let's play around a bit with Windows Explorer so that you can get comfortable with it and you know exactly what you're dealing with.

Windows Explorer lets you see disk drives and folders in one fell swoop.

The Folders list

The Contents list

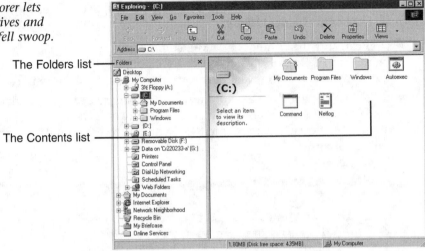

First, click the **Desktop** item at the top of the Folders list. In the next figure, notice that the contents of the Desktop item are precisely the same doodads that appear on the Windows 98 desktop! Well, at least that makes sense.

With Desktop high-lighted, notice that the items in the Contents list exactly match the items on the desktop itself.

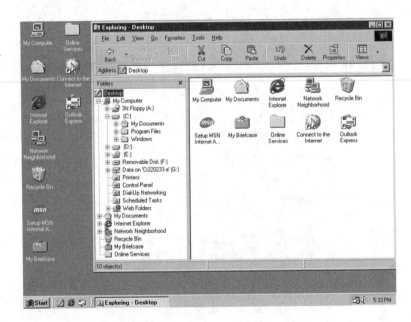

Okay, time for experiment number two. See the minus sign (–) to the left of My Computer in the Folders list? Go ahead and click that. You just simplified the Folders list so that it looks like the one shown in the following figure.

134

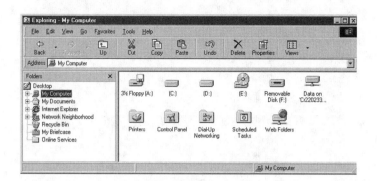

The simplified Folders list.

Notice in this figure that I highlighted the My Computer item. You can see in the Contents list that the contents are exactly the same as they were in the My Computer window I showed you earlier. In other words, Explorer is just a different way of looking at the same thing.

To see how this difference can come in handy, click the plus sign (+) beside the My Computer item. This returns you to your original Explorer view. Notice, though, that when Explorer opens My Computer, its contents appear in the Folders list and they branch off from the My Computer item. This is the fundamental way you work with the Folders list. To summarize:

> **To expand a branch,** click the plus sign (+) to the left of the folder's name. (If the plus sign is too small a target, you can also double-click the folder's name.)

> **To collapse a branch,** click the minus sign (–) beside the folder's name. (You can also double-click the folder's name.)

The advantage of this approach is that instead of getting where you want to go by navigating through all kinds of folders and subfolders in My Computer, you can just open the appropriate "branch" in the Folders list and then highlight it. The subfolders and files contained in that folder then appear in the Contents list.

Customizing Windows Explorer

One last thing to note: Most of the options I told you about earlier for My Computer apply also to Windows Explorer. In particular, you can display large icons, small icons, or file details in the Contents list, you can sort the Contents list in various ways, and you can adjust column widths in Details view.

Windows Explorer also enables you to adjust the width of the Folders list and the Contents list. To do this, point your mouse at the divider bar that separates the two lists. As you can see in the next figure, the pointer changes to a two-headed arrow. Now drag the pointer left or right to adjust the widths as necessary.

You adjust the list widths by dragging the divider bar left or right.

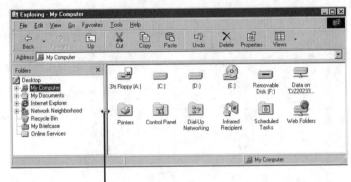

The pointer changes to a two-headed arrow on the divider bar.

Chapter 13

Routine File Maintenance

In This Chapter

➤ Copying and moving files

➤ Renaming and deleting files

➤ Searching for files

➤ Drag–and–drop demystified

➤ A slew of file maintenance shortcuts and speedups

We keep our cars looking good by performing routine maintenance chores such as washing the exterior, vacuuming the interior, and cleaning out any detritus that has accumulated in our travels. You keep the disks and folders on your computer looking good by performing various file-maintenance chores such as copying and moving files to different locations, renaming files, and deleting files you no longer need. This chapter gives you step-by-step instructions for performing all of these chores.

First Things First: How to Select Files

Before you can do anything to a file, you have to select it. For a single file, use one of the following methods:

➤ If Web integration is on, point at the file until it's highlighted.

➤ If Web integration is off, click the file.

SEE ALSO

➤ *For the full scoop on this Web integration business, see the "Turning Web Integration On and Off" section, p. 94, in Chapter 9, "Webtop Windows: Web Integration and the Active Desktop."*

If you need to work with multiple files, Windows 98 lets you select them all and then work with the selected files as a unit. Here are three methods you can use:

➤ If the files you want to work with are all in a row, select the first file, hold down the **Shift** key, and then select the last file.

➤ If the files aren't displayed consecutively, you can select files randomly by holding down the **Ctrl** key and selecting each file. Release Ctrl after you've selected all the files.

➤ To select a group of files, "lasso" them with your mouse. Move the mouse pointer beside the first file (make sure that it's not over the file's name or icon), and then drag the mouse to form a box around the files. As you're dragging, Windows 98 displays a dotted box, and every file that falls within that box becomes highlighted (see the following figure). When you have all the files you need, release the mouse button.

You can select a group of files by dragging your mouse over them.

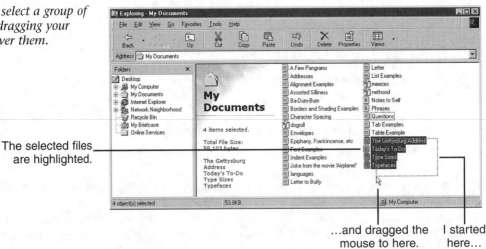

The selected files are highlighted.

...and dragged the mouse to here.   I started here...

Selecting Everything

To select everything inside a folder, either run the **Edit, Select All** command or press **Ctrl+A**.

A Few File Chores

With all those handy selection tricks up your sleeve, you can now turn your attention to some file fiddling. Here's a rundown of the various chores I'll take you through in this section:

Copying files: In an office, photocopying memos, reports, and various parts of one's anatomy (after hours, of course) is a big part of the everyday routine. In your computer, you'll find that copying files, whether you copy them from one part of your hard disk to another or between your hard disk and a floppy disk, is one of your most common chores. Check out the next section, "From Here to There: Copying and Moving Files."

Moving files: When you copy a file, the original stays put, and Windows 98 creates an exact replica in the new location. If you don't want to keep the original, however, you need to pack up the file and *move* it instead of copying it. Fortunately, as you'll see soon enough, moving stuff in Windows 98 doesn't require hunting down boxes and tape or hiring big, beefy guys to sweat all over your possessions.

Renaming a file: If you don't like the name of one of the files you've created, you can easily rename it to something you can live with. For example, if you have a Christmas present wish list document named "Christmas Goodies 1998" that you want to reuse in 1999, you can rename the file to "Christmas Goodies 1999." See "A File By Any Other Name: Renaming a File," later in this chapter.

Deleting files: In real estate, it's taken for granted that property values will always rise because nobody's making any more land. This is true in hard disk real estate, as well. As applications (especially Windows applications) become bigger and bigger, your hard disk becomes more and more cramped. (Remember how huge it seemed when you first got it?) In the "Deleting a File (and Undeleting It, Too)" section, you learn how to free up disk space by deleting files you no longer need. And just in case you delete a vital file by accident, I also show you how to use the Recycle Bin to get a file back.

From Here to There: Copying and Moving Files

Let's begin by looking at three different methods for copying and moving files:

➤ Using the Copy or Cut commands
➤ Using drag-and-drop
➤ Using the Send To command

Here are the steps to follow to copy or move one or more files, using the Copy or Cut method:

1. Select the file or files you want to work with.

139

2. Pull down the **Edit** menu and select one of the following commands:

    Copy: Select this command if you want to copy the files.

    Cut: Select this command if you want to move the files.

3. Open the folder or disk drive that you want to use as the destination.

4. Run the **Edit, Paste** command. Windows 98 then copies or moves the files to the destination. Depending on the size of the file and the destination you chose, this may take as little as a few seconds or as much as a few minutes.

Shortcuts for Moving and Copying

Note that the Copy, Cut, and Paste commands are all available from the shortcut menus. (For example, right-click the selected files and then click Copy or Cut.)

Also, here's a summary of the toolbar and keyboard shortcuts you can use instead of the Copy, Cut, and Paste commands:

Click This	Or Press This	To Do This
✂]	Ctrl+X	Cut the selected file
📄]	Ctrl+C	Copy the selected file
📋]	Ctrl+V	Paste the cut or copied file

Okay, let's see how the drag-and-drop method works. Note, first of all, that you need to use Windows Explorer for this. Here's a blow-by-blow account of the steps to follow:

1. In the Folders list, open the branches until the destination folder is visible.

2. In the Contents list, select the file or files you want to copy or move.

3. Now hold down one of the following keys:

    Ctrl: Hold down this key to copy the files.

    Shift: Hold down this key to move the files.

4. Drag the selected files toward the destination folder. If you're copying the files, the mouse pointer shows a little square with a plus sign (+) attached to it. (The next figure shows a file in mid-drag.) The plus sign is Windows 98's way of telling you that you're copying the file.

5. Move the mouse over the destination folder, release the mouse button, and then release **Ctrl** or **Shift**. Windows 98 copies or moves the files to the destination.

Right-Drag to Be Sure

If you have trouble remembering which key to hold down for a copy or a move, you can avoid them altogether by right-dragging the selected files. When you drop them on the destination, Windows 98 displays a shortcut menu with Move Here and Copy Here commands. Just click the command you want.

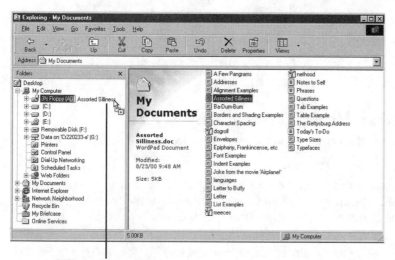

When you drag a file, the mouse pointer shows the file name. The little square with the plus sign (+) tells you that you're copying the file.

A file in the process of being dragged.

A good chunk of your file-maintenance labors involve copying files to a floppy disk to make backup copies of important data or for transportation to another machine. Here's an easy way to go about this:

1. Make sure that there's a disk in the floppy drive.

2. Select the file or files you want to copy.

3. Run the **File, Send To** command (or right-click the selected files and click **Send To** in the shortcut menu that appears). As you can see in the following figure, selecting **Send To** produces a submenu that lists, among other things, your floppy drive (or drives, if you have more than one).

4. Click the floppy drive command from this menu. Windows 98 copies the file to the floppy without further prodding.

The File menu's Send To command displays a list of locations where you can copy a file.

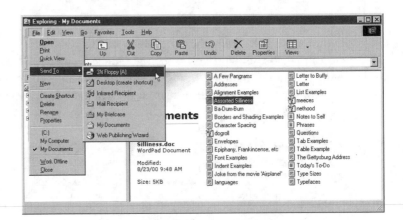

A File by Any Other Name: Renaming a File

Renaming is easy, as you'll see when you follow this procedure:

1. Select the file you want to rename.

2. Open the filename for editing by either running the **File, Rename** command or by pressing **F2**. Windows 98 creates a text box around the filename, highlights the name, and throws in an insertion point cursor for good measure (see the next figure).

3. Edit the name just as you would any text in a text box.

4. When you're finished, press **Enter** to remove the text box and confirm the new name.

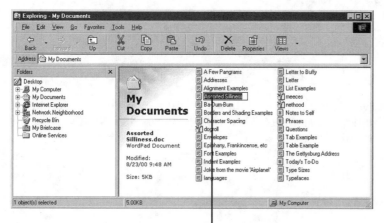

When you tell Windows 98 that you want to rename a file, a text box shows up so that you can edit the name as you see fit.

A filename ready for editing.

Some Renaming Caveats

When renaming your files, you need to watch out for a couple of things. First of all, remember that although Windows 98 is happy to accept long filenames (up to 255 characters) with spaces in them, it chokes on names that include the following characters: \ | ? : * " < >

Also, rename only those files that you've created yourself. Any other files on your computer are probably used by your programs (or Windows 98 itself), and those programs can be quite picky about what names these files have. If you mess around with the wrong file, your program may refuse to play with you anymore.

Deleting a File (and Undeleting It, Too)

Okay, it's time to take out the garbage, electronically speaking. Here are the steps you follow to delete a file:

1. Select the file or files you want to delete.

2. Run the **File, Delete** command. Windows 98 displays the Confirm File Delete dialog box (shown here) to ask whether you're sure you want to go through with the deletion.

143

Windows 98, ever cautious, asks whether you're sure you want to delete the poor file.

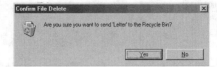

3. After giving the whole thing a second thought (and maybe even a third, just in case), click **Yes** to delete the file. (Alternatively, you can click **No** if you get cold feet at the last second.)

Shortcuts for Deleting

Here's a summary of the toolbar and keyboard shortcuts you can use to delete a file (and to get it back if you make a mistake):

Click This	Or Press This	To Do This
✕]	Delete	Delete the selected file
↩]	Ctrl+Z	Undo the last action

One of the sad realities of computing life is that sometime, somewhere, you'll accidentally delete some crucial file that you would give your eyeteeth to get back. Well, I'm happy to report that you can keep your teeth where they are because Windows 98's Recycle Bin is only too happy to restore the file for you.

 You should know, first off, that if the deletion was the last thing you did, you don't have to bother with the Recycle Bin. Just pull down the **Edit** menu and select the **Undo Delete** command to salvage the file.

You should know, second off, that if you have Windows 98 Second Edition, you can reverse the last *ten* actions you performed. Again, you pull down the **Edit** menu and select the **Undo *Whatever*** command (where *Whatever* is the name of the command, such as Delete).

Otherwise, you have to trudge through these steps:

1. Open the Recycle Bin folder. If you're in Explorer, click **Recycle Bin** in the Folders list. Otherwise, open the desktop's **Recycle Bin** icon.

2. Select the file or files you want to undelete.

3. Run the **File, Restore** command. (Note that you can also right-click the selected files and then click Restore in the shortcut menu.) The Recycle Bin instantly returns the file to its original location, safe and sound. (Insert sigh of relief here.)

The Inner Mysteries of the Recycle Bin

Holy Lazarus! How the heck can the Recycle Bin restore a deleted file?

Good question. You can get part of the answer by looking at the Recycle Bin icon on your Windows 98 desktop. It looks like a garbage can, and that's sort of what the Recycle Bin is. Think about it: if you toss a piece of paper in the garbage, there's nothing to stop you from reaching in and pulling it back out. The Recycle Bin operates the same way: It's really just a special hidden folder (called Recycled) on your hard disk. When you delete a file, Windows 98 actually moves the file into the Recycled folder. So restoring a file is a simple matter of "reaching into" the folder and "pulling out" the file. The Recycle Bin handles all this for you (and even returns your file *sans* wrinkles and coffee grounds).

Keep in mind that the Recycle Bin has a finite size. When the Recycle Bin gets full, Windows 98 gets rid of the oldest deleted files to make room for new ones. If you want, you can adjust the size of the Recycle Bin and a few other settings. To do this, right-click the Recycle Bin and click Properties to get the Recycle Bin Properties dialog box, shown in the following figure.

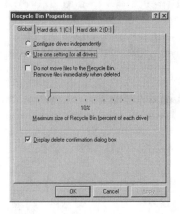

Use this dialog box to set some Recycle Bin properties.

For starters, you need to decide whether you want separate Recycle Bin settings for each of your hard disks (assuming, of course, that your system has multiple hard disks):

➤ **Configure drives independently:** Activate this option to use separate settings for each disk. For example, if you have a disk that's perilously low on free space, you'll probably want to configure that disk with a smaller Recycle Bin.

➤ **Use one setting for all drives:** Activate this option to use one set of options for all your hard disks.

After that's done, you can manipulate the rest of the settings. Each tab has the following options:

➤ **Do not move files to the Recycle Bin. Remove files immediately when deleted**: Activate this option to bypass the Recycle Bin for all deletions. Activating this command is living dangerously, so I do not recommend doing so!

Bypassing the Recycle Bin

Even if you leave the **Do not move files to the Recycle Bin. Remove files immediately when deleted** check box deactivated, you can still bypass the Recycle Bin by holding down the **Shift** key while you delete a file.

Note, too, that files deleted from removable disks—such as floppy disks and Zip disks—are *not* sent to the Recycle Bin.

➤ **Maximum size of Recycle Bin (percent of each drive):** This slider controls the maximum amount of hard disk acreage that the Recycle Bin usurps on all the drives. The default is 10%, which is probably a bit high (100 megabytes on a 1 gigabyte drive!). Note, however, that the lower the value, the fewer files the Recycle Bin can store.

Finally, the Global tab also has a **Display delete confirmation dialog box** check box. If you deactivate this option, Windows 98 doesn't prompt you for confirmation when you select the Delete command or press the Delete key.

Easier File Maintenance with the Open and Save As Dialog Boxes

When you're working in an application, you'll find you often need to perform one or two quick file-maintenance jobs (such as renaming or deleting a file). It often feels like overkill, however, to have to crank up My Computer or Windows Explorer, find the folder you want, select the file, and then run the necessary commands. Fortunately, Windows 98 gives you a more convenient way to handle these kinds of quickie tasks.

If the application is built specifically for Windows 95 or Windows 98 (as are, say, WordPad and Paint) and you have a mouse, you can handle a good chunk of your file labors in the program's Open and Save As dialog boxes. All you do is open either dialog box, find the file you want to work with, and then right-click it. As you can see in the next figure, the shortcut menu that appears sports all kinds of file-related commands, including Send To, Cut, Copy, Delete, and Rename.

SEE ALSO

➤ *For more information about the Open and Save As dialog boxes, refer to Chapter 6, "A Few Workaday Document Chores," p. 63.*

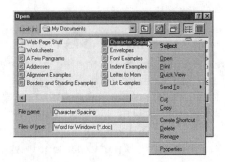

In the Open or Save As dialog boxes, right-click a file to get a handy menu of file-maintenance commands.

Finding File Needles in Hard Disk Haystacks

Today's behemoth hard disks can easily hold hundreds or even thousands of files. If you use your computer a lot, you know it's no sweat to add to this hard disk overpopulation by creating dozens of your own documents. It's inevitable that you'll misplace the odd file from time to time. Instead of wasting time scouring your folders, however, why not let Windows 98's Find program do the work for you?

Find is available from the Windows Explorer and My Computer windows as well as from the Start menu. Here are the three methods you can use to fire it up:

➤ In Windows Explorer, highlight the disk or folder in which you want to search, and then select the **Tools, Find, Files or Folders** command.

147

▶ In My Computer, highlight the disk or folder in which you want to search, and then select the **File, Find** command.

▶ Select **Start, Find, Files or Folders**.

In each case, the Find window leaps onto the desktop (see the following figure).

Use the Find program to scour your computer for a particular file.

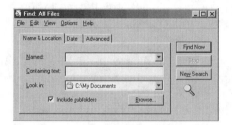

Now let's examine the steps you need to follow to get Find on the trail of your long-lost file:

1. Use the **Look in** drop-down list to tell Find where you want it to snoop for the files. Either select a location from the list or click **Browse** to choose the location from the Browse for Folder dialog box.

2. If you want Find to look also inside whatever subfolders might exist in your selected location, make sure that the **Include subfolders** check box is activated.

3. Use the **Named** text box to tell Find the name of the file you want to track down. Fortunately, you don't have to type the entire name (a blessing if the file you're looking for has a lengthy moniker). Your best bet is to enter only one word or part of a word from the filename. (The problem with entering multiple words is that Find matches any files that contain one word *or* the other.)

4. If you know that the file you want contains a particular word, type that word in the **Containing text** box.

5. Click the **Find Now** button. Find forages through the drive or folder you selected and displays its results in the box at the bottom of the window. The following figure shows an example.

If Find locates one or more matching files, it displays them in a list at the bottom of the window.

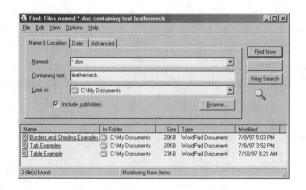

148

6. From here, you can use the commands on Find's File and Edit menus to do what you will with the file. (If you want Windows 98 to open the selected file's folder, run the **File, Open Containing Folder** command.)

7. When you're finished with Find, you can shut it down by selecting the **File, Close** command.

Here are a few notes to bear in mind when using Find:

➤ To give your searches extra flexibility, the **Named** text box also accepts wildcard characters. Use the question mark (?) to substitute for a single character and the asterisk (*) to substitute for multiple characters. For example, ***.doc** finds all files that use the .DOC extension. Similarly, **?o?ato.doc** finds file names such as potato.doc and tomato.doc (but not potatoe.doc).

➤ If you know, more or less, when the file was created or when it was last modified, you can narrow your search criteria even further. Select the Date tab to display the controls shown in the next figure. Activate the **Find all files** option and then work with the following controls:

between: Activate this option and then use the two calendar boxes to select a date range.

during the previous *x* month(s): Activate this option to narrow the search to the previous number of months you enter in the spin box.

during the previous *x* day(s): Activate this option to narrow the search to the previous number of days you enter in the spin box.

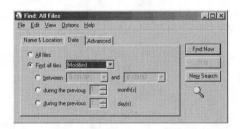

Use the Date tab to search for files by date.

➤ The Advanced tab gives you two more options:

Of type: This drop-down box contains a list of all the file types that Windows 98 knows how to deal with.

Size is: Use these controls to specify a file size. In the drop-down list, select either **At least** or **At most**; in the spin box, enter a value in kilobytes.

Chapter 14

Storage Solutions: Working with Folders and Floppy Disks

In This Chapter

➤ Creating new folders

➤ Copying, moving, and deleting folders

➤ How to format a disk

➤ Creating an emergency startup disk

➤ More drag-and-drop shenanigans

Now that you've got files all figured out, it's time to tackle two more Windows 98 "F" words: *folders* and *floppies* (floppy disks). To that useful end, this chapter shows you various techniques for fiddling with folders, including how to make 'em, move 'em, and even delete 'em. No rest for the weary, however, because then you'll head right into a few floppy disk chores, including copying and formatting disks, and how to create that all-important "emergency startup disk" thingy.

Folder Folderol: Working with Folders

Way back in Chapter 6's "Saving Your Work for Posterity" section, I told you that your hard disk is the home that your documents return to when they've finished walking the Windows 98 streets. Like any cozy house, your hard disk haven is divided into separate rooms. These are called *folders*, and you use them as storage areas for related documents.

Now you may be saying to yourself (you aren't' talking out loud while reading this book, are you?)...

Wait just a second, bucko. Didn't you also say in Chapter 6 that Windows 98 has a My Documents folder or something? Why don't we just use that?

Oh, you will. But you don't store all your house stuff in a single room, do you? You've got utensils and appliances in the kitchen, tools in the workshop, and things you can't deal with right now off in a corner of the basement. So why not bring a bit of organization to your hard disk home, as well? For example, you could start off with the My Documents folder, and then create a Memos subfolder to hold your office notes. You could also erect a Letters subfolder for your correspondence, a Shocked and Appalled subfolder to hold your letters to the editor, and so on. And if several people (such as your spouse and kids) have access to your computer, you can set up a separate subfolder for each person.

On the downside, this will require a bit of folder maintenance on your part, but nothing that's too onerous. The next few sections tell you everything you need to know: how to create a new folder, how to copy and move a folder, how to rename a folder, and how to delete a folder you no longer need.

Creating a Shiny, New Folder

There's no time like the present, as they say, so let's get right to the steps you need to follow to create a bouncing baby folder:

1. In My Computer or Windows Explorer, select the folder in which you want to create your new folder. For example, if you want to put your new folder in My Documents, select the **My Documents** folder.

2. Select the **File, New, Folder** command. (You can also right-click inside the folder and then click **New, Folder** in the shortcut menu.) Windows 98 tosses a new subfolder onto the screen and displays **New Folder** in a text box.

3. Because "New Folder" isn't a particularly descriptive name, use the text box to type a new name (as shown in the next figure) and then press Enter. Folder names follow the same rules as file names: 255 characters max, and spaces are okay but the following characters are not: \, ? : * " < >

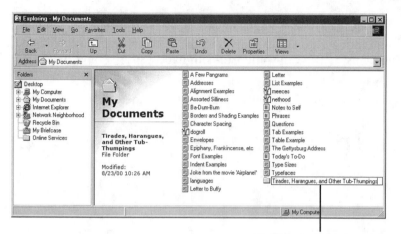

When you create a new folder, Windows 98 provides you with a text box so that you can enter a proper name for the folder.

Use this text box to enter a
catchy name for the new folder.

Remember when I showed you how to use the new Open and Save As dialog boxes for file maintenance in the last chapter? Interestingly, you can use these same dialog boxes to create new folders, as well. This is particularly handy if you create a new document in a Windows program, select the Save command, and then realize that you need to store this particular document in a new folder. Instead of firing up Windows Explorer and running through the rigmarole outlined above, you simply click the New Folder button (shown in the next figure), type the name of the folder, and then press Enter.

SEE ALSO

➤ *For that information, refer to the "Easier File Maintenance with the Open and Save As Dialog Boxes" section in Chapter 13, "Routine File Maintenance," p. 147.*

When you click the
New Folder button...

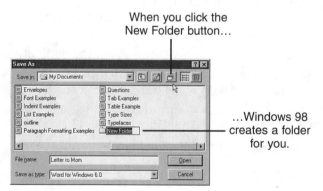

...Windows 98
creates a folder
for you.

You can convince Windows 98 to build a new folder right from the Save As or Open dialog boxes.

Copying and Moving a Folder in a Single Bound

Just as you can copy and move files, as I explained in the last chapter, you can also copy and move folders by using the Copy and Cut commands, or by doing the drag-and-drop thing.

Here are the instructions for copying or moving one or more folders, using the Copy or Cut commands:

1. Select the folder or folders you want to work with.

Selecting Folders

You can select folders by using the same file-selection techniques I made you suffer through in Chapter 14's "First Things First: How to Select Files" section. Note, too, that you can also use Windows Explorer's Folders list to select a folder to work with. You can only select one folder at a time in the Folders list, however.

2. Pull down the **Edit** menu and choose one of these commands:

   Copy: Select this command if you want to copy the folders. (Alternatively, you can press **Ctrl+C** or right-click the selected folders and then click **Copy** in the shortcut menu.)

   Cut: Select this command if you want to move the folders. (You can also either press **Ctrl+X** or right-click the folders and then click **Cut** in the shortcut menu.)

3. Open the folder or disk drive that you want to use as the destination.

4. Select the **Edit, Paste** command. Windows 98 then copies or moves the folders to the destination. This may take a while if the folders contain lots of files.

Here's how the drag-and-drop technique works:

1. In Windows Explorer's Folders list, open the branches until the destination folder is visible.

2. In the Contents list, select the folder or folders you want to copy or move.

3. Now hold down one of the following keys:

   Ctrl: Hold down this key to copy the folders.

   Shift: Hold down this key to move the folders.

4. Drag the selected folders, drop them on the destination folder, and then release **Ctrl** or **Shift**. Windows 98 copies or moves the folders to the destination.

Renaming Your Folders

After you've created a new folder, you may decide that you don't like the name you gave it. That's not a problem because you can rename a folder just as easily as you rename a file. Here's what you do:

1. Select the folder you want to rename.
2. Put the folder name inside a text box for editing, either by selecting the **File, Rename** command or by pressing **F2**.
3. Edit the name as you see fit.
4. Press **Enter** when you're finished.

A Warning for Would-Be Movers and Renamers

You should only move or rename those folders and subfolders that were created with the sweat of your own brow. All the other folders on your system were put there either by Windows 98 or by the programs you use. Changing even a single letter of one of these folders can put an application in a huff and make it refuse to run.

Deleting Your Folders

When a folder you created has outlived its usefulness, you should delete it to keep your hard disk free of clutter. Here's how it's done:

1. Select the folder or folders you want to blow away.
2. Run the **File, Delete** command (or just press the **Delete** key). Windows 98 displays the Confirm Folder Delete dialog box, which asks whether you're sure you want to remove the poor folder.
3. To get on with the deletion, click **Yes**. If you change your mind, click **No**, instead.

Can a killed folder be resurrected from the dead? Absolutely. If deleting the folder was the last thing you did, select the **Edit, Undo Delete** command to get the folder back. (Remember that Windows 98 Second Edition lets you reverse up to the last 10 things you did.)

If that doesn't work, you can pluck the nuked folder from the Recycle Bin, like so:

1. If you're in Windows Explorer, click **Recycle Bin** in the Folders list. Otherwise, open the desktop's **Recycle Bin** icon.

2. Select the folder you want to undelete.

3. Run the **File, Restore** command. (You can also right-click the folder and then click **Restore** in the shortcut menu.) The Recycle Bin escorts the folder back to its original location.

Disk Driving: Working with Floppy Disks

So far, all our file and folder labors have taken place inside the spacious confines of the computer's hard disk. Every one of the techniques you've been subjected to over the last couple of chapters can also be performed with a floppy disk, however. Things run a lot slower, and a typical floppy can hold only a fraction of the data held by even a small hard disk, but the principles are the same.

In this section, though, I want to look some floppy-specific chores:

➤ **Copying a floppy disk:** If you've saved some files on a floppy disk and you want to make an exact copy of the disk, Windows 98 has a Copy Disk command that makes the process easy.

➤ **Formatting a floppy disk:** In most cases, you can't just stick any old piece of plastic in a disk drive and expect it to read and write information. Floppy disks often need to be *initialized* first so that you can store information properly on the disk. This initialization process is called *formatting*.

➤ **Creating an emergency startup disk:** If your hard disk goes kaput, you may be able to recover it by using an emergency startup disk. You just insert the disk in drive A and reboot your computer. Because the startup disk tells Windows 98 to boot from the floppy disk instead of the hard disk, you regain at least some control over your machine. You (or some nearby computer wiz) can then proceed to investigate the problem. Not only that, but the start-up disk also contains some programs that you (or your troubleshooting guru) can use to diagnose the problem. For example, the startup disk includes the ScanDisk program.

SEE ALSO

➤ *For more about the ScanDisk program, check out the "Using ScanDisk to Avoid Hard Disk Hard Times" section in Chapter 23, "Tools for Keeping Your System in Tip-Top Shape," p. 309.*

How to Copy a Floppy

If you need to make a copy of a floppy disk, Windows 98 is up to the task. Here are the steps you need to follow:

1. Insert the disk you want to copy (Windows 98 calls this the *source disk*). If your system has a second drive of the same type, insert the disk you want to use for the copy (this is the *destination disk*) in the other drive.

2. Right-click the source disk drive and click **Copy Disk** in the context menu. Windows 98 displays the Copy Disk dialog box, shown in the following figure.

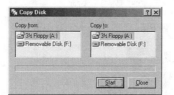

Use the Copy Disk dialog box to make a copy of a floppy disk.

The Source and Destination Must Be the Same Type

Make sure that the destination drive uses disks of the same type as the source disk:

➤ If your system has only one floppy drive, select that drive in both **Copy from** and **Copy to**.

➤ If your system has two drives of different types, you can use the same drive for the copy procedure. For example, suppose that drive A is 3 1/2-inch and drive B is 5 1/4-inch, and you want to copy a 3 1/2-inch disk. In this case, you'd select the 3 1/2-inch drive (drive A) in both **Copy from** and **Copy to**.

3. The **Copy from** box lists the floppy and removable drives on your system. Click the drive that contains the source disk.

4. The **Copy to** box also lists the floppy and removable drives on your system. Click the drive you want to use for the destination disk.

5. Click **Start**. Windows 98 reads the data from the source disk. If you're using the same drive for the copy, Windows 98 prompts you to insert the destination disk.

6. Insert the destination disk and click **OK**. Windows 98 copies the data to the destination disk.

7. When the copy is complete, click **Close**.

Starting Over: Formatting a Floppy Disk

Windows 98 makes disk formatting a relatively painless affair. The following steps show you how to format a new or used disk:

1. Insert the disk you want to format in the appropriate drive.

Formatting a Used Disk? Be Careful!

If you plan to format a used disk, you need to bear in mind that this will erase absolutely everything on the disk! Therefore, you probably should check the contents of used disks beforehand to make sure they don't contain anything important.

If formatting is so destructive, why would you want to do it? Well, for one thing, it's a quick way to erase all the files and folders on a disk. For another, formatting can help protect you against computer *viruses*, those nasty programs that like to terrorize innocent machines. Because most viruses transmit from computer to computer via floppy disks, the best thing to do if you inherit some old disks is format each one to eradicate everything on the disk, including any viruses lurking in the weeds.

2. In Windows Explorer or My Computer, right-click the drive and then click **Format** in the shortcut menu. Windows 98 displays the Format dialog box, as shown here.

Use the Format dialog box to set some formatting options.

158

3. Choose your formatting options:

   Capacity: Use this drop-down list box to select the proper capacity of the disk. (You probably don't have to change anything here.)

   Format type: For a new disk, select the **Full** option button. For a used disk, select the **Quick (erase)** option. (You can safely ignore the **Copy system files only** option.)

   Label: Fill in this text box (11 characters maximum) if you want to give the disk a name. This option is, well, optional.

4. When you've set up your options, click **Start** to get the formatting show on the road. When Windows 98 is finished, it displays a dialog box full of incomprehensible data about the disk.

5. Click **Close** to return to the Format dialog box.

6. Click **Close** to return to Explorer or My Computer.

What's the Quick (erase) Option All About?

The **Quick (erase)** option is a real time-saver because it cuts format time from a minute or so to a few seconds. The only problem with the Quick (erase) option is that it doesn't check the disk for damage. If you're dealing with a really old disk or if you've had problems with the disk, use the **Full** option instead.

Just in Case: Creating an Emergency Startup Disk

I mentioned earlier that if something goes awry with your hard disk, you can regain control of your computer by inserting an emergency startup disk in drive A and rebooting. When your computer detects that drive A has a startup disk, it bypasses your hard disk altogether and boots instead to drive A. (That is, you see the **A:\\>** prompt instead of the usual Windows 98 screen.)

Here are the steps to follow to create one of these disks:

1. Select **Start, Settings, Control Panel** to get the Control Panel window onscreen.

2. Open the **Add/Remove Programs** icon to display the Add/Remove Programs Properties dialog box.

3. Select the **Startup Disk** tab, shown in the following figure.

Not surprisingly, you use the Startup Disk tab to create a startup disk.

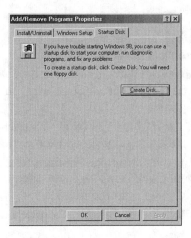

4. Click the **Create Disk** button. Windows 98 displays a dialog box asking you to insert the Windows 98 installation disc.

5. Insert the disc and click **OK**. After a few seconds, you're prompted to insert a disk in drive A, as shown in the next figure.

When you see the Insert Disk dialog box, insert a disk in drive A.

6. Pick out a disk that doesn't have any files on it that you need (Windows 98 will obliterate all the current info on the disk), insert it, and click **OK**. Windows 98 chugs away for a minute or two while it creates the startup disk. When it's finished, it returns you to the Add/Remove Programs Properties dialog box.

7. Click **Cancel** to return to the Control Panel, and then close the Control Panel window.

8. Remove the disk, label it so that you know what it is, store it in a safe place, and keep your fingers crossed that you never have to use it!

To be safe, you should probably give the startup disk a whirl to make sure that it works properly. To do this, follow these steps:

1. Make sure that the startup disk is in drive A.

2. Select **Start**, **Shut Down** to display the Shut Down Windows dialog box.

3. Activate the **Restart** option and then click **OK**.

4. Windows 98 shuts down and then restarts the system. After a while, you'll see the following menu:

```
Microsoft Windows 98 Startup Menu
====================================

    1. Start computer with CD-ROM support.
    2. Start computer without CD-ROM support.
    3. View the Help file.


Enter a choice:
```

5. If you have a CD-ROM drive, press **1**. Otherwise, press **2**.

6. Press **Enter**. You eventually end up at the A:\> prompt.

7. Remove the startup disk.

8. Press **Ctrl+Alt+Delete** to restart your machine and get back to Windows 98.

Disk Do's and Don'ts

Here are a few things to bear in mind when you're working with floppy disks.

Do:

➤ Label your disks so that, six months from now, you can figure out what they contain.

➤ Buy cheaper, no-name disks for everyday use.

➤ Buy top-quality disks for important needs, such as backing up your hard disk.

➤ Try to get out more.

Don't:

➤ Touch the magnetic surface of a disk.

➤ Expose a disk to direct sunlight, cigarette smoke, or excessive temperatures.

➤ Place a disk near a strong magnetic or electronic source.

➤ Fold, spindle, or mutilate a disk.

➤ Try to remove a disk from a disk drive if the drive's light is still on.

➤ Use the floppy disk as a drink coaster.

➤ Take any wooden nickels.

Zip and Jaz: Floppy Disks on Steroids

Between your floppy disk islands and your hard disk continent lies the nether realm of the Zip and Jaz disks. These are special disks that have hard disk-like storage capacities (100 megabytes for a Zip disk and a whopping 1,000 megabytes for a Jaz disk) and yet are removable like a floppy disk. The disks are housed in special drives—called, you guessed it, Zip drives and Jaz drives—that are connected by a cable to the back of your computer. (Many computer manufacturers are now shipping their machines with Zip drives built right in.)

Windows 98 supports these types of disks right out of the box and you can use all the file, folder, and floppy disk techniques discussed in the previous two chapters. (Except that you can't set up a Zip or Jaz disk as a startup disk.) The following figure shows that the File menu sprouts a new **Eject** command that you can use to eject disks from a Zip or Jaz drive.

Windows 98 "knows"
Zip and Jaz drives.

Part V
It's a Small World: Communications and the Internet

Has anyone else noticed that we seem to have turned into a nation of chatterboxes overnight? It seems like only yesterday that educators and other takers of the public pulse were complaining that the twin arts of letter writing and good conversation had fallen by the wayside in favor of channel surfing and other solitary practices. Now, however, it seems that folks have more to say than ever. And thanks to technologies such as modems, e-mail, computer-based faxing, and the omnipresent Internet, it's easier than ever to get your two cents' worth in. Well I say, if you can beat them, e-mail them! The chapters here in Part 5 will show you not only how to set up your modem, but also how to send out e-mail epistles,, get on the Internet, put up your own Web pages, and lots more.

Chapter 15

How to Get Connected to the Internet

In This Chapter

➤ Telling Windows 98 about your modem

➤ Signing up for a new Internet account

➤ A complete list of all the info you need to set up your account by hand

➤ Getting connected to the Internet

➤ Your personal on-ramp to that information expressway thing

It's official: the Internet is now a Big Deal. Television shows by the dozen talk about it; magazines as diverse as *Time*, *Business Week*, and *GQ* gush over it; and newspapers from every state in the union send out bemused "technology" reporters to figure out just what the heck is happening out there. Meanwhile, millions of ordinary citizens who wouldn't wear a pocket protector if you paid them, and whose heads are decidedly unpointy, are flocking to the Internet like so many swallows heading for Capistrano.

If you'd like to join the migration, this chapter can help. It's the first of a four-part series on Windows 98's Internet baubles and bangles. This chapter gets you off the ground by telling you what you need to make things happen and how to get your Internet account established. The next three chapters show you how to mess around with Internet goodies such as email and newsgroups, the World Wide Web, and publishing your own web pages. Surf's up!

Setting Up a Modem from Scratch

A modem is a little chunk of hardware that attaches to your computer. This handy device makes it possible for two or more computers to communicate through telephone lines—which are known to the online cognoscenti as *POTS*: Plain Old Telephone Service. Phone lines aren't built to carry computer data, though; they're built to carry sounds. The modem's job is to convert computer data to sounds that can be sent across the phone lines. On the receiving end, the other modem captures the incoming sounds and converts them back to computer data.

Modems are characterized by how quickly they can squirt data from here to there and back again. The speed of modem transmissions is measured in *bits per second* (bps). (A *bit* is the fundamental unit of all computer data. To give you a frame of reference, it takes 8 bits to make up a single character, such as the letter *A* or the number *2*.) Older modems trickle along at a measly 1,200 or 2,400 bps. Newer modems, however, offer more impressive velocities ranging from 28,800 bps to 56,000 bps.

Before you can get on the Internet, you need to tell Windows 98 what kind of modem you have. To that end, this section takes you through the rigmarole of installing your modem.

Assuming your modem is connected to your PC and is turned on (if it's an external modem, that is), begin by cracking open the **Start** menu and selecting **Settings, Control Panel**. When the Control Panel window appears, launch the **Modems** icon. At this point, one of two things will happen:

➤ **The Modems Properties dialog box appears:** If this happens, the dialog box should show that you already have a modem installed. Shout "Woo hoo" and high five yourself because it means you don't have to bother with the rest of this section.

➤ **The Install New Modem Wizard appears:** This wizard will guide you through the modem installation process. Click **Next** to get started. The wizard takes a few seconds to interrogate your system into revealing its modem secrets. If the wizard was successful, you'll see the Verify Modem dialog box. Click **Next** to install the modem and then click **Finish** when Windows 98 tells you that the modem has been set up.

If, on the other hand, the wizard fails in its quest to find your modem, all is not lost. In this case, you need to follow these steps:

1. Click **Next** to get a list of all the modems that Windows 98 knows about.

2. Use the **Manufacturers** and **Models** lists to highlight your modem. If you don't see your modem, select **(Standard Modem Types)** in the **Manufacturers** list, and then choose the standard model that corresponds to your modem's speed.

3. Click **Next**. The next wizard dialog box asks you to select the port for your modem.

4. Highlight the port (if you're not sure, try COM1) and then click **Next**. Windows 98 installs your modem.

5. Click **Finish**.

When the Add New Modem Wizard completes its labors, it displays the Modems Properties dialog box, shown next. This dialog box also appears the next time you launch the Modems icon in Control Panel. In this dialog box, you can do any of the following:

➤ To install a second modem, click **Add** to use the Add New Modem Wizard once again.

➤ To delete a modem you don't use, highlight it and then click **Remove**.

➤ To change the way Windows 98 dials the modem, click **Dialing Properties** and then, using the dialog box that shows up, make your changes. See Chapter 27, "Keeping in Touch: Mobile Computing with Dial-Up Networking," for an in-depth look at the options in the Dialing Properties dialog box.

SEE ALSO

➤ *See "Using Locations with Dial-Up Networking," p. 369.*

When you're finished, click **Close** to return to Control Panel.

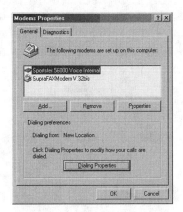

This dialog box shows you the modem you installed.

Using the Internet Connection Wizard to Set Up Your Account

You can take two (or possibly three) routes to set up an Internet connection:

➤ If you don't have an Internet account, use the Internet Connection Wizard to create and configure a new account automatically.

➤ If you have an existing Internet account, use the Internet Connection Wizard to do a step-by-step setup.

167

➤ If you have an existing account and you have Windows 98 Second Edition, you may be able to get the Internet Connection Wizard to transfer your account data automatically.

There are a couple of ways to launch the Internet Connection Wizard:

➤ Open the icon named **Connect to the Internet** on your Windows 98 desktop. (Note that this method works only once. After you've completed the wizard, this icon is deleted.)

➤ Select **Start, Programs, Internet Explorer, Connection Wizard**. (If you have Windows 98 Second Edition, the correct procedure is **Start, Programs, Accessories, Internet Tools, Internet Connection Wizard**.)

The initial wizard dialog box that you see depends on which version of Windows 98 you're running. If you're running the original version, you'll see the dialog box shown in the following figure, and it presents you with your first fork in the road. Here are the long-winded choices presented in this dialog box:

➤ **I want to sign up and configure my computer for a new Internet account:** Activate this option if you don't have an existing Internet account.

➤ **I have an existing Internet account through my phone line or a local area network (LAN):** Activate this option if you have an existing Internet account and you want to tell Windows 98 about it.

➤ **My computer is already set up for the Internet:** Activate this option if you know you already have an Internet connection set up on your computer.

Make your choice and click **Next**.

Use this dialog box to tell the wizard which route you want to take.

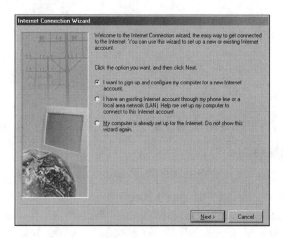

If you have Windows 98 Second Edition, you get the wizard dialog box shown next. Here are your choices:

➤ **I want to sign up for a new Internet account:** Activate this option if you don't have an existing Internet account.

➤ **I want to transfer my existing Internet account to this computer:** Activate this option if you have an existing Internet account that Windows 98 can transfer to your machine. Note that this only works with certain Internet service providers (ISPs). See "Transferring an Existing Internet Account," later in this chapter.

➤ **I want to set up my Internet account manually, or I want to connect through a local area network (LAN):** Activate this option if you have an existing Internet account that you need to set up by hand.

Make your selection and click **Next**.

This is the wizard dialog box you see if you have Windows 98 Second Edition.

Setting Up a New Internet Account

If you need to set up a new Internet account, here are the hoops you'll have to jump through:

1. At this point, you may trip over one of the following:

   ➤ If you see the Installing Files dialog box, it means Windows 98 has to populate your computer with a few more files that it needs for this Internet business. In this case, click **OK**, follow the prompts that come your way, and then click **OK** when Windows 98 tells you that it has to restart your machine.

   ➤ If you were negligent in your modem setup duties, Windows 98 will launch the Install New Modem wizard so that you can set up a modem. Note that you may have to restart your computer when the dust clears.

169

➤ If you have multiple modems set up on your computer, the wizard will display the Choose Modem dialog box. Use the list box to pick out the modem you want to use for connecting to the Internet, and then click **OK**.

2. The Wizard dials your modem and proceeds to grab a list of the Internet service providers in your area. When that's done, the Wizard displays a list of some Internet service providers in your area, as shown in the next figure.

You'll eventually see a list of possible providers.

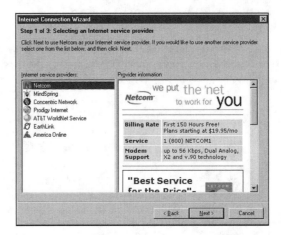

3. When you decide which one you want, click the provider and then click **Next**.

4. The Wizard then prompts you for your name, rank, and serial number (actually, it's your name, address, and phone number). Fill in the data and then click **Next**.

5. From here, the Wizard connects you with the provider so that you can complete the sign-up procedure. (This varies from provider to provider.)

Transferring an Existing Internet Account

If you have Windows 98 Second Edition and you activated the **I want to transfer my existing Internet account to this computer** option, the wizard sees if it can convince your ISP to fork over your account data. Here's what happens:

1. The wizard dials your modem and comes back with a list of providers in your area.

2. If you see your provider, highlight it and click **Next**. The wizard dials your modem once again, this time to connect to the provider. When that's done, you see the dialog box shown in the following figure.

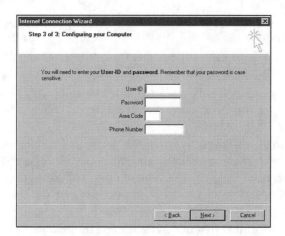

To transfer your existing account data, you need to enter some particulars for your account.

3. Enter your **User-ID** and **Password**, as well as the provider's **Area Code** and **Phone Number**.

4. Click **Next**. The wizard logs in to your provider, retrieves your account settings, and then sets up your Internet connection. When that's done, you see a dialog box showing your account data.

5. Click **Next**.

6. Click **Finish** in the last wizard dialog box.

Setting Up an Existing Internet Account

If you already have an Internet account, the Internet Connection Wizard can take you step by step through the long and winding road of setting up your connection by hand. There's a good deal of information you'll need to fill in as you go along. Your ISP should have provided you with some or all of this data when you signed up for your Internet account. Here's a list of all the possible things you'll need (but bear in mind that you likely won't need all of this info):

➤ Your *username* (or *logon name*) and password.

➤ The phone number you use to dial in to the provider.

➤ Whether you have to type your username and password each time you log on.

➤ Whether your connection is "PPP" or "SLIP."

➤ Whether your ISP assigns an *IP address* automatically when you log on. (Your IP address identifies your computer to the Internet community. When you request information—such as a web page—the data is sent to your IP address.)

➤ If an IP address isn't assigned automatically, you need to know the permanent IP address (for example, 123.45.67.89) that has been assigned to your account.

➤ Whether your ISP automatically assigns the address of their *DNS server* when you log on. (A DNS server routes your requests to the appropriate Internet site.)

➤ If the DNS server address isn't assigned automatically, you need to know the permanent address of the DNS server (for example, 123.45.67.1). Most ISPs have a secondary DNS server, as well.

➤ For Internet email, you need to know the name of your account and your account password (these are usually the same as your logon name and password). You also need to know the type of email account you have (POP3 or IMAP) and the addresses of your service provider's incoming (POP3 or IMAP) email server and outgoing (SMTP) email server.

➤ For Internet newsgroups (Usenet), you'll need the name of your service provider's *news server* (also called an *NNTP server*) and whether you must log on to this server. If you do log on, you'll also need your logon name and password.

➤ Whether your service provider provides an *Internet directory service* (often called *LDAP*—Lightweight Direct Access Protocol—service). If they do, you'll need the name of the *directory server* and whether you must log on to this server. If you do log on, you'll also need your logon name and password.

➤ If you're connecting over your company's network, whether that network uses a "proxy server" and, if so, the name of the proxy server. Your network administrator can tell you about his.

The exact operation of the wizard is different depending on which version of Windows 98 you're running. This section shows you what to do if you're running the original flavor of Windows 98. If you have the Second Edition, skip to the section titled "Setting Up an Existing Account in Windows 98 Second Edition."

Here's what happens:

1. After you select the **I have an existing Internet account through my phone line or a local area network (LAN)** option, click **Next**. The next wizard dialog box presents you with a choice:

   ➤ **Connect using my phone line:** Activate this option if you'll be using your modem to connect to the Internet.

   ➤ **Connect using my local area network (LAN):** Activate this option only if your computer is attached to a network and the network has an Internet connection. If you choose this option, the wizard will ask whether your network uses "proxy server" and, if it does, will ask you for the name of that server.

2. Click **Next** to continue.

3. As explained earlier, the wizard may now tell you that it's going to install some files, or it may ask you to choose one of your installed modems, or it may run the Install New Modem wizard. Follow the onscreen prompts, as described earlier.

4. The next wizard dialog box, shown in the following figure, asks for the **Area code**, **Telephone number**, and **Country name and code** of the ISP's dial-in phone number. If the call isn't long distance, make sure that you deactivate the **Dial using the area code and country code** check box. When you're finished, click **Next**.

Use this dialog box to enter your provider's dial-in phone number.

5. The next item on the wizard's to-do list is to ask for the **User name** and **Password** you use to log on to your service provider (see the next figure). Fill in the boxes and click **Next**.

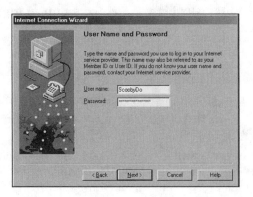

Tell the wizard the user-name and password that your service provider assigned to you.

6. Now the wizard wonders whether you want to work with the "advanced settings." Select **No** if you don't, or select **Yes** if you need to specify any of the information in the following wizard dialog boxes:

   ➤ **Connection Type:** Whether your service provider uses a PPP or SLIP connection.

   ➤ **Logon Procedure:** Whether you need to log on manually (that is, by typing your username and password at your service provider's logon screen).

   ➤ **IP Address:** Whether your service provider automatically assigns you an IP address or you have a permanent IP address (see the following figure).

   ➤ **DNS Server Address:** Whether the IP address of your service provider's DNS server is assigned automatically or they use a specific address.

The advanced settings include such arcane things as your IP address.

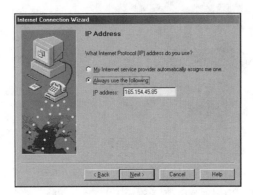

7. You'll eventually end up at the Dial-Up Connection Name dialog box. Enter a name for your new connection and then click **Next**.

8. The Wizard now asks whether you want to set up an Internet email account. Activate the **Yes** option if you do, or the **No** option if you don't, and then click **Next**.

9. If you told the wizard that you want to set up your email account, the following dialog boxes will come your way:

   ➤ **Your Name:** This is the name people see when you send them a message.

   ➤ **Internet E-mail Address:** This is the email address your service provider assigned to you.

   ➤ **E-mail Server Names:** In this dialog box, you specify whether your provider's email server uses POP3 or IMAP. You also enter the names of the incoming mail server and the outgoing mail server (see the following figure).

   ➤ **Internet Mail Logon:** Enter the account name and password for your email account.

   ➤ **Friendly Name:** Enter a name that you want to use to refer to this email account.

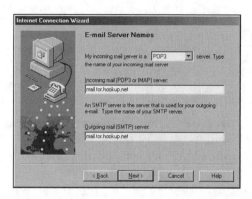

This is one of the dialog boxes you'll have to deal with if you're setting up your Internet email account.

10. Next on the wizard's agenda is whether you want to set up an Internet news account. Again, either activate **Yes** or **No**, and then click **Next**.

11. If you told the wizard that you want to set up your news account, you'll be pestered with another series of dialog boxes:

   ➤ **Your Name:** This is the name people see when you send a message to a newsgroup.

   ➤ **Internet News E-mail Address:** This is the email address that people in your newsgroups can use to send you a message. This will almost certainly be the same as the Internet email address you specified earlier.

   ➤ **Internet News Server Name:** Enter the name of the news server that your provider uses (see the next figure). If you have to log on to this server, activate the **My news server requires me to log on** check box.

   ➤ **Internet News Server Logon:** If you have to log on to the news server, this dialog box enables you to enter the account name and password for your news account.

   ➤ **Friendly Name:** Enter a name that you want to use to refer to this news account.

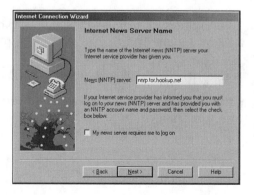

This is one of the dialog boxes from the Internet news portion of the wizard's show.

12. The infuriatingly curious Internet Connection Wizard next asks whether you want to set up your Internet directory service. Again, select **Yes** or **No**, and then click **Next**.

13. If you selected Yes in the previous wizard dialog box, it will come as absolutely no surprise that you'll have to trudge through another host of dialog boxes. Here's a summary:

    ➤ **Internet Directory Server Name:** Enter the name of your service provider's Internet directory server. If you have to log on to this server, activate the **My LDAP server requires me to log on** check box.

    ➤ **Internet Directory Server Logon:** If you have to log on to the directory server, use this dialog box to enter the account name and password for your directory server account.

    ➤ **Check E-mail Addresses:** This dialog box wonders whether you want to check the email addresses you use in your outgoing messages with the email addresses in the Internet directory service. You'll probably want to select **No** here, but if you're sure you want to perform this check, select **Yes**, instead.

    ➤ **Friendly Name:** Use this dialog box to type the name you want to use to refer to this Internet directory account.

14. Break out the virtual champagne because you're finally finished! In the Complete Configuration dialog box, click **Finish**. If the Wizard prompts you to restart your computer, click **Yes**.

When you get back to Windows 98, you'll find a new connection in your Dial-Up Networking folder. To use this connection to establish an Internet session, see "Dialing Up Your Service Provider" later in this chapter.

Setting Up an Existing Account in Windows 98 Second Edition

Windows 98 Second Edition offers a streamlined version of the Internet Connection Wizard that doesn't make you jump over as many hoops. Here are the steps you go through:

1. The next wizard dialog box presents you with a choice:

    ➤ **I connect through a phone line and modem:** Activate this option if you'll be using your modem to connect to the Internet.

➤ **I connect through a local area network (LAN):** Activate this option only if your computer is attached to a network and the network has an Internet connection. If you choose this option, the wizard will next ask you about a "proxy server." Your best bet here is to activate the **Automatic discovery of proxy server** check box.

2. Click **Next**.

3. As explained earlier, the wizard may now tell you that it's going to install some files, or it may ask you to choose one of your installed modems, or it may run the Install New Modem wizard. Follow the onscreen prompts, as described earlier.

4. The next wizard dialog box asks for the **Area code**, **Telephone number**, and **Country/region name and code** of the ISP's dial-in phone number. If the call isn't long distance, make sure that you deactivate the **Dial using the area code and country code** check box.

5. If you have to enter advanced settings such as your IP address or DNS server addresses, click **Advanced**. Use the Advanced Connection Properties dialog box to enter your settings, and then click **OK**.

6. When you're ready to rumble, click **Next**.

7. The next thing the wizard wonders about is the **User name** and **Password** you use to log on to your ISP. Fill in the text boxes and click **Next**.

8. In the next wizard dialog box, enter a snappy name for your new connection and then click **Next**.

9. The wizard now asks whether you want to set up an Internet email account. Activate **Yes** if you do, or **No** if you don't, and then click **Next**.

10. If you told the wizard that you want to set up your email account, the following dialog boxes will come your way:

    ➤ **Your Name:** This is the name people see when you send them a message.

    ➤ **Internet E-mail Address:** This is the email address your service provider assigned to you.

    ➤ **E-mail Server Names:** In this dialog box, you specify whether your provider's email server uses POP3 or IMAP. You also enter the names of the incoming mail server and the outgoing mail server.

    ➤ **Internet Mail Logon:** Enter the account name and password for your email account.

11. In the last of the wizard incessant dialog boxes, deactivate the **Connect to the Internet immediately...** check box, and then click **Finish**.

No Account? Try the Online Services Folder

Another way to get your Internet connection happening is to sign up with one of the big *online services*, such as CompuServe, America Online, the Microsoft Network, or Prodigy. These services offer not only a path to the goodies on the Internet, but also lots of useful and interesting attractions (and, of course, a few useless and dull ones, too) assembled by the company that owns the service. You normally have to pay a monthly fee (and sometimes additional hourly charges) to hook up to an online service.

In most cases, the connection to the service is handled by special software supplied the company, and you need to contact them to get everything you need. Windows 98 boasts a new **Online Services** icon on the desktop, however. Opening this icon displays the Online Services folder shown in the following figure. From here, you have a couple of ways to proceed:

➤ Open the **About the Online Services** icon to find out a bit more about the services.

➤ Open one of the other icons to set up a trial account with a service.

Opening Windows 98's Online Services desktop icon displays this Online Services folder.

Dialing Up Your Service Provider

With your Internet connection set up and ready for action, you can establish your net session at any time. If you're accessing the Internet via your network, the connection is established automatically when you log on to the network. For dial-up connections, however, you need to do the following:

1. Select **Start, Programs, Accessories, Communications, Dial-Up Networking**. The Dial-Up Networking window that shows up will have an icon for the connection you just created (see the following figure).

The icon for your Internet connection is stored in the Dial-Up Networking folder.

2. Highlight the icon for your Internet connection and then either select the **Connections, Connect** command, or click the Dial button in the toolbar. The Connect To dialog box appears, as shown in the next figure.

Bypassing the Connect To Dialog Box

Most of the time you won't use the Connect To dialog box for anything other than slamming the Connect button. If you'd rather avoid this dialog box altogether, select **Connections, Settings** in the Dial-Up Networking window. In the dialog box that appears, deactivate the **Prompt for information before dialing** check box, and then click **OK**.

This dialog box shows up when you launch your Internet connection.

3. Click **Connect**. Windows 98 uses your modem to dial your service provider. You may hear all kinds of strange, other-worldly beeps and screeches from the speakers as the two modems exchange pleasantries.

4. If you have to log on manually, you'll see the Post-Dial Terminal Screen shown in the next figure. Depending on the ISP, you may have to enter some or all of the following:

   ➤ If you just see a blank terminal window, try pressing **Enter**.

   ➤ Your username.

   ➤ Your password.

➤ The connection type. In some cases, you'll enter a command (such as **ppp**); in other cases, you'll select the connection type from a menu of choices.

To connect to an ISP you often need to enter a little information in the terminal window.

You Get the Pre-Dial Terminal Screen

After you click Connect, Windows 98 may display the Pre-Dial Terminal Screen instead of the Post-Dial Terminal Screen. To fix this, in the Dial-Up Networking folder, highlight the icon for your connection and then select **File, Properties**. In the General tab of the dialog box that appears, click **Configure** and then display the **Options** tab. Deactivate the **Bring up terminal window before dialing** check box and activate the **Bring up terminal window after dialing** check box. Click **OK** and then click **OK** again.

5. After you've entered all your options, click the terminal window's **Continue** button (or press **F7**).

If you want to keep an eye on your connect time, double-click on the Dial-Up Networking icon in the taskbar. This displays a dialog box like the one shown in the following figure. Note that you can disconnect from the Internet by displaying this dialog box and clicking the **Disconnect** button.

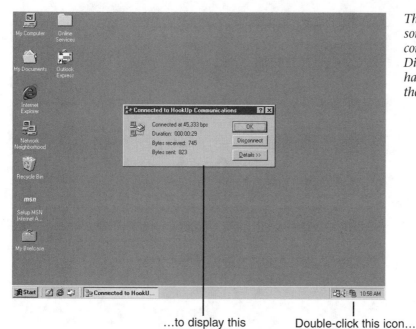

This dialog box shows some stats about your connection. Click Disconnect when you've had just about enough of the Internet for one day.

...to display this dialog box.

Double-click this icon...

All right, you're on the Net and ready for some serious surfing! Here's where to find info on using the various Internet services:

Email: I show you how to use Outlook Express to send and receive email messages in the "Express Yourself I: Using Outlook Express for Email" section of Chapter 16, "Can We Talk? Email, Newsgroups, and Internet Phone Calls, " p.184.

Newsgroups: To learn how to participate in Usenet newsgroups, head for the "Express Yourself II: Using Outlook Express for Newsgroups" section of Chapter 16, p. 194.

Internet phone calls: Using NetMeeting to make "phone calls" over the Internet is the subject of Chapter 16's "Phone Free: Using NetMeeting to Place Calls over the Internet" section, p. 199.

The World Wide Web: Surfing the web is the subject of Chapter 17, "Wandering the Web with Internet Explorer," p. 205.

Publishing web pages: To learn how to put your own material on the web, give Chapter 18, "Becoming a Webmaster with FrontPage Express and Other Page Publishing Tools," p. 227, a thorough going-over.

Chapter 16

Can We Talk? Email, Newsgroups, and Internet Phone Calls

In This Chapter

➤ Sending and receiving email with Outlook Express

➤ Using Outlook Express to participate in Usenet newsgroups

➤ Using NetMeeting to make voice calls over the Internet

➤ An excellent extroverted excursion that'll help you survive in the have-your-people-email-my-people world

Over the past few years, we've seen many a pondering pundit rail against the perceived evils of technology. "People are going to spend all their time hunkered down in front of a computer screen and never talk to each other," they cry. Hah! These digital Chicken Littles should spend some time on the Internet, where everybody talks to everybody! And I don't just mean the naturally loquacious and garrulous, either. Even folks who are usually shy and reticent enjoy shipping out an email and contributing to a newsgroup discussion. That's not too surprising, considering that the Internet was designed with this kind of give-and-take in mind. And, bonus of bonuses, Windows 98 comes with some great new tools that make it even easier to communicate with your fellow *Netizens* (Net citizens). If you're looking to shoot the electronic breeze, this chapter shows you how to use Outlook Express for Internet email and newsgroups. I'll even show you how to use NetMeeting to place phone calls over the Internet's airwaves.

Express Yourself I: Using Outlook Express for Email

Windows 98's Outlook Express program was built from the ground up to handle the rigors of Internet email. (It also does newsgroups, as you'll see a bit later.) Whether you're sending out an e-memo, dishing e-gossip with friends, or sending e-compliments to your favorite author (wink, wink), Outlook Express is up to the challenge.

Before the brass tacks come out, it's worth mentioning at this point that I'm assuming you've set up both your Internet connection and your email and newsgroup accounts. (One thing, though: if you're running Windows 98 Second Edition, the Internet Connection Wizard doesn't take you through the process of setting up a newsgroup account. I'll show you how you can do this from Outlook Express a bit later.) Also, you may want to check out my online email primer to learn more about this email thing before going any further:

```
http://www.mcfedries.com/Ramblings/email-primer.html
```

SEE ALSO

➤ *If you haven't set up these accounts, head back to Chapter 15, How to Get Connected to the Internet,"* *p. 165, to get the nitty-gritty details.*

To get started with Outlook Express, you have no less than three choices:

➤ Select **Start, Programs, Internet Explorer, Outlook Express**. (Windows 98 Second Edition users need only choose **Start, Programs, Outlook Express**).

➤ Open the **Outlook Express** icon on the desktop.

➤ Click the **Launch Outlook Express** icon in the taskbar's Quick Launch area.

When you first launch Outlook Express, you'll see the Browse for Folder dialog box shown here. (This dialog box is nowhere to be seen in Windows 98 Second Edition.) This dialog box wants to know where you'd like your email messages stored. The default folder is fine, so click **OK**.

When you first start the program, Outlook Express wonders where you want to store your stuff.

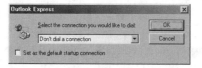

For the last of the startup chores, Outlook Express displays the dialog box shown in the following figure to ask what Internet connection you want to dial. (You'll see a slightly different dialog box in Windows 98 Second Edition.) You have two choices:

➤ If you don't want to connect to your service provider just now, make sure that **Don't dial a connection** is selected in the list.

➤ If you want to connect, use the list to select the connection you created in the previous chapter.

If you want Outlook Express to use your selection automatically each time you start the program, activate the **Set as the default startup connection** check box. Click **OK** when you're finished.

Outlook Express also offers to establish a connection to your Internet service provider.

With all that hoo-ha out of the way, the Outlook Express window finally shows its face. The next figure points out some of the more important features of the window. (If the window you see looks completely different than the one shown here, it probably means you have the new version of Outlook Express that ships with Internet Explorer 5 and Windows 98 Second Edition—it's version 5, if you're keeping score. See "What's New in Outlook Express 5," later in this chapter, for a closer look at this new version.)

A few features of the Outlook Express landscape.

The Inbox folder is where the messages you receive are stored.

The Folders list contains various Outlook Express storage areas.

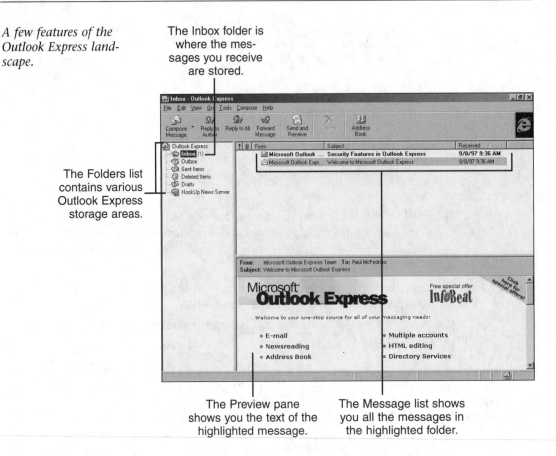

The Preview pane shows you the text of the highlighted message.

The Message list shows you all the messages in the highlighted folder.

If you select the Inbox folder and if you had an email program installed on your machine when you installed Windows 98, Outlook Express will now offer to import the messages and address book from the old program (see the following figure). This is a good idea; if you decide to go ahead, you'll need to follow these steps:

1. Make sure that your old email program is highlighted in the **Import from** list.

2. Make sure that both the **Messages** and **Address Book** check boxes are activated.

3. Click **Next**.

4. If Outlook Express prompts you to choose a profile, click **OK**.

5. When Outlook Express asks you to select the folders to import, make sure that **All folders** is activated, and then click **Finish**.

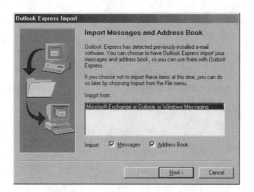

Outlook Express may offer to import your old messages and address book.

Working with the Windows Address Book

When you start shipping out email messages to the four corners of the Internet world, you'll probably find that you have a few recipients you contact frequently—perhaps your boss, a colleague or two, your wired friends, or just a pen-pal you picked up along the way. Windows 98 has an address book that you can use to store addresses and retrieve them with just a couple of mouse clicks, instead of having to constantly type the addresses of these regulars.

To get to the Windows Address Book, use either of the following techniques:

➤ In Outlook Express, either select **Tools, Address Book** or click the **Address Book** toolbar button. (Keyboard fans can also slam **Ctrl+Shift+B**.)

➤ In Windows 98, select **Start, Programs, Internet Explorer, Address Book**. (If you have Windows 98 Second Edition, select **Start, Programs, Accessories, Address Book**.)

Either way, the Address Book window shows up. Here are the steps to plow through to add a recipient:

1. Either select **File, New Contact** or click the New Contact toolbar button. (Keyboardists may prefer to tickle the **Ctrl+N** key combo.) The Properties dialog box, shown here, appears.
2. In the **Personal** tab, use the **First** and **Last** text boxes to enter the person's name.
3. Enter the person's email address in the **Add new** text box, and then click **Add**.
4. Outlook Express enables you to send messages that contain fancy fonts and other formatting. If you know this person's email software doesn't display the fancy stuff, activate the **Send E-Mail using plain text only** check box.
5. If you want to use the Windows Address Book as an all-purpose contact database, feel free to fill in the data in the **Home**, **Business**, and **Other** tabs.
6. Click **OK**. The new contact is added to the list.

Use the Properties dialog box to fill in the details for your recipient.

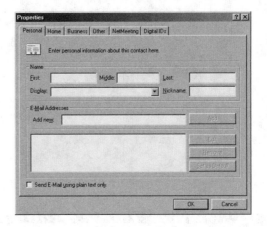

Extroverts in the crowd may enjoy sending out their missives not just to one person, but to several. You'll see a bit later that it's easy to specify multiple email addresses when you're sending a message. If you have a group of recipients that you use consistently, however, it's easier to define these recipients as a *group* in the Windows Address Book. Then you can specify just the group name when you send a message, and Outlook Express will be happy to make sure that every member of the group gets a copy. Here's how to forge a new group in the Windows Address Book:

1. Either select **File, New Group** or click the New Group toolbar button. (The **Ctrl+G** key combination will do the trick as well.)

2. In the Properties dialog box that appears, use the **Group Name** text box to enter a catchy name for the group.

3. To add new members to the group, you have two choices:

   ➤ To add a member who already exists in the Windows Address Book, click the **Select Members** button to display the Select Group Members dialog box. Highlight the name of each person you want in the group, and then click **Select**. When you're finished, click **OK**.

   ➤ To add a member who doesn't exist in the Windows Address Book, click **New Contact** and then fill out the dialog box, as described earlier.

4. When you're finished, click **OK**.

Sorting the Contacts

By default, the Windows Address Book sorts the contacts by first name. You may prefer something more sensible, such as sorting the contacts by last name. To change the sort order, select **View, Sort By** and then choose the order you want from the submenu that appears.

The Two-Cents-Worth Department: Composing a New Message

When you feel the urge to get something off your chest, or if you just feel like foisting your unmatched prose on certain lucky members of the Internet community, here are the steps to follow to compose a new message:

1. In Outlook Express, either select **Compose, New Message** or click the **Compose Message** toolbar button. (In Outlook Express 5, select **Message, New Message** or click **New Message**. Keyboard diehards may prefer pressing **Ctrl+N**.) The New Message window appears, as shown in the following figure.

Click here to select a recipient from your address book.

Use the New Message window to compose your email missive.

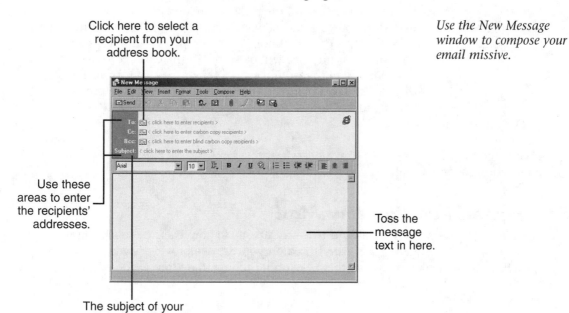

Use these areas to enter the recipients' addresses.

Toss the message text in here.

The subject of your tirade goes here.

2. Use the **To** box to specify the message recipient. You have the following choices:

   ➤ Type in the email address by hand.

   ➤ If you want to type multiple addresses, separate each address from the next with a semicolon (;).

   ➤ To send your message to an address book contact, click the icon at the beginning of the To line. In the Select Recipients dialog box, highlight a name and click **To**. Repeat to taste, and then click **OK**.

3. To send a courtesy copy to a different recipient, use the **Cc** box.

   4. To send a blind courtesy copy to a different recipient, use the **Bcc** box. (*Blind courtesy copy* means that the other people who receive this message won't see the addresses listed on the Bcc line. To see the Bcc box in Outlook Express 5, activate the **View, All Headers** command.)

5. Use the **Subject** box to enter a short-but-meaningful description of your message.

6. In the large blank box at the bottom of the window, enter the text of your message. If the recipient can see formatting such as fonts and colors, feel free to use the Formatting toolbar to gussy up your message.

7. When your message is ready to send, you have two ways to proceed:

   ➤ To send the message right away, select **File, Send** (it's **File, Send Message** in Outlook Express 5) or click the **Send** toolbar button. (The **Alt+S** keyboard shortcut is also available.)

   ➤ If you'd prefer to send the message later (say, when you're connected to your Internet service provider), select **File, Send Later**. In this case, Outlook Express displays a message telling you that your message will be stored in the Outbox folder. Click **OK**. When you're ready to send all your messages for real, select the **Tools, Send** command in Outlook Express. (The proper command in Outlook Express 5 is **Tools, Send and Receive, Send All**.)

If you aren't already connected to your service provider, Outlook Express makes the connection for you and then sends the messages.

Getting and Reading Your Mail

Good email conversations are always two-way streets, so you'll also have messages coming your way. These messages are stored on your service provider's mail server until such time as you go and get them. To do so, follow these steps:

1. Start Outlook Express if you haven't done so already.

2. Either select the **Tools, Send and Receive** command, or click the **Send and Receive** toolbar button. (In Outlook Express 5, select **Tools, Send and Receive, Receive All** or drop down the **Send/Recv** button and then click **Receive All**.) Outlook Express then asks whether you want to go online to get the messages.

3. Click **Yes**. Outlook Express makes the connection and then convinces the mail server to pass along your waiting messages.

4. Disconnect from the Internet.

Sending and Receiving

 Outlook Express 5 also gives you a method to send your outgoing messages and receive your incoming messages in one fell swoop. Either select **Tools, Send and Receive, Send and Receive All** or drop down **Send/Recv** and then click **Send and Receive All**. The keyboard crowd may prefer to press **Ctrl+M**.

The new messages that Outlook Express grabs are stored in the program's Inbox folder. They're displayed in a list that shows the name of the person or company that sent each message, the Subject line of each message, and the date and time you received each message.

To read a message, you have a couple of options:

➤ Highlight the message and then use the Preview pane to read the text.

➤ Highlight the message and then select **File, Open** (you can also press **Ctrl+O** or just press **Enter**.)

The next figure shows the window that appears. After you've read the message, you can either close the window or use the following techniques to check out your other messages:

➤ To open the next message in the list, either select **View, Next, Next Message** or click the Next Message toolbar button (**Ctrl+>** works, too).

➤ To open the previous message in the list, either select **View, Next, Previous Message** or click the Previous Message toolbar button (you can also try on **Ctrl+<** for size).

➤ To open the next *unread* message, select **View, Next, Next Unread Message** (or press **Ctrl+U**).

When you open a message, it appears in a window like this one.

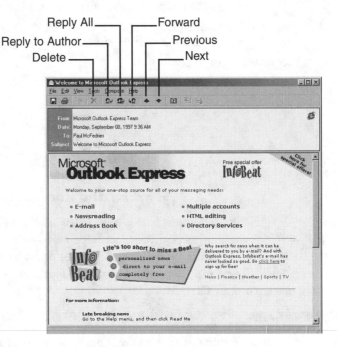

Now What? Replying to, Forwarding, and Deleting Messages

After you've read your messages, there's a whole whack of things you can do with them:

➤ **Send a reply:** To send back a retort to the author of the message, either select **Compose, Reply to Author**, or click the **Reply to Author** toolbar button. (The keyboard shortcut is **Ctrl+R**. In Outlook Express 5, select **Message, Reply to Sender**.) Enter your reply in the window that appears, and then send the message as described earlier.

➤ **Send a reply to all the recipients:** If the message was sent to several people, you can send a rejoinder to all the recipients by selecting **Compose, Reply to All**, or by clicking the **Reply All** toolbar button. (From the keyboard, press **Ctrl+Shift+R**. In Outlook Express 5, select **Message, Reply to Sender**.)

➤ **Forward the message:** If you'd like someone else to eyeball the message, you can forward it to them by either selecting **Compose, Forward**, or clicking the **Forward** button. (Keyboard mavens can press **Ctrl+F**. In Outlook Express 5, select **Message, Forward**.)

➤ **Delete the message:** To get rid of the message, either select **File, Delete**, or click the **Delete** button (or press **Ctrl+D**; in Outlook Express 5, select **File, Delete Message**.). In this case, Outlook Express moves the messages to the Deleted Items folder. (If you change your mind, there's no problem moving the message back to the Inbox, using the technique described next.)

➤ **Move it to another folder:** You probably won't want to leave all your messages cluttering the Inbox folder. Any messages you want to keep should be stored in a separate folder. To move a message to another folder, select **File, Move To Folder** (**Edit, Move to Folder** in Outlook Express 5), use the Move dialog box to highlight the destination folder, and then click **OK**. (If you want to create a new folder along the way, click the **New Folder** button in the Move dialog box.)

What's New in Outlook Express 5

 You've seen in quite a few places so far in this chapter that Outlook Express 5—the version of Outlook Express that comes with Windows 98 Second Edition and Internet Explorer 5—makes a few changes to the way you work with messages.

Here's a quick review of some of the more usual new features in Outlook Express 5:

➤ **Easier access to addresses:** As pointed out in the figure, Outlook Express 5 adds a new Contacts list to the main window. This enables you to send a message to any contact simply by double-clicking their name.

➤ **Fast, free account signup:** Hotmail is a free email provider that's run by Microsoft. To sign up for a Hotmail account, select **Tools, New Account Signup, Hotmail**.

➤ **Work with identities:** If you share your computer with someone else, email can be a real problem because it's tough to hide your messages from the other person. Outlook Express 5 solves that by enabling each user to set up a separate *identity* which essentially gives each person their own Outlook Express configuration. To create a new identity, select **File, Identities, Add New Identity**. Enter your name, activate the **Ask me for a password when I start** check box (if you want the added security), and click **OK**.

➤ **Improved searching:** The Outlook Express Find feature has been beefed up so that you can search across folders, examine the message Subject and text, and more. Select **Edit, Find, Message**.

➤ **Easier filtering:** Outlook Express 5 has new options for filtering incoming messages. My favorite is the **Message, Block Sender** command, which tells Outlook Express to automatically delete any future messages that come in from the person who sent the highlighted message. It's great for blowing away bozos. You can also use **Message, Create Rule From Message** to make a new filtering rule based on the author of the current message.

Express Yourself II: Using Outlook Express for Newsgroups

Usenet is an Internet service that, in essence, is a collection of topics available for discussion. These discussion groups—or *newsgroups*, as they're called—are open to all and sundry, and they won't cost you a dime (aside from the usual connection charges, of course).

Will you find anything interesting in these discussion groups? Well, let's put it this with way: with literally thousands of groups to choose from, if you can't find anything that strikes your fancy, you'd better check your pulse.

Assuming that you've set up your news account for your service provider's news server (as explained in the last chapter), follow these steps to get started:

Creating a News Account in Outlook Express 5

As I mentioned earlier, the Windows 98 Second Edition version of the Internet Connection Wizard doesn't ask you to set up a new account. To do this from Outlook Express 5, select **Tools, Accounts** and display the **News** tab. If you don't see an account listed (your ISP may have set one up automatically), click **Add, News** to create the account.

1. In the Outlook Express Folders list, click the news account. The first time you do this, Outlook Express will display the dialog box shown here.

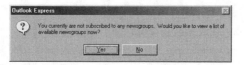

You'll see this dialog box the first time you access your news account.

2. You'll need to see the list of newsgroups, so click **Yes**.

3. If you aren't online already, Outlook Express asks whether you want to go online now. Click **Yes**. Outlook Express then connects to the news server and begins downloading the newsgroup names. Note that this may take quite some time if you have a slow connection.

Subscribing to a Newsgroup

When the newsgroups are loaded, you'll see the Newsgroups dialog box shown in the next figure. (In subsequent news sessions, you can get to this dialog box either by selecting the **Tools, Newsgroups** command, or by clicking the **Newsgroups** toolbar button.)

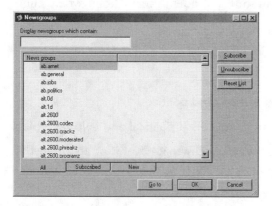

Use this dialog box to subscribe to the newsgroups that look interesting.

Here's how to view or subscribe to a newsgroup:

1. To find a newsgroup, either scroll through the list or use the **Display newsgroups which contain** text box to enter part of the newsgroup name.

2. When you've found the newsgroup you want, you may prefer just to check out the newsgroup to see whether you like it. To do so, highlight the newsgroup name and click **Go to**. Note that when you click this button Outlook Express closes the dialog box.

3. If, instead, you want to subscribe to the newsgroup, highlight the newsgroup name and click **Subscribe**. (*Subscribing* means that Outlook Express adds the newsgroup to your news account so that later on you can view the newsgroup from the Folders list.)

4. To continue subscribing, repeat step 3 as often as you like.

5. To see a list of the subscribed newsgroups, click the **Subscribed** tab.

6. When you're finished, click **OK** to return to Outlook Express.

What's with Those Weird Newsgroup Names?

Usenet divides its newsgroups into several classifications, or *hierarchies*. There are seven so-called *mainstream* hierarchies:

comp	Computer hardware and software
misc	Miscellaneous stuff that doesn't really fit anywhere else
news	Usenet-related topics
rec	Entertainment, hobbies, sports, and more
sci	Science and technology
soc	Sex, culture, religion, and politics
talk	Debates about controversial political and cultural topics

There's also a huge **alt** (alternative) hierarchy that covers just about anything that either doesn't belong in a mainstream hierarchy, or is too whacked out to be included with the mainstream stuff.

Newsgroup names have three parts: the hierarchy to which they belong, followed by a dot, followed by the newsgroup's topic. For example, check out the following name:

```
rec.juggling
```

Here, the hierarchy is **rec** (recreation), and the topic is **juggling**. (To be hip, you'd pronounce this name as *reck dot juggling*). For more info on Usenet, please see the following page on my Web site:

```
http://www.mcfedries.com/Ramblings/usenet-primer.html
```

Getting and Reading Newsgroup Messages

Here are the steps to march through to get the current messages in a newsgroup:

1. In the Outlook Express Folders list, open the news account branch and click the newsgroup you want to check out. (In Outlook Express 5, the program connects to the Internet and starts downloading the message headers. This means you can skip the rest of these steps and just start reading the messages. Note, however, that you need to stay online to do this.)

2. Select the **Tools, Download this Newsgroup** command. Outlook Express displays the Download Newsgroup dialog box, shown next.

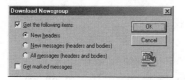

Outlook Express wants to know how much it should download.

3. Activate the **Get the following items** check box, make sure that the **New headers** option is activated, and then click **OK**.

4. As usual, if you aren't online already, Outlook Express asks whether you want to go online now. Click **Yes**. Outlook Express then connects to the news server and begins downloading the newsgroup message headers.

5. When you have all the headers, you need to mark the interesting ones for downloading. To do this, highlight each message you want and then select **Tools, Mark for Retrieval, Mark Message**.

6. To download the marked messages, select the **Tools, Download this Newsgroup** command to display the Download Newsgroup dialog box again.

7. Activate the **Get marked messages** check box and click **OK**.

8. Click **Yes** if Outlook Express asks whether you want to go online.

9. After the messages have been downloaded, you can read them just as you read email messages.

The *modus operandi* of most newsgroups is that someone sends an original message to the group, someone else responds to that message, a few other folks respond to the response, and so on. These related messages constitute a *thread*.

When you get the messages for a newsgroup, you'll see that Outlook Express has organized them by thread. You can tell that a thread has multiple messages by looking for a plus sign (+) beside a message. Highlight that message, press the plus sign key on your numeric keypad, and Outlook Express will display all the other thread messages.

Getting Connected

If you get sick to death of Outlook Express always asking whether you want to "go online," there's a way to avoid these incessant prompts. Just select **File, Connect** or click the Connect button in the toolbar. Outlook Express, relentless beast that it is, will get one last shot in and ask whether you want to go online. Grrr. Click **Yes**.

Joining in the Fun: Posting a Message

When it's time to dazzle the other newsgroup participants with your brilliant prose, you need to send a message to the newsgroup. (This is called *posting* to the group.) There are various ways to go about this:

➤ To send a new message, make sure that the newsgroup is highlighted in the Folders list and then either select **Compose, New Message** or click the **Compose Message** toolbar button. (In Outlook Express 5, select **Message, New Message** or click **New Post**.)

➤ To send a response to the newsgroup, highlight the original message and then either select **Compose, Reply to Newsgroup** or click the toolbar's **Reply to Group** button. (In Outlook Express 5, select **Message, Reply to Group** or click **Reply Group**.)

➤ To reply only to the person who sent a message, highlight the message and then either select **Compose, Reply to Author** or click the **Reply to Author** button in the toolbar. (In Outlook Express 5, select **Message, Reply to Sender** or click **Reply**.)

➤ To reply both to the newsgroup and to the person who sent a message, highlight the message and then select **Compose, Reply to Newsgroup and Author**. (In Outlook Express 5, select **Message, Reply All**.)

➤ To forward a message to an email recipient, either select **Compose, Forward** or click the **Forward** button in the toolbar. (In Outlook Express 5, select **Message, Forward** or click **Forward**.)

Phone Free: Using NetMeeting to Place Calls over the Internet

Email is a great way to keep in touch without having to bother with a phone call. What happens, however, if you really need to have a true conversation with someone, but that person is too far away to meet face-to-face? Well, there's always your old and sadly neglected friend the telephone, of course. But what if I told you that it's possible to use your Internet connection to "call" someone and have a real live voice-to-voice powwow? It's true: you can turn the Internet into a giant phone booth that enables you to chat amiably with someone across town, across the country, or even across the ocean. And get this: *no long-distance charges apply*! The "cost" of the call is just your Internet connection time.

But you've gotta have some kind of high-falutin' equipment installed, right? Nope. All you (and the person you're calling) need is the following:

➤ A sound card in your computer. (For best results, make sure that you have a sound card that supports something called *full-duplex audio*. This just means that the sounds—that is, your conversations—can travel both ways at the same time.)

➤ A microphone attached to the sound card.

➤ Windows 98's NetMeeting program.

The rest of this chapter shows you how it's done.

Getting NetMeeting Ready for Action

Assuming that your Internet connection is up and running, let's stroll through the steps necessary to configure NetMeeting:

 1. Select **Start, Programs, Microsoft NetMeeting**. (In Windows 98 Second Edition, select **Start, Programs, Accessories, Internet Tools, NetMeeting**.) The first time you do this, Windows 98 launches the Microsoft NetMeeting Wizard.

2. The first wizard dialog box just gives you an overview of NetMeeting's capabilities; click **Next** to proceed.

 3. The next dialog box asks whether you want to log on to a "directory server." This server is like a giant white pages that lists all the people you can call who also have NetMeeting running. If this sounds like fun (remember that the server will show *your* name, as well), leave the **Log on to a directory server when NetMeeting starts** check box activated. (If you have Windows 98 Second Edition, you can gain some privacy by activating the **Do not list my name in the directory** check box.) Click **Next** when you're ready to proceed.

4. Now the wizard asks for a few particulars that help identify you in the NetMeeting world. Enter your **First name**, your **Last name**, and your **E-mail address**, and then click **Next**.

5. The wizard will next ask how you want to categorize the data you just entered: **For personal use**, **For business use**, or **For adults-only use**. Make the appropriate choice and click **Next**.

6. In the next dialog box, select the speed of your Internet connection and click **Next**. (In Windows 98 Second Edition, you now get a dialog box asking if you want to set up a couple of shortcuts for NetMeeting. These shortcuts are a good idea, so leave the check boxes activated and click **Next**.)

7. NetMeeting now launches the Audio Tuning Wizard, which will check your sound card to see whether it supports two-way sound transmission and to set the appropriate audio levels. Click **Next**. (Again, the Windows 98 Second Edition version of NetMeeting tosses in an extra step. This time, you click **Test** to set the volume level of your speakers. Click **Next** when you're done.)

8. Now you'll see the dialog box shown in the next figure. Make sure that you have your sound card microphone plugged in and at the ready. Then click **Start Recording** and speak into the microphone, using your normal voice. (In Windows 98 Second Edition, there's no button, so just start talking. The wizard suggests that you read the couple of paragraphs under the Start Recording button, but you can make up any old gibberish).

Click Start Recording and then speak into the microphone, using your normal voice.

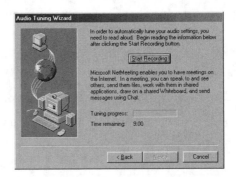

9. When the recording is complete, click **Finish** in the final Wizard dialog box to continue loading NetMeeting.

 After the Wizard has completed its labors (and each subsequent time you start NetMeeting, the Microsoft NetMeeting window, shown in the next figure, appears. (Note that you'll only see the long list of NetMeeting users if you elected to log on to the directory at startup. If you didn't, you can log on now at any time by selecting the **Call, Log On to server** command. Note, too, that the version of NetMeeting that comes with Windows 98 Second Edition has a different layout.)

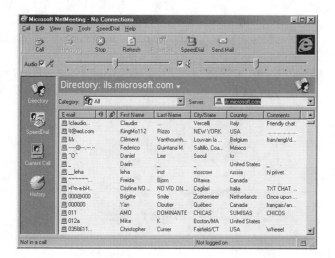

The NetMeeting window with an active conference.

Reach Out and Touch Someone: Placing NetMeeting Calls

Without further ado, let's get right to a NetMeeting phone call:

1. If you want to call someone in the directory list, highlight that name.

2. Select the **Call, New Call** command, or click the Call button in the NetMeeting toolbar. You'll see the New Call dialog box, shown in the following figure.

3. In the **Address** list (the **To** list in Windows 98 Second Edition), specify the person you want to call by entering one of the following:

   ➤ If the person is logged on to the same directory server as you, type his or her email address.

   ➤ If the person is logged on to a different directory server, type the server name, a slash (/) and then the person's email address (for example: **ils.microsoft.com/biff@newbie.net**).

➤ If you're on a network, type the name that the person's computer uses on the network.

➤ If the person is connected to the Internet, type the IP address of the person's computer.

4. Make sure that the **Call using** list says Automatic, and then click **Call**.

5. After NetMeeting finds the user and places the call, the other person hears a ring and sees a dialog box similar to the one shown in the next figure. The remote user clicks **Accept** to "answer" the call, or clicks **Ignore** to reject the call. (NetMeeting rejects an incoming call automatically if it isn't answered after five rings.)

Use this dialog box to tell NetMeeting who you gonna call.

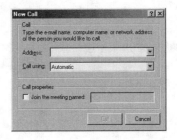

This dialog box appears when there is an incoming NetMeeting call.

6. To talk to the other person, just speak into your microphone.

When it's time to end a NetMeeting call, either select **Call, Hang Up** or click the Hang Up button in the toolbar.

If you call certain people frequently, you can use NetMeeting's SpeedDial feature to connect to these users with only a couple of mouse clicks or keystrokes.

To create a SpeedDial entry, follow these steps:

1. If you're already connected to the person you want to put on the SpeedDial list, highlight her name.

2. Select the **SpeedDial, Add SpeedDial** command to display the Add SpeedDial dialog box. (In Windows 98 Second Edition, select **Call, Create SpeedDial**.)

3. Use the **Address** text box to enter the address of the person. (If you highlighted a connected user in advance, the address will be filled in for you.)

4. Make sure that the **Call using** list says Automatic.

5. Click **OK**.

After you've added someone to the SpeedDial, you can call that person by pulling down the SpeedDial menu and selecting her name from the list that appears at the bottom of the menu.

Hanging Out a "Do Not Disturb" Sign

If you have NetMeeting running but you don't want to accept any new calls for a while, you can hang out an electronic "Do Not Disturb" sign by activating the **Call, Do Not Disturb** command, and then clicking **OK** in the dialog box that appears.

What Other Fun Can You Have in NetMeeting?

Internet phone calls are a lot of fun, but NetMeeting is no mere one-trick pony. After you've established a connection, there are all kinds of things you can do to take advantage of it. Here's a quick summary:

➤ **Sending files to and fro:** To send a file to the other person, select **Tools, File Transfer, Send File** (in Windows 98 Second Edition, select **Tools, File Transfer**), or press **Ctrl+F**. Use the dialog box that shows up to pick out the file, and then click **Send**.

➤ **Using Chat for text talk:** If you don't have a microphone, NetMeeting's audio features won't do you much good. That doesn't mean you can't communicate with remote callers, however. For simple text communications in real time, NetMeeting's Chat feature is perfect. To run Chat, either select **Tools, Chat** or click the Chat toolbar button. (You can also press **Ctrl+T**.) In the Chat window that appears, type your message and press **Enter**.

➤ **Collaborating with a whiteboard:** Whiteboards have become *de rigueur* in boardrooms and conference rooms across the land. Presenters, facilitators, and meeting leaders use them to record action points, highlight important information, and draw charts and diagrams. You can use NetMeeting's Whiteboard feature for the same purposes. The Whiteboard is basically a revamped version of the Paint window that enables you to enter text, highlight information, and draw lines and shapes. Everything you add to the Whiteboard is reflected on the other users' screens, and they see exactly what you're typing and drawing. To work with the Whiteboard, each person must display it either by selecting **Tools, Whiteboard** or by clicking the Whiteboard toolbar button. (You can also click **Ctrl+W**.)

➤ **Sharing programs:** Chat and the Whiteboard are handy features, but their functionality is limited to text and simple drawings. For truly collaborative computing, you need to be able to run a program on one computer and display what's happening on the other person's machine. To share a running application, either select **Tools, Share Application** (in Windows 98 Second Edition, select **Tools, Sharing**) or click the Share button in the toolbar. In the list that appears, click the name of the application you want to share and then click **OK**. If you want to give the other person the ability to work with the program as well, either activate the **Tools, Start Collaborating** command or click the **Collaborate** toolbar button, and then click **OK**.

Chapter 17

Wandering the Web with Internet Explorer

In This Chapter

➤ Getting comfy with the Internet Explorer window

➤ How to navigate pages

➤ Internet Explorer's Search, Favorites, and History features

➤ Setting up subscriptions and Active Channels

➤ How to watch online movies using NetShow

➤ Customizing Internet Explorer to taste

Email is the most popular Internet pastime, and newsgroups and Internet phone calls have their place in the wired world. But for sheer, unadulterated, no-holds-barred, time-wasting, finger-clicking, mega-JPMs (Jolts Per Minute) fun, you can't do much better than the World Wide Web. The *Web* (the aficionado's preferred short form) is home to millions of sites that display everything from simple "Hey, look at me!" personal home pages, to "Hey, buy me!" online shopping malls, to "Hey, surf me" corporate marketing efforts.

If the Web has a downside, it's that there may be *too* much eye candy. When people are first exposed to the Web's embarrassment of riches, they often can't get enough and spend endless hours *surfing* (as navigating from site-to-site is called). This addiction must have hit the Microsoft programmers, too, because it's clear that they built Windows 98 with the Web in mind. It's possible to access Web sites from just about anywhere in Windows 98.

SEE ALSO

> ➤ *In Chapter 9, "Webtop Windows: Web Integration and the Active Desktop," p. 93, you learned how to use basic Web techniques for interacting with the desktop and folders.*

Still, because the prime vehicle for your Web journeys is the Internet Explorer browser, that's what I'll talk about most in this chapter. I'll show you how to leap from page to page, how to store you favorite sites, and how to use some of the new Web goodies in Windows 98, including subscriptions, channels, and even how to view Web-based movies with NetShow. I'll also tell you about some of the stuff that's new and different in Internet Explorer 5, which is the Web browser that comes with Windows 98 Second Edition.

A Tour of the Internet Explorer Screen

Windows 98 offers a ton of ways to get Internet Explorer up and surfing. Here's the basic method:

1. If you're looking to burn off a few extra calories after dinner, here's the long way to start Internet Explorer: select **Start, Programs, Internet Explorer, Internet Explorer**. (If you're running Windows 98 Second Edition, you select **Start, Programs, Internet Explorer**.) Otherwise, Windows 98 gives you two ways to launch Internet Explorer with a single click:

   ➤ Click the desktop's **Internet Explorer** icon. (Remember to double-click if you have Web integration turned off.)

   ➤ Click the Launch Internet Explorer Browser icon in the taskbar's Quick Launch toolbar.

2. You may now see a dialog box telling you that something or other is "not available offline." If so, click **Connect**.

3. If you don't have a connection established with your Internet service provider, the connection dialog box shows up at this point. Go ahead and click **Connect** to reunite Windows 98 and the Internet.

The following screen shows the Internet Explorer window and points out a few interesting landmarks.

Here's a summary of the main features of the Internet Explorer window:

➤ **Page title:** The top line of the screen shows you the title of the current Web page.

➤ **Address bar:** This area shows you the address of the current page.

➤ **Links bar:** This toolbar gives you a few predefined *links*, which are connections to other locations on the Web. Click one of these links (I explain each of them later on) to head for that page.

Address bar   Page title

*Here's the Internet
Explorer window.*

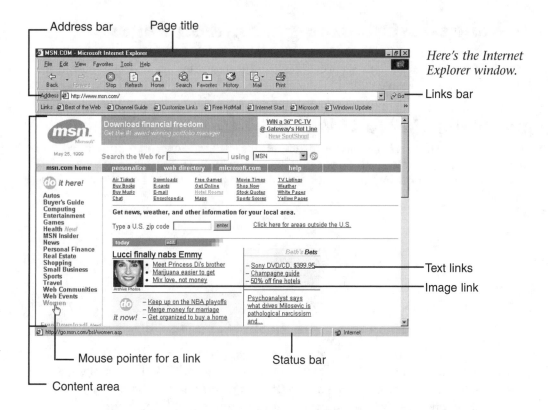

Links bar

Text links

Image link

Mouse pointer for a link   Status bar

Content area

➤ **Content area:** This area below the Address and Links bars takes up the bulk of the Internet Explorer screen. It's where the body of each Web page is displayed. You can use the vertical scroll bar to see more of the current document.

➤ **Image link/text link:** The content area for most Web pages also boasts a link or two (or 10). These links come in two flavors: images and text (the latter are usually underlined and/or in a different color than the rest of the text). You select a link by clicking it. When you point to a link, Internet Explorer does two things: it changes the mouse pointer to a hand with a pointing finger, and it displays in the Status bar the address of the document to which the link will take you.

➤ **Status bar:** This bar lets you know Internet Explorer's current status, displays a description of the links you point to, and tells you the progress of the current Internet Explorer operation (such as downloading a file).

Web Wanderlust: Working with Web Pages

Now that you're familiar with the lay of the Internet Explorer land, you can start using it to navigate sites. This section takes you through the various ways you can use Internet Explorer to weave your way through the Web.

Leaping from Link to Link: Navigating the Web

As you saw earlier, Internet Explorer displays links either as text in an underlined font that's a different color from the rest of the text, or as an image. To follow one of these links, you need do nothing more than click the link text or the image. What could be simpler?

Some Images Are All Show and No Go

Just to keep us all confused, not all of the images you see on a Web page are necessarily links. Some are there strictly for show—you can click them until your finger falls off, and nothing will happen. How can you tell links from nonlinks? The only surefire way is to point your mouse at the picture. If the mouse pointer turns into the little hand with the pointing finger, then you know you're dealing with a link.

If you want to strike out for a particular Web site, you can specify the address by following these easy steps:

1. Click inside the Address bar.
2. If the address is one you used recently, drop down the list and select the address. Otherwise, delete the current address.
3. Type the address for the new site.
4. Press **Enter**.

The Weirdness of Web Addresses

Internet addresses, with their "http" this and slash (/) that are strange beasts, indeed. If you'd like to know more about these addresses (which are called *Uniform Resource Locators*—URLs for short—in geekspeak), here's an example that illustrates the general format:

```
http://www.mcfedries.com/books/cigwin98/index.html
```

http://	This part identifies this as a Web address.
www.mcfedries.com	This is the "domain name" of the host computer where the Web page resides (www.mcfedries.com is my Web server).
/books/cigwin98/	This is the directory that contains the Web page.
index.html	This is the file name of the Web page.

This is probably as good a time as any to take a closer look at how much the Web has infiltrated the Windows 98 world. The next figure demonstrates two other ways to type a Web address:

➤ All folder windows in Windows 98 have an Address bar just like the one in Internet Explorer. For example, check out the My Computer window shown in the next figure. (If you don't see this bar on your own machine, right-click the toolbar or menu bar and activate the **Address Bar** command in the menu that appears.) You type the Web site address in the Address Bar and press **Enter**. In this case, the My Computer window magically transforms itself into the Internet Explorer window and the Web page appears!

➤ The taskbar also has its own Address bar (see the next figure). To display it, right-click an empty section of the taskbar, click **Toolbars** in the menu, and then activate the **Address** command. Again, you type the Web site address and press **Enter**. In this case, Windows 98 loads Internet Explorer and displays the page.

You can enter a Web page address here
to view the page inside this window.

*Windows 98 has Address
bars out the wazoo.*

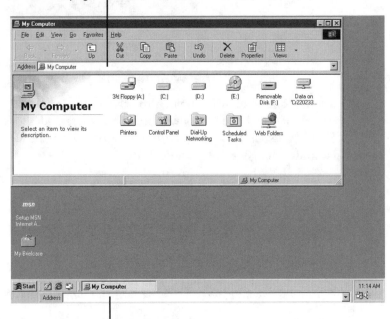

You can also enter the address here to
view the page inside Internet Explorer.

After you've started leaping and jumping through the Web's cyberspace, you'll often want to head back to a previous site, or even to your start page (the first page you see when you launch Internet Explorer). Here's a rundown of the various techniques you can use to move back and forth in Internet Explorer:

➤ To go back to the previous document, either click the **Back** toolbar button or select the **Go, Back** command. (With Internet Explorer 5, select **View, Go To, Back**.)

➤ After you've gone back to a previous document, you can move ahead to the next document either by clicking the toolbar's **Forward** button or by selecting the **Go, Forward** command. (With Internet Explorer 5, select **View, Go To, Forward**.)

➤ Both the Back and Forward buttons do double-duty as drop-down lists. When you click the little arrow to the right of each button, Internet Explorer displays a list of the sites you've visited (see the next figure). You can then click the site you want and jump straight there. Note that these lists are cleared when you return to the start page.

➤ To return to the start page, either click the **Home** button or select **Go, Start Page**. (With Internet Explorer 5, select **View, Go To, Home Page**.)

➤ To return to a specific document you've visited, pull down the **File** menu and select the document's title from the list near the bottom of the menu. (With Internet Explorer 5, select **View, Go To** and select the title from the menu.)

Click this arrow to display the list.

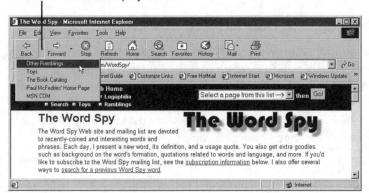

The Back and Forward buttons display a list of the current string of sites you've visited.

If you're not sure where you want to go on the Web, Internet Explorer's Links bar contains five prefab sites that you can try out to get your Web feet wet. (If you can't see the full Links bar, move the mouse pointer over the left edge of the bar and then drag it below the Address bar.) Here's a summary of each link:

➤ **Best of the Web:** This is a great place to start your Web explorations. Clicking this link takes you to the Web Directory page, which contains even more links arranged by category: Entertainment, Finance, News, Sports, and much more.

➤ **Channel Guide:** Click this link to display the Web Events page, which gives you access to pages that feature audio and video.

➤ **Customize Links:** This link takes you to a page that tells you how to customize the Links bar.

➤ **Free HotMail** (Internet Explorer 5 only): Clicking here takes you to a page where you can sign up for a free email account with Microsoft's HotMail service.

➤ **Internet Start:** This link returns you to Internet Explorer's startup page.

 ➤ **Microsoft** (Internet Explorer 5 only): This button takes you to the Microsoft home page.

➤ **Windows Update** (Internet Explorer 5 only): Click this link to go to the Windows Update Web site.

➤ **Windows** (Internet Explorer 5 only): This link takes you to the Windows home page.

➤ **Internet Explorer News** (Internet Explorer 4 only): **:** Click this link to get the latest Internet Explorer news and updates.

211

Dealing with Files in Internet Explorer

As you click your way around the Web, you'll find that some links don't take you to other pages but are, instead, tied directly to a file. In this case, Internet Explorer throws the File Download dialog box at you and asks whether you want to **Open this file** or **Save this file to disk**. Make sure that the latter option is activated, and then click **OK**. In the Save As dialog box that shows up next, choose a location for the file, and then click **Save**.

Can I Get There from Here? Using the Search Page

The navigation approaches you've tried so far have encompassed the two extremes of Web surfing: randomly clicking on links to see what happens, and entering addresses to display specific sites. What if you're looking for information on a particular topic, but you don't know any appropriate addresses and you don't want to waste time clicking aimlessly around the Web? In this case, you'll want to put the Web to work for you. That is, you'll want to crank up one of the Web's search engines to track down sites that contain the data you're looking for.

Conveniently, Internet Explorer contains a special Search feature that gives you easy access to a few of the Web's best search engines. Here's how you use this feature to perform a search:

1. Either click the toolbar's **Search** button or select the **View, Explorer Bar, Search** command. Internet Explorer adds a Search screen to the left of the content area.

2. The way you run the search depends on which search engine you have displayed. In all cases, however, there is a text box you use to enter a key word (or two) that represents the type of site you want to find.

3. When you've entered your search text, click the **Search** button. (This button may be called Seek, Submit, or Find, depending on the search engine.)

4. At this point, Internet Explorer may display a scary-looking Security Alert dialog box. This is just a warning that when you submit data to a site, other people may be able to view the data. That's no big deal here, so click **Yes**.

When you press this button...

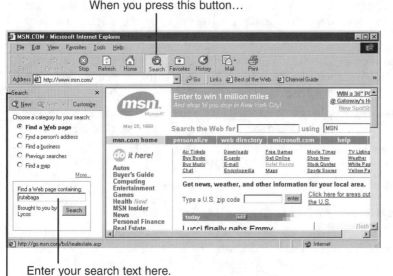

...Internet Explorer displays this Search bar.

Enter your search text here.

Windows 98's Internet Explorer has a new Search bar that gives you access to some of the Web's top search engines.

5. The search engine will rummage through its database of Web sites and then, hopefully, it will display a list of sites that contain the word or words you entered. If so, great: just click any of the offered links to check out the page (see the following figure). If no matches are found, repeat steps 4 and 5, using different search terms.

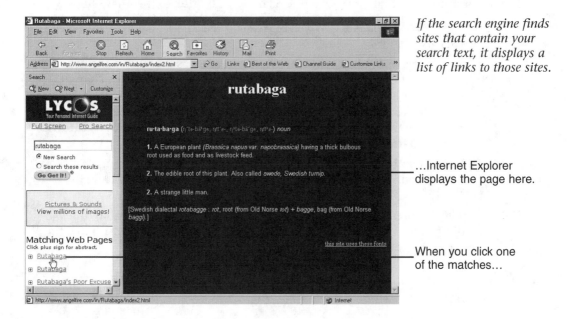

If the search engine finds sites that contain your search text, it displays a list of links to those sites.

...Internet Explorer displays the page here.

When you click one of the matches...

Internet Explorer's Search feature can use a different search engine if you aren't getting good results. How you change the search engine depends on which version of Internet Explorer you're running:

➤ **Internet Explorer 4:** The Search area usually displays a random search engine (this is called the *Provider-of-the-day engine*). To use a different search engine, click **Choose a Search Engine**.

 ➤ **Internet Explorer 5:** In the Search bar, click the **Next** button or drop down the **Next** button and select a search engine from the list. You can control the order of the search engines and the engines that appear on the list by clicking **Customize**.

The Favorites Folder: A Site to Remember

The sad truth is that much of what you'll see on the Web will be dreck that's utterly forgettable and not worth a second surf. However, there are all kinds of gems out there waiting to be uncovered—sites that you'll want to visit regularly. Instead of memorizing the appropriate addresses or plastering your monitor with sticky notes full of URLs, you can use Internet Explorer's handy Favorites feature to keep track of your choice sites.

The Favorites feature is really just a standard folder (you'll find it in your main Windows 98 folder) that you use to store shortcuts that point to Internet sites. The advantage of using the Favorites folder as opposed to any other folder is that you can add, view, and link to the Favorites folder shortcuts directly from Internet Explorer.

When you find a site that you'd like to declare as a favorite, follow these steps:

1. Select the **Favorites, Add To Favorites** command. The Add Favorite dialog box appears.

 2. This dialog box asks whether you want to subscribe to the page. I'll hold off on this subscription business until later in this chapter (see the "Hands-Free Surfing: Setting Up Subscriptions" section). For now, make sure that the **No, just add the page to my favorites** option is activated. (With Internet Explorer 5, you want **Make available offline** to be deactivated.)

3. The **Name** text box displays the title of the page. This is the text that appears later, when you view the list of your favorites. Feel free to edit this text if you like.

4. Internet Explorer enables you to set up subfolders to hold related favorites. If you don't want to bother with this, skip down to step 7. Otherwise, click the **Create in** button to expand the dialog box as shown here.

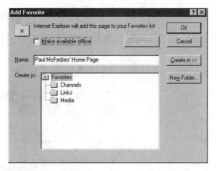

Clicking the Create in button gives you this enlarged version of the Add Favorite dialog box.

5. To create a new folder, click **New Folder** (there's a duh), type the name of the folder in the dialog box that shows up, and then click **OK**. Windows 98 takes you back to the expanded Add Favorite dialog box.

6. Click the folder you want to use to store the favorite.

7. Click **OK**.

Organizing Your Favorites

After you've worked with Internet Explorer for a while, you may find that your Favorites folder is getting a bit messy. To help relieve the clutter, you can work with the Favorites folder directly and use it to add more subfolders, move, rename, and delete favorites, and so on. To try this out, select the **Favorites, Organize Favorites** command to open the Organize Favorites folder dialog box.

The purpose of the Favorites folder, of course, is to give you quick access to those sites you visit regularly. To link to one of the shortcuts in your Favorites folder, you have three choices:

➤ Pull down Internet Explorer's **Favorites** menu and then select the page you want.

➤ Click the **Favorites** toolbar button, or select **View, Explorer Bar, Favorites**, to display the Favorites bar, as shown in the following figure. Click a link in the Favorites bar.

➤ In the taskbar, select **Start, Favorites** and then click the favorite you want from the submenu that appears.

The Favorites bar keeps your fave-rave links visible at all times.

When you press this button...

...the Favorites bar makes an appearance.

When you click a link...

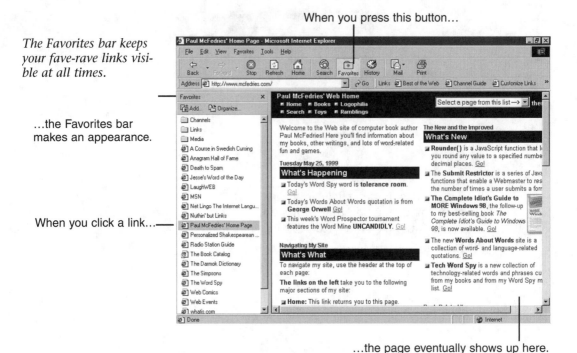

...the page eventually shows up here.

Taking Advantage of the History List

I showed you earlier how you can click the Back and Forward buttons to follow in your own Web footsteps. Internet Explorer wipes those lists clean, however, when you return to the start page or exit the program. What do you do when you want to revisit a site you checked out a few days ago? Well, you'll be happy to know that Internet Explorer keeps track of the addresses of all the pages you've perused during the last 20 days!

This is called the **History** list, and you can view it either by clicking the History button in the toolbar, or by selecting the **View, Explorer Bar, History** command. You'll then see the History bar on the left side of the window, as shown here. Click the day or week you want, and then click the link you want. It's that easy.

Hands–Free Surfing: Synchronizations and Subscriptions

The Web is in a constant state of flux. Not only do new sites pop up like mushrooms after a warm rain, but existing pages change regularly as Webmasters tweak their content. How's a poor surfer supposed to keep up with the latest and greatest? The hard way is to set up a site as a favorite and then check out the site regularly. That route quickly loses its luster as your Favorites folder fattens up.

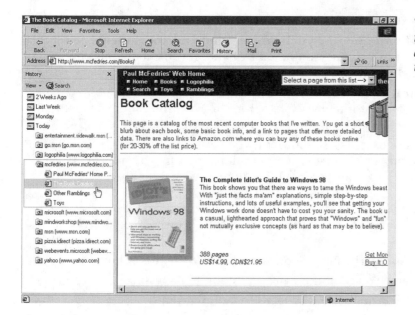

The History list keeps track of all the Web addresses you called on in the last 20 days.

Fortunately, Internet Explorer offers an easier way to do this, but the exact path you take depends on which version of the program you're using. The next two sections give you the specifics.

Synchronizing Pages with Internet Explorer 5

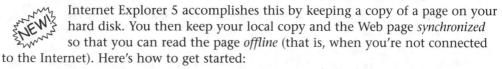

Internet Explorer 5 accomplishes this by keeping a copy of a page on your hard disk. You then keep your local copy and the Web page *synchronized* so that you can read the page *offline* (that is, when you're not connected to the Internet). Here's how to get started:

➤ **If the page is already set up as a favorite:** Pull down the **Favorites** menu, right-click the favorite, and click **Make available offline**.

➤ **If the page isn't yet a favorite:** Surf to the page and select **Favorites, Add to Favorites** to reacquaint yourself with the Add Favorite dialog box. Activate **Make available offline** and then click **Customize**.

Either way, you end up alongside the Offline Favorite Wizard. Here's what happens now:

1. The first wizard dialog box doesn't do much, so click **Next**.

2. The next dialog box asks if you want any pages that are linked to the favorite to be downloaded, as well. If you don't want the linked pages, activate **No**; otherwise, activate **Yes** and then use the **Download pages *x* links deep from this page** spin box to set the number of levels of links you want grabbed. Click **Next**.

3. The wizard next wonders how you want the page synchronized:

   ➤ **Only when I choose Synchronize from the Tools menu:** Select this option to run the synchronization by hand. If you choose this option, click **Next** and then skip to Step 5.

   ➤ **I would like to create a new schedule:** This is the option to choose if you'd prefer that Internet Explorer run the synchronization automatically on a preset schedule. In this case, click **Next** and then go to Step 4.

   ➤ **Using this existing schedule:** If you've already put together a schedule when setting up another synchronization, you can reuse it here by selecting it from this list. Click **Next** and jump to Step 5.

4. If you elected to set up a synchronization schedule, the next dialog box offers the following controls to set the schedule (click **Next** when you're ready to move on):

   ➤ **Every *x* days:** The number of days between synchronizations.

   ➤ **at:** The time you want the synchronization to happen.

   ➤ **Name:** The name for this synchronization schedule.

   ➤ **If my computer is not connected...:** If you activate this check box, Internet Explorer will connect your computer to the Internet in order to download the page (or pages).

5. The last dialog box asks if the Web page requires you to log on. If not, activate **No**; if so, activate **Yes** and then enter your **User name** and **Password** (twice). Then click **Finish**.

6. If you were adding a favorite, choose a folder and then click **OK** in the Add Favorite dialog box.

If you decided upon a manual synchronization, you download the pages for offline reading by selecting the **Tools, Synchronize** command. The Items to Synchronize dialog box appears. Deactivate the check boxes for any pages you don't want to synchronize, and then click the **Synchronize** button.

The Items to Synchronize dialog box also lets you do the following tasks:

➤ **Adjust the settings for a synchronized item:** Highlight the item and then click **Properties**. The dialog box that appears has three tabs:

Web Document: Enables you to stop synchronizing the page by deactivating **Make this page available offline**.

Schedule: Enables you to change the synchronization schedule for the page.

Download: Enables you to change the number of link levels you want downloaded. Also, if you activate **When this page changes, send e-mail to** check box and then fill in your **E-mail address** and **Mail Server (SMTP)** (the

Internet name of your ISP's outgoing mail computer), Internet Explorer will send you an email to let you know when the page has changed.

➤ **Adjust the settings for the Synchronize feature itself:** Click **Setup** to get to the Synchronization Settings dialog box. Once again, there are three tabs:

Logon: Enables you to set up a synchronization every time you log on to Windows 98.

On Idle: Enables you to set up a synchronization when your computer hasn't been used for a while.

Scheduled: Enables you to adjust the synchronization schedules that you've defined so far.

Setting Up Subscriptions with Internet Explorer 4

With Internet Explorer 4, you keep track of Web pages by using *subscriptions*. The idea is that you subscribe to a particular page, and Internet Explorer regularly checks that page for changes. If there's something new for you to see, Internet Explorer can either download the page for "offline" viewing or send you an email to let you know.

To set up a subscription, there are two paths you can take:

➤ If the page is already part of your Favorites folder, select **Favorites, Organize Favorites**, right-click the page in the Organize Favorites dialog box, and then click **Subscribe.**

➤ For any other site, first surf to the site you want to work with and then select the **Favorites, Add to Favorites** command to display the Add Favorite dialog box.

Either way, you'll be presented with the following two choices:

➤ **Only tell me when this page is updated:** If you activate this option, Internet Explorer sends you an email if it detects that the page has been updated.

➤ **Notify me of updates and download the page for offline viewing:** If you choose this option, instead, Internet Explorer not only sends you an email when it sees that the page is changed, but it also downloads the new page so that you can view the update without having to connect to the Internet.

When you've made your choice, click **OK**. Now, each midnight, Internet Explorer will connect to the Internet, check out your subscriptions, and then notify you about the updates. Note, too, that you can force Internet Explorer to update all your subscriptions at any time by selecting the **Favorites, Update All Subscriptions** command.

If you want to customize the way Internet Explorer deals with your subscriptions, select the **Favorites, Manage Subscriptions** command. In the Subscriptions window that appears, highlight a subscription and then select **File, Properties**. The dialog box that pops up contains three tabs:

➤ **Subscription:** This tab gives you a summary of the subscription settings. If you no longer want to subscribe to the Web page, click the **Unsubscribe** button.

➤ **Receiving:** Use this tab to specify a **Subscription type** (notification only or notification plus download). You can also use the **Notification** group to specify the email address used by Internet Explorer to notify you of updates.

➤ **Schedule:** Use this tab to set up a schedule for the subscription update. If you activate **Manually**, Internet Explorer doesn't check automatically for changes. Instead, you have to run the Update All Subscriptions command, as described earlier. If you activate the **Scheduled** option, instead, Internet Explorer will automatically check for changes. To set the frequency of those checks, click **Edit** and use the Custom Schedule dialog box to choose the frequency of the updates and the time of day they occur.

The Internet Show Must Go On: Using the NetShow Player

For those of us who use the Web every day for research, content is king. We don't give a hoot about fancy-schmancy graphics and other right-brain ticklers. "Show me the text!" is our battle cry.

When our work is done, however, fun becomes the operative word and our eyes and ears crave novelty in the form of well-made images, animations, and maybe a snippet or two of sound. With Windows 98, it's possible to take this search for Web-based entertainment to the next level. That's because the Windows 98 package includes NetShow, a tool that enables you to view Web-based movies, animations, and audio feeds.

So now you may be saying:

Wait a minute. Doesn't it take forever to download all that stuff?

Nope. NetShow's parlor trick is that it can handle video and audio on-the-fly. You wait just a few seconds and NetShow begins the show without further ado. It sounds like voodoo, I know, but it works pretty well. The only catch is that you need a reasonably fast Internet connection   28.8Kbps is usually the minimum. The faster the connection, the better the quality of the video and audio.

To get started with NetShow, type the following address into Internet Explorer:

```
http://www.microsoft.com/windows/windowsmedia/
```

The page that appears gives you a bit of background about NetShow. From there, click the Gallery link to get to the NetShow Gallery page, which includes NetShow samples, pointers to upcoming live events, past events, and much more.

Each NetShow extravaganza is presented inside the NetShow Player. As you mess around with the shows, you'll see that the NetShow Player comes in the following three guises:

➤ **Separate NetShow Player for video:** In some cases, activating a show displays a new NetShow Player window.

➤ **Separate NetShow Player for audio only:** This is basically the same as the NetShow Player in the preceding figure, except there's no video portion.

➤ **Embedded NetShow player:** Many NetShow-enhanced Web pages have the NetShow Player built right in.

Internet Explorer Your Way: Customizing the Internet Properties

To get the most out of Internet Explorer, you should set up the program to suit your own personal style. This includes not only cosmetic options such as the fonts and colors used by the program, but also more important concerns, such as the level of security that Internet Explorer uses.

 To display these options, select the **View, Internet Options** command. (With Internet Explorer 5, you select **Tools, Internet Options**.) You'll see the Internet Options dialog box, shown in the following figure. The rest of this chapter gives you the gory details on the various tabs found in this dialog box.

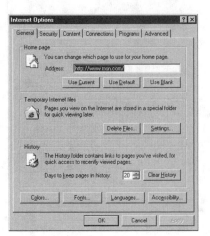

Use the Internet Options dialog box to customize Internet Explorer to suit the way you work.

The **General** tab contains a mixed bag of options:

➤ **Home page**: To change the Internet Explorer *home page* (the page that first appears when you launch the browser), first navigate to the page you want to use, and then click **Use Current** in this group. To revert to Internet Explorer's default home page, click the **Use Default** button. If you'd prefer that Internet Explorer not load a page at startup, click **Use Blank**.

➤ **Temporary Internet files**: The temporary Internet files folder is a cache of files that Internet Explorer stores on your computer as you visit pages. Then, when you revisit a page, Internet Explorer can display the page contents much more quickly. You can click **Delete Files** to clear this cache, and you can click **Settings** to adjust a few parameters. I recommend leaving these options as they are, however.

➤ **History:** This group controls various options related to the History list I talked about earlier. Use the **Days to keep pages in history** spin box to set the maximum number of days that Internet Explorer will store an URL in its History list. You can also click **Clear History** to remove all URLs from the History folder.

The **Security** tab in the Internet Options dialog box lets you customize the level of security used by Internet Explorer. I don't recommend changing any of the settings in this tab, however.

The **Content** tab, shown in the following figure, boasts a wide array of settings for dealing with the content you come across on the Web.

The Content tab lets you restrict access to certain Web sites as well as store information about yourself.

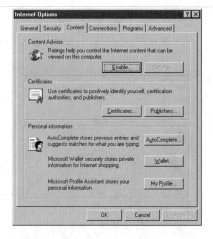

The buttons in the **Content Advisor** group let you control the type of content that appears in the browser:

➤ **Enable:** Clicking this button displays the Create Supervisor Password dialog box, which you use to enter a password for the Content Advisor. (With Internet Explorer 5, you go straight to the Content Advisor dialog box, described next. When you click **OK**, the Create Supervisor Password dialog box appears.) After you've done that, the name of this button changes to Disable. You can turn off the ratings by clicking this button and entering your password.

➤ **Settings:** Clicking this button displays the Content Advisor, which you use to set site restrictions for people who don't know the password. The idea is that you select a category (such as Language or Nudity) and then move the slider to set the maximum level that users who don't have a password can view. If a site is rated higher, users must enter the supervisor password to download the site.

Other Ways to Restrict Content

The Internet is bursting with other tools that can help parents restrict the content their children can view. These packages come with names such as CyberSitter, Net Nanny, and KinderGuard   you get the idea. The Yahoo! Service has a list of these software packages at the following address:

```
http://www.yahoo.com/Business_and_Economy/Companies/Computers/Software/
Internet/Blocking_and_Filtering/Titles/
```

The **Certificates** group deals with site certificates that act as positive identifications on the Web. This is advanced stuff, and it can be safely ignored.

The **Personal information** group gives you a place to store some data about yourself. Here are the Internet Explorer 5 options:

➤ **AutoComplete:** This new feature enables Internet Explorer 5 to automatically enter some data for you, including form data. Click this button and then activate the check boxes for the features with which you want to use AutoComplete.

➤ **Wallet:** Click this button to enter data about yourself that can be entered automatically when you're shopping online. (Note, however, that not all sites support this feature.)

➤ **My Profile:** Click this button to enter more data about yourself that Web sites can grab automatically.

Here are the Internet Explorer 4 options:

➤ **Edit Profile:** Click this button to enter info about yourself, such as your name, email address, home and business addresses, and more. With this data in place, Web sites that would normally pester you for your name, rank, and serial number can be told to just grab what they need from your profile.

➤ **Reset Sharing:** After you've given a site permission to access your profile, that site will be able to get this data without prompting each time you visit the site. To prevent this access, click the **Reset Sharing** button to clear the list of sites that have access to your profile.

➤ **Addresses:** If you plan to shop online, you can use Microsoft Wallet to make things easier. For starters, use the **Addresses** button to store one or more addresses. You can then supply the online retailer with an address from the wallet instead of typing the info manually.

➤ **Payments:** Similarly, you can click this button to add data about your credit cards to the wallet.

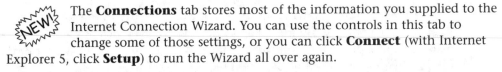 The **Connections** tab stores most of the information you supplied to the Internet Connection Wizard. You can use the controls in this tab to change some of those settings, or you can click **Connect** (with Internet Explorer 5, click **Setup**) to run the Wizard all over again.

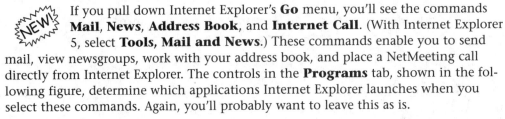 If you pull down Internet Explorer's **Go** menu, you'll see the commands **Mail**, **News**, **Address Book**, and **Internet Call**. (With Internet Explorer 5, select **Tools, Mail and News**.) These commands enable you to send mail, view newsgroups, work with your address book, and place a NetMeeting call directly from Internet Explorer. The controls in the **Programs** tab, shown in the following figure, determine which applications Internet Explorer launches when you select these commands. Again, you'll probably want to leave this as is.

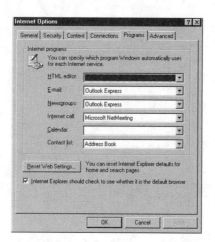

Use the Programs tab to set the default programs that Internet Explorer uses for things like email and reading Usenet news-groups.

Finally, the **Advanced** tab boasts a huge list of check boxes and option buttons that control numerous aspects of the way Internet Explorer interacts with the Web. For example, if you're sick of those lame MIDI files that so many Webmasters play when you visit their sites, you can turn them off by deactivating the **Play sounds** check box.

Unfortunately, there are just way too many options to go through here. Most are straightforward, however. If you're not sure what a particular control is used for, right-click the control and then click **What's This?** to get a brief explanation.

Chapter 18

Becoming a Webmaster with FrontPage Express and Other Publishing Tools

One of the most interesting of Web phenomena is the startling fact that people from all walks of life are clamoring to publish their own pages. I'm sure there are as many reasons for this as there are would-be Web weavers. Some folks are tired of being passive Internet consumers and want to produce their own content rather than merely digesting it. Others have information (essays, stories, jokes, diatribes, shopping lists) that they want to share with the world at large, but they have never before had the opportunity to do so. And there are other poor souls whose boss has told them, "Get our company on the World Wide Web *now*, before it's too late!", and who have to get up to speed before it's too late for *them*.

Whatever the reasons, if you'd like to carve out your own chunk of Web real estate, Microsoft has two tools that can help. One is Windows 98's FrontPage Express, which you use to create Web pages using more or less the same commands you use to pound out memos and letters in a word processor. The other is the Web Publishing Wizard, which helps you get your pages on the Web by using the wizardly step-by-step approach you've come to know and love. This chapter shows you how to wield these Windows Web page wonders.

Using FrontPage Express to Forge Web Pages

 Web pages are really just simple text files that contain extra instructions that tell a Web browser how to display a page. These extra instructions are called *tags,* and together they constitute the *Hypertext Markup Language* (HTML). There's nothing difficult about HTML, but it's fussy, fiddley stuff that requires patience and a keen eye for detail.

Instead of messing around with the intricacies of HTML, you can use FrontPage Express, which enables you to build Web pages using simple menu commands, toolbar buttons, and dialog boxes. It's a lot like using a program such as WordPad because you'll be using fonts, alignment options, bulleted lists, and so on. Of course, there are also commands for creating things like links and tables.

Downloading FrontPage Express

For some reason, Microsoft dropped FrontPage Express from the lineup in Windows 98 Second Edition. You can still get it, though. Just head to the Windows Update Web site (http://windowsupdate.microsoft.com/), activate the **FrontPage Express** check box, and start the download.

 To launch FrontPage Express, select **Start, Programs, Internet Explorer, FrontPage Express**. (If you installed FrontPage Express from the Web, you need to select **Start, Programs, Accessories, Internet Tools, FrontPage Express**.)

Getting a Web Page Off the Ground

As you'll see, FrontPage Express has all the bits and pieces you need to create top-notch Web pages. To make your Web weaving even easier, the program also boasts several wizards and templates that you can use to get your pages off to a fine start. Here's how you create a new page in FrontPage Express:

1. Select the **File, New** command, or press **Ctrl+N**. FrontPage Express tosses the New Page dialog box onscreen (as shown in the following figure).

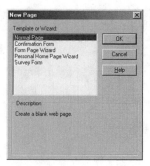

FrontPage Express has a few templates and wizards.

2. Select one of the following templates and wizards:

   ➤ **Normal Page:** This option just creates an empty Web page.

   ➤ **Confirmation Form:** After the user submits a form this option creates a page suitable for display.

   ➤ **Form Page Wizard:** This wizard helps you build a form for gathering data.

   ➤ **New Web View Folder:** Use this wizard to create a template for displaying a folder in Web view.

   ➤ **Personal Home Page Wizard:** This wizard helps you put together a simple home page.

   ➤ **Survey Form:** This template not only creates a form, but also takes the data submitted in the form and stores it in a file.

3. Click **OK.**

4. If you selected a wizard, fill in all the dialog boxes.

5. Many of the pages created using these templates and wizards contain *placeholders*, which are fields where you need to fill in your own data. For example, in the next figure (a Web page created by using the Personal Home Page Wizard), you need to edit the data with your own email address, Web address, and telephone number. Just use the normal text editing techniques to delete the existing information and type your own.

A Few Formatting Features

The pages created by the wizards and templates are an easy way to get a head start on your Web page chores. You'll probably find, however, that you have to make extensive modifications to these pages to end up with the design you prefer. Alternatively, you can start with a blank page and create everything from scratch. Either way, you have to know how to wield the myriad Web page layout and formatting tools that ship with FrontPage Express.

You need to enter your own data in the placeholders created by the templates and wizards.

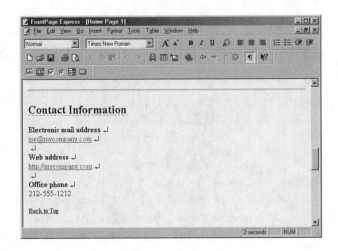

Got a Hankering for HTML?

If you know HTML, you may want to take a gander at the tags created by FrontPage Express. To do so, select the **View, HTML** command. In the View or Edit HTML window that appears, feel free to edit the tags as necessary, and then click **OK** to return to the FrontPage Express window.

Here's a quick look at a few basic techniques:

➤ **Adjusting the page title:** To adjust the title of the Web page, select the **File, Page Properties** command. In the dialog box that appears, use the **Title** text box to enter a new title for the page, and then click **OK**.

➤ **Formatting fonts:** The basic formatting options—bold, italic, underline, font, font size, font color, and so on   can be had by selecting the **Format, Font** command. Use the Font dialog box (shown in the next figure) to make your selections, and then click **OK**. (Note, however, that any typefaces you use will be visible on the user's browser only if the appropriate font is also installed on the user's computer.) As you can see in the following figure, many font options are available via the Format toolbar.

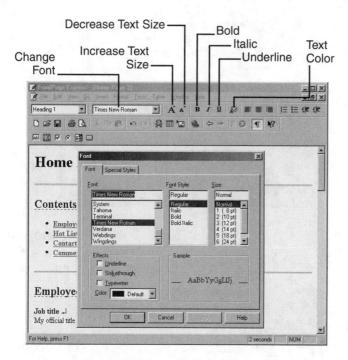

You can use either the Font dialog box or the Format toolbar to set some character-formatting options.

➤ **Setting the page background:** To specify the page background, select the **Format, Background** command to display the Background tab of the Page Properties dialog box (shown next). To set a background image, activate the **Background Image** check box and then enter the image filename (or click **Browse**). Alternatively, use the **Background** list to choose a background color.

➤ **Setting the default colors for text and links:** While you're using the Background tab, you can also use the **Text** list to set the default color for the page text. You can use the other color lists to set the default colors for each **Hyperlink**, **Visited Hyperlink**, and **Active Hyperlink**. (The latter is a link that has been clicked and that the user is waiting for the page to load.)

➤ **Working with headings:** Headings are separate paragraphs that are used most often for section titles. HTML defines six heading styles (Heading 1 to Heading 6) in decreasing order of font size. To apply a heading style to a paragraph, either use the Change Style list in the Format toolbar, or select **Format, Paragraph** and choose the style you want in the Paragraph properties dialog box that appears (see the following figure).

231

Use the dialog box to set the page background. You use it also to set the default colors for text and links.

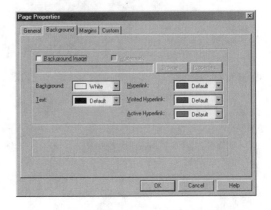

You can select a heading style by using this dialog box or by using the Change Style list.

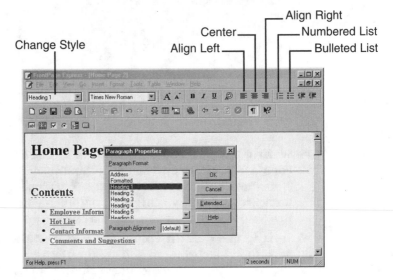

➤ **Aligning paragraphs:** FrontPage Express gives you three paragraph alignment options: Left, Center, and Right. To set the alignment, either use the **Paragraph Alignment** list in the Paragraph Properties dialog box (see the preceding figure), or click the appropriate alignment button in the Format toolbar.

➤ **Formatting bulleted and numbered lists:** If you have a list of things to present, a bulleted list is usually the best way to present the items. Similarly, if you have a ranked list or a series of steps, a numbered list is the way to go. To start one of these lists, select the **Format, Bullets and Numbering** command, and then use the List Properties dialog box to choose the style you want. Alternatively, you can set a basic list style by clicking either the Bulleted List or the Numbered List toolbar button. Either way, you then type each item and press **Enter** to move to the next item. To end the list, press **Enter** twice.

Tossing In a Few Links

It's a rare Web page that doesn't come equipped with a link or two for surfing fun. If want to add links to your page, here are the steps to follow:

1. Type the link text you want to use, and then highlight it.

2. Select the **Insert, Hyperlink** command (or press **Ctrl+K**). FrontPage Express displays the Create Hyperlink dialog box, shown in the next figure, so that you can define the particulars of the hyperlink.

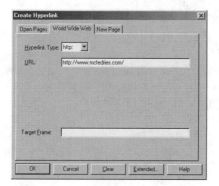

Use the Create Hyperlink dialog box to set up your hyperlink.

3. Use the **Hyperlink Type** list to choose the type of link you want. In most cases, you'll use the default **http:** selection, but several others are available also. For example, you can select **mailto:** if you want to create an email link.

4. Now enter the link address in the **URL** text box.

5. Click **OK** to insert the link.

Adding Multimedia to Your Page

If you feel like enhancing your page with a nice graphic or two, a background sound, or even a video, FrontPage Express is up to the challenge.

To insert an image, position the insertion point where you want the image to appear, and then select the **Insert, Image** command. Use the Image dialog box to pick out the GIF or JPEG file you want to use, and then click **OK**.

With the image in place, you can make a few adjustments by clicking the image and then selecting the **Edit, Image Properties** command. The Image Properties dialog box that pops up contains several controls, but only these few are all that useful:

➤ **Setting alternative text:** Many Web users either have browsers that can't handle graphics, or else they surf with graphics turned off to speed things up. For these graphically challenged folks, you should provide a text alternative so that they know what your image represents. To do so, enter the text in the General tab's **Text** area.

➤ **Creating a link:** If you want to turn the image into a link, use the General tab's **Location** text box to enter the URL you want to use.

➤ **Setting alignment and spacing:** Use the Appearance tab's **Alignment** list to set the image alignment relative to the surrounding text. You can also use the **Horizontal Spacing** and **Vertical Spacing** controls to set the distance between the image and the nearby text and give the image a bit of breathing room.

➤ **Specifying a size:** Web page text loads much quicker when the browser knows how much room each image on the page takes up. Therefore, you should always activate the Appearance tab's **Specify Size** check box.

Store HTML and Other Files in the Same Folder

Later, you'll be sending all your files   the HTML file, the image files, the sound files, and so on   to your Web server. When you do, it's likely that you'll store all the files in one place: your home directory on the server.

Whatever file you refer to in your page, your life will be infinitely simpler if you copy or move the file into the same folder you're using to store your Web page. That way, when you specify the file in the Image dialog box (or wherever), you need only enter the name of the file and not the drive and folder. Otherwise, you'd have to strip out the extra drive and folder info before sending your files to the server.

The next task on the multimedia hit parade is to specify a background sound—a sound file that automatically plays in the background when the surfer loads your page.

To insert a background sound, select the **Insert, Background Sound** command, enter the name of the sound file in the Background Sound dialog box that appears, and then click **OK**.

As with images, there are a few properties you can set for background sounds. To plop these properties onto the screen, select **File, Page Properties**. In the Page Properties dialog box that shows up, the General tab has a **Background Sound** group. In this group, use the **Loop** spin box to set the number of times the sound should play. Alternatively, activate the **Forever** check box to have the sound play indefinitely. (Boy, that better be a *nice* sound!)

I don't recommend adding a video file to a Web page because they're normally huge files and take far too long to download. If you know that your visitors will have a fast connection (if they're on your corporate intranet, for example), a slick video can add a nice touch, however.

Again, the inserting part is criminally easy. First, position the insertion point where you want the video to play. Then select **Insert, Video**, enter the file name in the dialog box that flies in for the occasion, and click **OK**.

Are there video properties you can set? Of course! Click the video to select it, and then run the **Edit, Image Properties** command. FrontPage Express loads up the Image Properties dialog box and selects the Video tab for you (check out the following figure). Here's a look at the cast of options featured in this tab:

➤ **Video Source:** This text box holds the filename for your video.

➤ **Show Controls in Browser:** If you activate this check box, FrontPage Express sets things up so that the video displays simple controls that enable the visitor to start and stop the video.

➤ **Repeat:** These controls determine how many times the video plays. Use the **Loop** spin box to set the number of showings, and use the **Loop Delay** spin box to set the amount of time between each showing. If you'd prefer that your video play *ad nauseum*, activate the **Forever** check box.

➤ **Start:** When the **On File Open** check box is turned on, Internet Explorer starts playing the video as soon as anyone surfs to your page. If you activate the **On Mouse Over** check box, the video will start up again when the user puts his or her mouse pointer over the video.

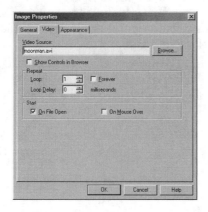

Use the Video tab to customize your Web page video.

Building Web Page Tables

A *table* is a rectangular grid of rows and columns. The intersection of each row and column is a *cell*, and you use the cells to enter text, images, lists, or anything else you can think of. Tables are a great way to display data, but many Webmasters also use them to define the overall layout of the page. In other words, they create one giant table and insert *all* their Web page stuff in the table's cells. This method gives you precise control over the horizontal and vertical positioning of the various page elements.

If all you want to do is create a simple table without any fancy features, the easiest way to go is to click the Insert Table button in the Standard toolbar. FrontPage Express displays a grid, and you drag your mouse into this grid to select the number of rows and columns you want, as shown in the next figure. When you release the mouse, FrontPage Express cranks out the new table.

Click the
Insert Table
button.

Hold down the left
mouse button and
move the pointer into
the grid.

Simple tables are a snap to build when you use the handy Insert Table button.

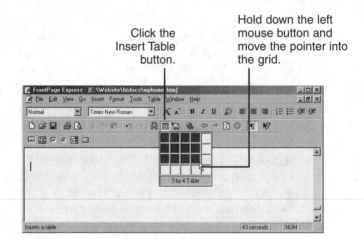

You can get a bit more control over the finished table if you follow these steps, instead:

1. Move the insertion point to where you want the new table to appear.

2. Select the **Table, Insert Table** command. FrontPage Express displays the Insert Table dialog box, shown in the following figure.

3. In the **Size** group, use the **Rows** and **Columns** spin boxes to set the number of rows and columns you want in the table. (If you're not sure about this, don't sweat it too much because you can always add and delete rows and columns later.)

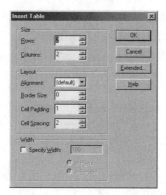

The Insert Table dialog box lets you specify a few extra table tidbits.

4. The **Layout** group offers up the following goodies:

   ➤ **Alignment:** Use this list to specify the table's horizontal alignment within the page.

   ➤ **Border Size:** This spin box determines the size of the border that surrounds the table.

   ➤ **Cell Padding:** This spin box sets the amount of white space that surrounds the data in each cell.

   ➤ **Cell Spacing:** This spin box sets the amount of space between table cells.

5. To set the width of the table, activate the **Specify Width** check box, and then use the text box to enter the width you want. (Note that you can enter a value either **in Pixels** or **in Percent**.)

6. Click **OK** to insert the table.

   When your table is in place, the FrontPage Express **Table** menu boasts an impressive array of commands for table touch-ups. Here's a quick summary (make sure that the insertion point is inside the table):

   ➤ **Insert Rows or Columns:** Use this command to add rows and columns to the table.

   ➤ **Insert Cell:** This command adds a new cell to the table.

   ➤ **Insert Caption:** When you select this command, FrontPage Express moves the insertion point just above the table. You can type a caption that describes or names the table.

   ➤ **Merge Cells:** If you selected two or more cells in advance, you can use this command to merge those cells into a single cell.

   ➤ **Split Cells:** Use this command to split a single cell into two or more rows or columns.

   ➤ **Select Cell:** This command selects the current cell.

   ➤ **Select Row:** This command selects the current row.

237

➤ **Select Column:** This command selects the current column.

➤ **Select Table:** This command selects the entire table.

➤ **Caption Properties:** Use this command to display the caption at either the top or at the bottom of the table. (Note that you need to put the insertion point into the caption before you can select this command).

➤ **Cell Properties:** Selecting this command displays the Cell Properties dialog box shown in the next figure. Use the controls in this dialog box to set the cell alignment and width, specify a background image or color, set the border colors, and more.

➤ **Table Properties:** When you select this command, the Table Properties dialog box appears. Many of the options in this dialog box are the same as those you saw in the Cell Properties dialog box. (The difference is that the Table Properties options apply to the entire table.)

The Cell Properties dialog box is chock-full of controls for customizing individual table cells.

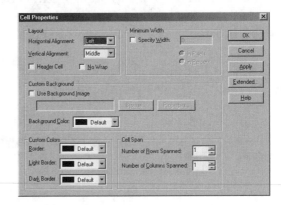

Creating a Scrolling Text Marquee

A *marquee* is a special text box in which the text scrolls (usually) from right to left. (It's somewhat reminiscent of a theater marquee, hence the name.) FrontPage Express makes it a snap to set up one of these marquee things. To try it, position the insertion point and then select the **Insert, Marquee** command. FrontPage Express coaxes the Marquee Properties dialog box (shown in the following figure) onto the screen. Here's a rundown of the options you get to play with:

➤ **Text:** Use this text box to enter the text you want to display.

➤ **Direction:** These options set whether the text moves right-to-**Left** or left-to-**Right**.

➤ **Movement Speed:** Use these controls to set the speed of the scrolling text. The **Delay** spin box determines the number of milliseconds before the text starts scrolling. The **Amount** spin box determines the number of pixels that the text moves each time. (The larger the amount, the faster the text will scroll.)

➤ **Behavior:** These options determine the way the text moves in the box. Select **Scroll** to make the text move from one end of the box to the other and then repeat; select **Slide** to have the text move once from one end of the box to the other; select **Alternate** to have the text move back and forth in the box.

➤ **Align with Text:** These options set the way the marquee is aligned relative to the surrounding text.

➤ **Size:** Activate the **Specify Width** and **Specify Height** check boxes to set custom values for the marquee's width and height. (In both cases, you can enter a value either **in Pixels** or **in Percent**.)

➤ **Repeat:** These controls determine the number of times the text scrolls. Activate **Continuously** for a never-ending scroll, or deactivate this check box and then use the spin box to set the number of times the text scrolls by.

➤ **Background Color:** Use this list to set the background color of the scroll box.

When you're finished, click **OK** to add the marquee.

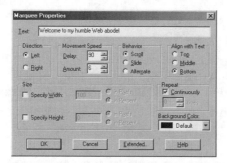

Use this dialog box to set up a scrolling marquee on your page.

Inserting Lines, Symbols, Comments, and Other Odds and Sods

To round out our look at FrontPage Express Web-page creation techniques, this section shows you how to insert a few more bits and pieces, including horizontal rules, special symbols, and more. All these items are available when you use the following **Insert** menu commands:

➤ **Break:** This command inserts a *line break*. A line break forces the browser to start a new line, but it doesn't create a new paragraph.

➤ **Horizontal Line:** This command inserts a horizontal line across the page.

➤ **Symbol:** This command displays the Symbol dialog box, which contains a list of special characters you can insert into the page. Highlight the character you want, and then click **Insert**.

➤ **Comment:** Use this command to add *comments* to your Web page. A comment is text that appears in the file but isn't displayed by the browser. Comments are handy for things like writing explanatory notes about the page contents.

➤ **File:** You can use this command to insert the contents of another file into your Web page. You'll use this most often to insert other HTML files, but you can also insert text files, WordPad files, and more.

➤ **Other Components:** This advanced command displays a submenu of components you can insert, including ActiveX controls and Java applets.

➤ **Form Field:** This command displays a list of form controls you can insert. In most cases, you're better off using one of the form-related wizards to set up a Web page form.

Painless Page Publishing: Using the Web Publishing Wizard

After you've polished your pages to a beautiful shine, it's time to put your creation on the Web. You normally use some kind of FTP program to send all the files to your home directory on your Web server, but a Windows 98 tool—the Web Publishing Wizard—can make this chore a bit less onerous.

Here's how you run the Web Publishing Wizard:

1. Select **Start, Programs, Internet Explorer, Web Publishing Wizard**. (In Windows 98 Second Edition, select **Start, Programs, Accessories, Internet Tools, Web Publishing Wizard**.)

2. The first wizard dialog box just gives you an overview; click **Next** to display the Select a File or Folder dialog box (see the following figure).

Use this wizard dialog box to pick out the folders or files you want to publish on the Web.

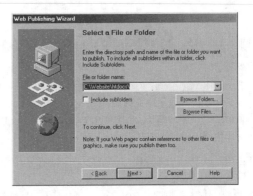

3. Type the name of the folder or file you want to publish (you'll need to include the drive and folder name). Alternatively, click either **Browse Folders** or **Browse Files** to pick out your would-be Web stuff from a dialog box. If you choose a folder, you can tell the wizard to publish all the subfolders, as well, by activating the **Include subfolders** check box. Click **Next** when you're ready to move on.

4. In the Name the Web Server dialog box that materializes, enter a descriptive name for your provider's Web server, and then click **Next**. The wizard now displays the Specify the URL and Directory dialog box, shown in the next figure.

5. Click **Next** after filling in the following text boxes:

   ➤ **URL or Internet address:** Enter the main URL for your Web site. This address usually takes the form http://*provider.domain*/~*user*, where *provider.domain* is the domain name of your Web provider, and *user* is your user name.

   ➤ **Local directory:** Enter the name of the folder on your computer that corresponds to the main directory on your Web server.

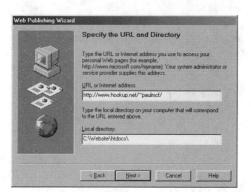

Use this dialog box to tell the wizard where to send your files and where to get them.

6. If the wizard can't make heads or tails of the Internet address you entered, you'll see the Specify a Service Provider dialog box. In this case, click **Next**. (If you don't see this dialog box, skip to step 8.)

7. The **Service provider** list (shown in the next figure) gives you the following choices (click **Next** when you've made your choice):

   ➤ **Automatically Select a Service Provider:** Choose this option if you're not sure where to send your files. The Wizard will ask you for the Internet address you use to access your files on the Web and the Internet address of your Web home. Given this information, the wizard will attempt to figure out the appropriate place to send your files.

   ➤ **FrontPage Extended Web:** Select this item if your Web server has FrontPage (the big brother of FrontPage Express) enabled. You'll need to provide the Internet address you use to access your files on the Web, and the Internet address of your Web home.

   ➤ **FTP:** This item publishes the files using the Net's FTP service. This is by far the most common choice.

241

➤ **HTTP Post:** Only select this command if your service provider accepts files submitted by using the HTTP Post method. You'll need to know the proper posting command.

➤ **Microsoft Content Replication System:** Choose this item if your Web server runs the Content Replication System (CRS). You'll need to enter the name of the CRS server and supply the name of the CRS project.

Use this wizard dialog to specify how you want to publish your files.

8. Now (assuming that you chose the FTP option in step 7) the wizard conjures up the Specify the FTP Server and Subfolder dialog box, shown in the following figure. Click **Next** after you supply the following info:

➤ **FTP server name:** Enter the domain name of your provider's FTP server.

➤ **Subfolder containing your Web pages:** Enter the full name of the directory assigned to you for file storage on the FTP site.

The wizard wants to know where to send the files on the FTP site.

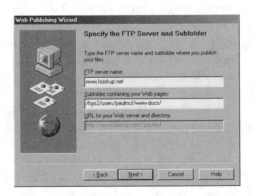

9. In the Publish Your Files dialog box that appears, click **Finish**. The wizard will likely display the Enter Network Password dialog box.

10. Enter your **User name** and **Password**, and then click **OK**. The wizard then connects to the provider, posts the files, and displays a dialog box to let you know that all went well.

11. Click **OK**.

The next time you run the wizard, you'll follow the first three steps outlined in the preceding list. Then the wizard will display the Select a Web Server dialog box so that you can choose the Web server name you entered in step 4. (If you want to define a new Web server, click **New**.) After you've done that, you can skip down to step 9 and publish your files without further ado.

Running Your Own Web Server

If you're feeling particularly brave, you might want to try running your own Web server. That sounds intimidating, I know, but Microsoft has a scaled-down Web server that's designed for small sites and will run under Windows 98. It's called *Personal Web Server* and my Web site has a tutorial that shows you how to set it up. Here's the address:

http://www.mcfedries.com/books/cightml/pws4.html

Advertising Your Site

Okay, your page is floating out there in Webspace. Now what? How are people supposed to know that your new cyberhome is up and running and ready for visitors? Well, people won't beat a path to your door unless you tell them how to get there. For starters, you can spread the news by word of mouth, email notes to friends and colleagues, and by handing out your shiny, new business cards that have your home page URL plastered all over them. Also, it's worth checking to see whether your hosting provider has a section devoted solely to announcing new customer pages.

For the Internet at large, however, you'll need to engage in a bit of shameless self-promotion. There's no central database of Web pages, but there are a few spots you can use to get some free publicity for your new page. These include Usenet newsgroups, "What's New" pages, Web directories, Web search engines, mailing lists, and more. The best place to get a complete rundown of all these sources is an article—"FAQ: How to Announce Your New Web Site"—that you can eyeball in either of the following locales:

➤ In the `comp.infosystems.www.announce` newsgroup

➤ On the Web at `http://ep.com/faq/webannounce.html`

Part VI
Putting Windows 98 to Work

Human eyes crave novelty and are quick to focus on shiny things. So it's natural that we've spent the last few chapters focusing on some of the more lustrous aspects of the Windows 98 package. However, computers aren't all gleam and glitter. There's work to be done and you'll see here in Part 6 that Windows 98 is ready for action when it's time for your nose and the grindstone to get reacquainted. And just to show you that this section isn't all work and no play, I've thrown in some fun multimedia tidbits that will keep your eyes (and ears) happy.

Chapter 19

The Write Stuff: Windows 98's Writing Tools

In This Chapter

➤ Using Notepad for "no–frills" writing

➤ Getting around in WordPad

➤ WordPad techniques for editing and formatting text

➤ How to get your words down on paper (sort of)

So far in your Windows 98 world tour, you've seen some pretty amazing sights: from Web integration to fancy customizing features, to Internet phone calls and the World Wide Web. These toys represent the more glamorous side of Windows 98. You'll spend most of your time, however, dealing with Windows 98 without its makeup on: the mundane but vital tasks you perform day in and day out. In particular, you'll likely use Windows 98 most often for writing: to-do lists, letters, memos, stories, résumès, ransom notes, and what have you. When it comes to writing stuff, Windows 98 has the right stuff: Notepad for simple text files, and WordPad for more ambitious word processing chores.

This chapter gives you a basic introduction to both of these not-overly-powerful-but-hey-whaddya-want-for-nothing writing tools. We'll cover all the must-know word pro tasks, including entering and editing text and navigating a document. For WordPad, you'll also learn about formatting text and paragraphs, setting tab stops, finding and replacing text, and more.

Using Notepad for Simple Text Tasks

Not all the documents you work with will have (or need) fancy character and paragraph formatting. Many documents are pure *text files*, which means that they contain only the letters, numbers, and symbols you can peck out on your keyboard. Although you can use WordPad to work with these simpler document specimens, doing so is probably overkill. A better choice is to use Notepad, which is designed specifically for text files.

To get Notepad on the desktop, select **Start, Programs, Accessories, Notepad**. The following figure shows the Notepad window that appears. There's not much to see, is there? That's in keeping with Notepad's nature. It's just a simple tool for making quick edits to text-only documents. No one expects you to use it to write your next novel.

Notepad's window redefines "Spartan."

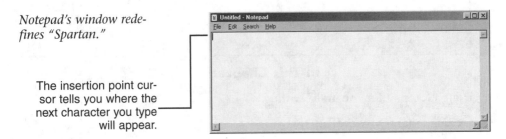

The insertion point cursor tells you where the next character you type will appear.

Some Basic Document Editing Chores

After you've launched Notepad, no further preparation is required. A quick crack of the knuckles and then you can just starting typing away. Notepad displays a blinking, vertical bar—called the *insertion point cursor*, or more often just the *cursor*—that shows you where the next character you type will appear.

As you create your document, you may have to delete text, move text chunks to different locations, and so on. To make your electronic writing life easier, it's crucial to get these basic editing chores down pat. To that end, here's a summary of the editing techniques you can use not only in Notepad, but also in WordPad:

➤ **Highlighting text with the mouse:** Before you can work with text, you need to *highlight* it. To highlight text with a mouse, simply drag the mouse over the characters you want. That is, you first position the mouse pointer ever so slightly to the left of the first character you want to highlight. Then you press and hold down the left mouse button and move the mouse to the right. As you do, the characters you pass over become highlighted (see the following figure). While you drag, you can also move the mouse down to highlight entire lines. When you release the mouse button, the text remains highlighted.

Keyboard Calisthenics

Typing teachers always suggest limbering up your fingers before you get down to heavy typing. One of the best ways to do this is to type *pangrams*—sentences that use all 26 letters of the alphabet. The standard pangram that everybody (sort of) knows is *The quick brown fox jumps over the lazy dog.* This is fine, but it's a bit dull. Try some of these on for size:

Pack my box with five dozen liquor jugs.
The five boxing wizards jump quickly.
Judges vomit; few quiz pharynx block.
Sexy zebras just prowl and vie for quick, hot matings.
Five Windows wizards jump thru dialog box hoops quickly.

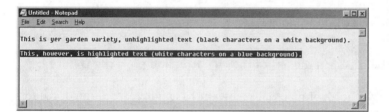

The difference between highlighted and unhighlighted text.

Accidentally Deleting Highlighted Text Is Really Easy

If you highlight some text and then press a letter on your keyboard, you'll be dismayed to see your entire selection disappear and be replaced by the character on the key you pressed! (If you press the Enter key, the highlighted text just disappears entirely.) This, unfortunately, is normal behavior that can cause trouble for even experienced document jockeys. To get your text back, immediately select the **Edit, Undo** command. (I'll talk a bit more about the life-saving Undo command a little later in this list.)

➤ **Highlighting text with the keyboard:** To highlight text by using the keyboard, position the cursor to the left of the first character, hold down the **Shift** key, and then press the right-arrow key until the entire selection is highlighted. Use the down-arrow key (or even Page Down if you have a lot of ground to cover) when you need to highlight multiple lines.

➤ **Copying highlighted text:** To make a copy of the highlighted text, select the **Edit, Copy** command (or press **Ctrl+C**). Then position the cursor where you want to place the copy, and select the **Edit, Paste** command (or press **Ctrl+V**). A perfect copy of your selection appears instantly.

➤ **Moving highlighted text:** When you need to move something from one part of a document to another, you *could* do it by making a copy, pasting it, and then going back to delete the original. If you do this, however, your colleagues will certainly make fun of you because there's an easier way. After you highlight what you want to move, select the **Edit, Cut** command (or press **Ctrl+X**). Your selection disappears from the screen, but don't panic; Windows 98 saves it for you. Position the cursor where you want to place the text, and then select **Edit, Paste**. Your stuff miraculously reappears in the new location.

➤ **Deleting text:** Because even the best typists make occasional typos, knowing how to delete is a necessary editing skill. Put away the White-Out, though, because deleting a character or two is easier (and less messy) if you use either of the following techniques:

> Position the cursor to the right of the offending character and press the **Backspace** key.

> Position the cursor to the left of the character and press the **Delete** key.

If you have a large chunk of material you want to expunge from the document, highlight it and press the **Delete** key.

➤ **To Err Is Human, to Undo Divine:** What do you do if you consign a vital piece of an irreplaceable document to deletion purgatory? Happily, Notepad, WordPad, and many other Windows 98 programs have an Undo feature to get you out of these jams. Select the **Edit, Undo** command (or press **Ctrl+Z**) to restore everything to the way it was before you made your blunder. (I've had some relationships where an Undo command would have come in *very* handy!)

Some Notepad Notes

The austere layout of Notepad's window is matched by its frugal collection of commands and features. Check out the File and Edit menus, for example, and you'll see that, for the most part, they contain only the standard commands available in most programs: New, Open, Save, Save As, and Print on the File menu; Undo, Cut, Copy, Paste, and Delete on the Edit menu. Yawn.

Notepad is not without its unique features and quirks, however. I've summarized the most important ones in the following list:

➤ Notepad assumes that the documents you'll open are text files with names that end with .TXT. There are, however, lots of text files that don't have this extension. To see these other files in the Open dialog box, select the **All Files (*.*)** option in the **Files of type** drop-down list.

➤ One of Notepad's biggest limitations is that it chokes on documents that are larger than a certain size. If you try to open such a file, you'll see the dialog box shown in the next figure. In this case, you'll probably want to select **Yes** to open the file in WordPad.

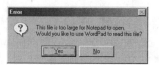

Some documents are too big for Notepad's britches.

➤ If you hit the right edge of the window as you're typing, Notepad may not wrap your text onto the next line. It'll just keep you on the same line for a thousand characters or so! To avoid this bizarre (and annoying) behavior, activate the **Edit, Word Wrap** command.

➤ The **File, Print** command doesn't display a Print dialog box. Instead, without even so much as a how-do-you-do, it just fires the document right to the printer.

➤ To find some text in a Notepad file, select the **Search, Find** command to display the Find dialog box shown in the following figure. Use the **Find what** text box to enter the text you want Notepad to look for. You can also specify the search direction as either **Up** or **Down**, and you can perform a case-sensitive search by activating the **Match case** check box. When you're ready, click **Find Next** to run the search.

Use the Find dialog box to scour your file for a word or phrase.

➤ The **File, Page Setup** command displays the dialog box shown in the following figure. You can use this dialog box to set various page layout and printing options, including the paper size and orientation, the size of each margin, and text that you want printed in each page's **Header** and **Footer**. (The **&f** thingy tells Notepad to print the name of the file, and the **&p** combo tells it to print each page number. You can also enter **&d** to print the current date, **&t** to print the current time, and **&l**, **&c**, or **&r** to align the header or footer text on the left, center, or right, respectively.)

251

Use the Page Setup dialog box to spell out various page layout and printing options for Notepad.

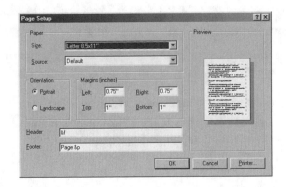

Full-Fledged Word Processing with WordPad

The WordPad word processor comes free with Windows 98. Granted, WordPad may not have all the fancy-schmancy features you get in the more glamorous word processors (such as Microsoft Word or WordPerfect for Windows), but it can handle simple day-to-day chores without a complaint. Unless you're a professional word jockey, WordPad can do the job. The rest of this chapter gets you up to speed with this useful little writing tool.

To start WordPad, select **Start, Programs, Accessories, WordPad**. The following figure shows the WordPad window and points out a few landmarks.

The WordPad window.

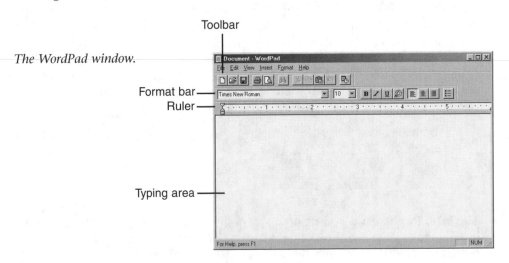

As with Notepad, you can start typing as soon as the WordPad window is onscreen. You can also use all the highlighting and editing techniques I made you sit through earlier. WordPad also has a few other text-selection tricks you can stuff up your word processing sleeve:

➤ **To select a word,** double-click it.

➤ **To select a line,** click inside the narrow strip of white space to the left of the line (that is, between the line and the WordPad window's left border). This area is known in the word pro trade as the *selection area*.

➤ **To select a paragraph,** double-click to the left of the paragraph. If you're feeling athletic, you can also select a paragraph by *triple*-clicking anywhere inside the paragraph. (I'd suggest a good half-hour finger warm up before attempting this maneuver.)

➤ **To select the entire document,** hold down **Ctrl** and click anywhere in the selection area.

Now that you know how to select text, you're ready to add formatting. The next few sections show you how to use formatting to dress up your WordPad prose so that it looks respectable.

Using Fonts to Spruce Up Your Text

The words you type in WordPad are displayed in a plain style that's serviceable but won't turn anybody's crank. To make your documents look their best, you need to spruce up your text by applying different fonts.

Fonts are distinguished by a unique set of features and patterns, including the following:

➤ **The typeface:** Any related set of letters, numbers, and other symbols has its own distinctive design called the *typeface*. Typefaces, as you can see in the following figure, can be wildly different depending on the shape and thickness of the characters, the spacing, and the designer's imagination. However, it's possible to categorize typefaces into three types (see the figure): *serif* typefaces that have tiny strokes (called *feet*) on the extremities of each character; *sans serif* typefaces that don't have the tiny strikes; and *decorative* typefaces that use fancy-schmancy effects.

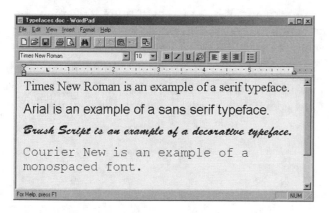

Some examples of typefaces.

➤ **The type size:** The *type size* indicates a font's height. The standard unit of measurement, just so that you know, is the *point*, and there are 72 points in an inch. So, for example, the individual letters in a 24-point font would be twice as tall as those in a 12-point font.

The True Measure of a Font

Technically, type size is measured from the highest point of a tall letter, such as *f*, to the lowest point of an underhanging letter, such as *g*.

➤ **The type style:** The *type style* of a font refers to enhancements such as **bold** and *italic*. Other type styles (often called type *effects*) are <u>underlining</u> and ~~overstrike~~ (sometimes called "strikethrough" or "strikeout") characters. These styles are normally used to highlight or add emphasis to sections of your documents.

➤ **The character spacing:** The *character spacing* of a font can take two forms: monospaced or proportional. *Monospaced* fonts reserve the same amount of space for each character. For example, take a look at the Courier New font shown in the earlier figure. Notice that skinny letters such as *i* and *l* take up the same amount of space as wider letters such as *y* and *w*. This is admirably egalitarian, but these fonts tend to look as though they were produced by a typewriter (in other words, they're *ugly*). By contrast, in a proportional font such as Arial or Times New Roman, the space allotted to each letter varies according to the width of the letter.

As my mother used to say, "You'll never plow a field by turning it over in your mind." In other words, that's enough theory. Let's get down to business and see how you go about selecting different fonts in WordPad. Here are the steps to run through:

1. To apply the font to existing text, highlight the text. If you don't highlight any text, WordPad will apply the new font to the subsequent characters you type.

2. Select the **Format, Font** command. WordPad displays the Font dialog box shown here.

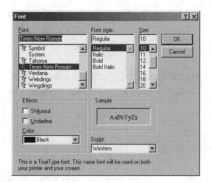

WordPad's Font dialog box.

3. Use the **Font** list box to select the typeface. (Yeah, I know, it should be called the "Typeface" list. Ah, well....)

4. Use the **Font style** list to select a type style.

5. Use the **Size** list to select a type size.

6. Use the **Effects** group to toggle the **Strikeout** and **Underline** effects on and off, and to select the text **Color**.

7. When you're finished, click **OK** to return to WordPad.

If you just want to throw a little bold or italic at a word or two, it's a bit of a hassle to fire up the Font dialog box every time. (Lazy? Moi? Nah. Merely efficient!) To make your text-formatting tasks faster, WordPad offers all kinds of shortcut methods.

For mouse mavens, the following figure shows the various buttons available on the Format Bar.

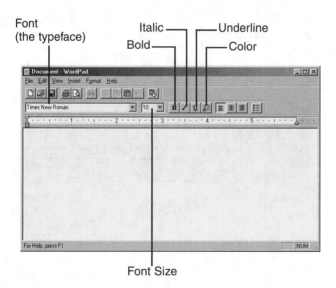

The Format Bar has all kinds of buttons you can use to fancy up some text quickly.

255

For keyboard connoisseurs, the following table summarizes some shortcut key combinations you can use.

Shortcut Key Combos for Formatting Text

Press	To Get
Ctrl+B	**Bold**
Ctrl+I	*Italics*
Ctrl+U	Underline

It's worth noting here that a given typeface covers not only the letters, numbers, and symbols you can eyeball on your keyboard, but dozens of others besides. For example, there's the ö in *Dag Hammarskjöld*. How do you add such characters to your documents?

You can do it with the Character Map accessory that comes with Windows 98. To check it out, follow these steps:

1. Select **Start, Programs, Accessories, System Tools, Character Map** to display the Character Map window shown in the next figure.

2. Use the **Font** list to choose the typeface you want to work with. (Hint: for foreign characters, select any regular typeface; for other symbols, try the Webdings, Wingdings, or Symbol typefaces.)

3. Select the symbol you want by clicking it and then clicking **Select** (you can also double-click the symbol). The symbol appears in the **Characters to copy** box.

4. Click the **Copy** button to copy the character to the Clipboard.

5. Return to WordPad, position the cursor where you want the character to appear, and select the **Edit, Paste** command.

The Character Map window gives you access to the full spectrum of Windows 98 characters.

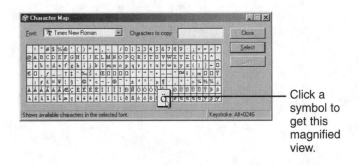

Click a symbol to get this magnified view.

Polishing Your Paragraphs

Although the content of your documents is important, the look of the documents is equally (if not more) important. Why? Because in these busy times, people will simply ignore (or trash) a document that looks cramped and uninviting. This section helps you avoid such a fate by showing you how WordPad's paragraph-formatting options can make you look good on paper. To try them out, follow these steps:

1. Place the cursor in the paragraph you want to format. (If you want to format multiple paragraphs, select the text for each paragraph.)

2. Select the **Format, Paragraph** command to display the Paragraph dialog box, shown in the following figure.

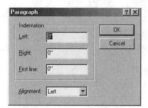

Use the Paragraph dialog box to format your paragraphs.

3. Use the Paragraph dialog box to work with the following controls:

   ➤ **Left:** Use this text box to control how far (in inches) the paragraph is indented from the left margin. For example, if you enter **1**, the paragraph is indented one inch from the left margin; entering **.5** indents the paragraph one-half inch.

   ➤ **Right:** Use this text box to control how far the paragraph is indented from the right margin.

   ➤ **First line:** Use this text box to control how far the first line (and only the first line) of the paragraph is indented from the left margin.

   ➤ **Alignment:** Use this drop-down list to adjust the alignment of the paragraph's lines. If you select **Left**, all lines in the paragraph are aligned with the left margin; if you select **Right**, all lines in the paragraph are aligned with the right margin; if you select **Center**, all lines in the paragraph are centered between the margins. You can also pick out an alignment by using the **Align Left**, **Center**, and **Align Right** buttons in the Format Bar.

Just so that you have some idea of what the heck I'm talking about, the following figure shows examples of the paragraph-formatting options.

WordPad's paragraph formatting options.

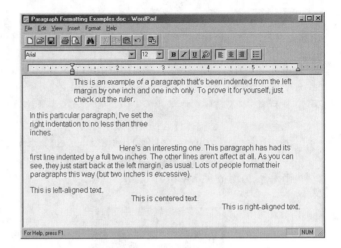

Creating a Bulleted List

If you have a list of things to present in your document, you might want to think about displaying them in a *bulleted list* with a small, round dot (called a *bullet*) to the left of each paragraph. To start a bulleted list, activate the **Format, Bullet Style** command. When your list is complete, deactivate this command. (Note, too, that you can toggle the bullet style on and off by clicking the Bullets button in the Format Bar.)

Setting Tab Stops

Documents look much better if they're properly indented and if their parts line up like soldiers on parade. One easy way to do this is to use *tabs* whenever you need to create some room in a line. Tabs are useful because they're meticulously precise. When you press the Tab key, the insertion point moves ahead to the next tab stop, no more, no less. (If you don't have any tab stops set, pressing Tab moves the insertion point ahead exactly half an inch.)

If you don't like the tab stops currently set in WordPad, don't just boycott tabs alto-gether—change 'em! After all, you're the one who's running the show around here. You'll need to make your way through the following steps to set your own tab stops.

1. Place the insertion point inside the paragraph you want to format. If you want to set the same tab stop for multiple paragraphs, select them all. (Keep in mind that if you set some tab stops for the current paragraph, each new paragraph you create below it will use those same tab stops.)

2. Select the **Format, Tabs** command. The Tabs dialog box appears.

3. In the **Tab stop position** text box, enter a location for the tab stop. For example, if you want the tab stop to be one inch from the left margin, enter **1**.

4. Click the **Set** button, and WordPad adds the tab to the list.

5. If you're feeling gung-ho, repeat steps 3 and 4 to enter any other tabs you want to set.

6. When you've had enough, select **OK**. WordPad adds the tab stops to the document and displays them in the ruler.

Faster Tab Stops

Instead of entering tab stop positions blindly in the Tabs dialog box, you can set your tabs visually in WordPad. As usual, place the cursor in the paragraph you want to work with; then move your mouse into the ruler, point at the position where you want your tab stop, and click. A tab stop appears instantly. If the tab isn't quite in the right spot, just drag it to the left or right with your mouse. To get rid of a tab, drag it off the ruler.

Finding Lost Text in Humongous Files

Finding a particular word or phrase is usually no problem in small WordPad files. But as your competence with WordPad grows, so will your documents. When you start dealing with 10- and 20-page extravaganzas, you'll find yourself singing "Where, oh, where has my little text gone? Where, oh where can it be?"

To help out (and to prevent your family or coworkers from thinking you've gone completely off the deep end), WordPad has a Find feature that does the searching for you. Here's how it works:

1. Select the **Edit, Find** command (or press **Ctrl+F**). The Find dialog box appears, as shown in the following figure.

Use the Find dialog box to search for a word or phrase in your document.

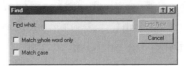

2. In the **Find what** text box, enter the word or phrase you want to locate.

3. You can refine your searches by using the two check boxes provided:

   ➤ **Match whole word only:** WordPad normally tries to find partial matches for your search text. For example, if you enter **waldo**, WordPad finds *Waldorf, Gottwaldov* (a city in the Czech Republic), and, of course, *Waldo*. If *Waldo* is all you want, activate the **Match whole word only** check box, and WordPad ignores partial matches.

   ➤ **Match case:** Activate this check box to make WordPad's searches *case-sensitive*. For example, if you enter **Curt** as your search text and you activate this check box, WordPad ignores the word *curt* and finds only the name *Curt*.

4. When you're ready to go, click the **Find Next** button. If WordPad finds the text, it highlights it in the document's typing area. If that's not the occurrence of the text you're looking for, keep clicking **Find Next** until you locate it. When you do, click the **Cancel** button to return to the document. If WordPad can't locate a match, a dialog box shows up to tell you that it has finished searching the document.

5. After you're back in the document, you may realize that you have to locate another occurrence of the search text. Instead of going through the hassle of the Find dialog box, you can continue the search by selecting the **Edit, Find Next** command (or you can simply press **F3**). WordPad remembers the last word(s) you were searching for.

A slightly different kettle of searching fish involves finding text and *replacing* it with something else. For example, you might want to change each occurrence of *Ave.* to *Avenue,* or some occurrences of *affect* to *effect* (yeah, I have a hard time remembering which is which, too). To do this, follow these marching orders:

1. Select the **Edit, Replace** command (or press **Ctrl+H**). The Replace dialog box that appears is almost identical to the Find dialog box you saw earlier.

2. As before, in the **Find what** text box enter the text you want to locate.

3. In the **Replace with** text box, enter the replacement text.

4. You now have two ways to proceed:

➤ If you know you want to replace every occurrence of the search text with the replacement text, click the **Replace All** button. WordPad trudges through the entire document, finding and replacing as it goes. When it's finished, it displays a dialog box to let you know. Select **OK** to return to the Replace dialog box, and then select **Close** to return to the document.

➤ If you want to replace only *certain* occurrences of the search text, click the **Find Next** button. Whenever WordPad finds an occurrence you want to replace, click the **Replace** button.

Replacing All? Be Careful!

You need to exercise a bit of caution before using the **Replace All** feature willy-nilly. For example, suppose that your search text is *ave* and your replacement text is *avenue*. Because *ave* matches *avenge* or *average* also, **Replace All** changes these words into the nonsensical *avenuenge*, and *avenuerage*.

Some Notes About a Few More Basic WordPad Chores

Back in Chapter 6, "A Few Workaday Document Chores," I took you through a few routine tasks that are more or less the same in most Windows applications. Just about all of those techniques are applicable to WordPad, but WordPad does have a few minor quirks you should know about:

➤ To make our lives more complicated, every word processor has its own format for the documents it creates. The format WordPad uses is the same as that used by an older version of Microsoft's high-end word processor: Word for Windows 6.0. So, when you run the Open command, WordPad's Open dialog box shows only those documents that conform to the Word for Windows 6.0 format. If you want to open a different type of document (such as a straight text file), you need to use the Open dialog box's **Files of type** drop-down box, which lists various other document types.

➤ If you select the **File** menu's **New** command, WordPad displays the New dialog box. Here, WordPad wants to know what kind of document you want to create: **Word 6** (the normal WordPad type, and the type you'll use most often), **Rich Text** (a special text file that lets you add formatting), or **Text Only** (a pure text file that can't contain any formatting).

➤ WordPad has a Print Preview feature that can save you lots of time (and paper). What Print Preview does is give you a bird's-eye view of your document so that you can see whether your formatting looks the way you want it to. To give it a go, select the **File, Print Preview** command.

➤ The WordPad window can display only one document at a time. If you need to copy or move a chunk of text between two WordPad documents, just start up a second copy of WordPad and open the other document in it. Then cut or copy the text from the original WordPad window, switch to the second window, and paste it.

SEE ALSO

➤ *For instructions on switching between open applications, see the "Belly Up to the Bar: How the Taskbar Works" section, p. 34, in Chapter 3, "Making Something Happen: Launching and Switching Programs."*

Chapter 20

Image Is Everything: Windows 98's Graphics Tools

Your left brain has a nice buzz going after all the writing you did in the previous chapter, but now your right brain is clamoring for some attention. Well, it'll get plenty to chew on in this chapter as I take you through some of Windows 98's graphics goodies. The bulk of the chapter shows you how to use the Paint program to create digital masterpieces. For those of you who don't have an artistic bone in your body, you'll also learn how to use a scanner and digital camera to get images from out here to in there, and then to use Windows 98's Imaging program to mess around with those images.

The Art of Windows 98: Using Paint

If you're looking for some enjoyment of the my-how-time-flies-when-you're-having-fun variety, look no farther than Windows 98's Paint program. What's that? Drawing was never your strong suit. Don't worry about it. Even if you're no Michelangelo, there are still plenty of wild things Paint can do to turn even the humblest drawing into a veritable *objet d'art*. This section gives you a brief explanation of Paint's basic drawing techniques, and then sends you to the master class so that you can play with Paint's *really* fun features.

A Look Around the Paint Canvas

To get your Paint studio open, select **Start, Programs, Accessories, Paint**. The following figure shows the Paint window that appears.

A few key facts about the Paint window.

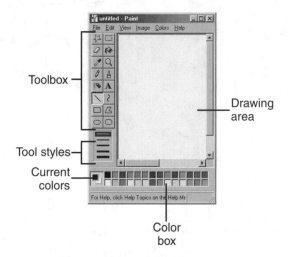

As you can see, the Paint window is chock-full of artistic goodies you can play with:

➤ **Toolbox:** This area contains the tools you use to create or edit your drawings. You get a Pencil, a Brush, an Airbrush, an Eraser, and all kinds of utensils for drawing lines and shapes. The toolbox and its treasures are shown in the next figure. I'll describe each tool in more detail a bit later.

➤ **Tool styles:** Some of the tools give you a selection of styles so that you can add some variety to your drawings. When you select one of these tools (such as the Brush tool or the Line tool), the available styles appear in the area below the toolbox.

➤ **Color box:** This section shows the available colors and patterns you can use for drawing or filling shapes. Think of this as your own personal 28-box of Crayola crayons (sans that icky flesh-colored crayon) that never need sharpening.

➤ **Current colors:** These two boxes display the currently selected foreground color (the top box) and background color (the bottom box). To select a new foreground color, click one of the color rectangles in the color box. To select a new background color, right-click a color.

➤ **Drawing area:** This is the large blank area that takes up most of the Paint window. The drawing area is your Paint canvas: it's where you perform the mouse moves that lead to the creation of your digital drawings. It is, in short, the place where all the fun happens.

Wielding the Paint Tools

The best way to approach Paint is simply to have a good time fooling around with the various tools, styles, and colors. Go on, let loose; toss off those inhibitions, free yourself from the shackles of adult responsibilities, and allow yourself to revert to an immature, to-heck-with-it-I'm-going-to-be-at-one-with-my-inner-child state. (You may want to close the door for this.)

When you're suitably juvenile, you can pick a tool and start playing. There *is* a basic four-step method you use for each tool, however:

1. Select the tool you want to work with by clicking it in the toolbox.
2. Click one of the available tool styles (if the tool has any, that is).
3. Select a foreground and background color from the color box.
4. Move the pointer into the drawing area and draw the shape you want.

Bailing Out of Your Mistakes

Before you start, you probably should know how to get rid of the botched lines and mutinous shapes that inevitably appear when you learn to use each tool:

➤ If you make a mess during the drawing, you can start again by simply clicking the other right button *before* you release the button you're using.

➤ f you've already finished drawing the shape, select the **Edit, Undo** command (or press **Ctrl+Z**).

➤ If the drawing is a total disaster, you can start over by selecting the **Image, Clear Image** command (or by pressing **Ctrl+Shift+N**).

The Paint window offers you lots of cool tools to get your creative juices flowing.

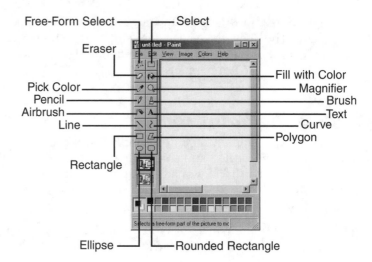

Here's a review of the drawing-related tools you can pluck out of the toolbox:

➤ **Pencil:** Use this tool to draw freehand lines. That is, after selecting this tool, you move the mouse into the drawing area, hold down the left mouse button, and then wiggle the mouse around. Paint draws a freehand line that mirrors your every twitch.

➤ **Brush:** You also use this tool also to draw freehand lines. The difference (between it and Pencil) is that Brush gives you a selection of brush shapes and sizes.

➤ **Line:** Use this tool to draw straight lines of varying widths. Drag the mouse in the drawing area to create a line. To draw a perfect horizontal or vertical line, or to draw your line at exactly a 45-degree angle, hold down the **Shift** key while dragging the mouse.

➤ **Rectangle:** This tool enables you to draw rectangles. To draw a perfect square, hold down the **Shift** key while dragging the pointer. The Rectangle tool gives you three styles to choose from: a "border only" style that draws only the border of the shape; a "border and fill" style that draws a border and fills it with a color; and a "no border" style that leaves off the shape's border and draws only the fill.

➤ **Ellipse:** Use this tool for drawing ovals. To draw a perfect circle, hold down the **Shift** key while you drag the mouse.

➤ **Rounded Rectangle:** This tool draws a rectangle that has rounded corners.

➤ **Curve:** You use this tool for drawing wavy lines. To wield this tool, first drag the mouse until the line is the length you want, and then release the button. Now drag the mouse again to curve the line, and then release the button. If you want to add a second curve to the line, drag the mouse again and release the button when you're finished.

➤ **Polygon:** Use this tool to create a polygon shape. (*Polygon* is a highfalutin' mathematical term for a collection of straight lines that forms an enclosed object, such as a triangle.) To give it a whirl, drag the pointer until the first side is the length and angle you want, and then release the mouse button. Now position the pointer where you want the next side to end, and then click. Paint draws a line from the end of the previous line to the spot where you clicked. Repeat to taste. To finish the shape, connect the last side with the beginning of the first side.

➤ **Fill with Color:** This tool fills any enclosed shape with whatever color you select. It's really easy to use, too: just click the **Fill with Color** tool in the toolbox, and then click anywhere inside the shape. If you left-click, Paint fills the shape with the current foreground color; if you right-click, Paint uses the current background color.

➤ **Airbrush:** This fun tool is like a can of spray paint and it's useful for satisfying those graffiti urges without breaking the law. When you drag the mouse in the drawing area, Paint "sprays" the current color.

➤ **Text:** Use this tool to add text to your drawing. You first drag your mouse in the drawing area to create a box big enough to hold your text. When you release the mouse button, an insertion point cursor appears inside the box and the Text toolbar appears (see the following figure) Use the drop-down lists and buttons on the Fonts toolbar to establish a format for your text; then type your text in the box.

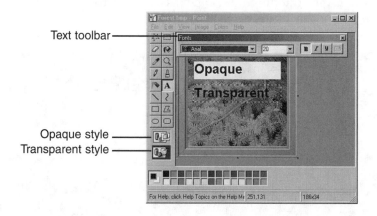

Text toolbar

Opaque style
Transparent style

You can add text to your drawing, using either an opaque or transparent style.

➤ **Pick Color:** Use this tool if the drawing you're working on has a particular color you want to use. To set a color as the current foreground color, select this tool and then left-click the color you want. Right-clicking sets the color as the current background color.

➤ **Eraser:** Use this tool to erase parts of your drawing. You select a width for the eraser, and then drag the mouse in the drawing area to wipe out everything in the mouse pointer's path. (This is not a tool to wield lightly!)

Erasing Colors

The Eraser tool has another personality: the *color eraser*. How does it work? Well, suppose that you want to preserve the outlines of a drawing but wipe out the color that fills it, or suppose that you want to replace one color with another. These sound like tricky operations, but the color eraser can do the job without breaking a sweat.

You use the color eraser just as you do the eraser, except that you right-drag the eraser box. When you drag the tool over your drawing, it replaces anything it finds in the current foreground color with the current background color.

➤ **Magnifier:** Use this tool to magnify your drawing so that you can get a closer look at a particular section. At the maximum magnification (a whopping 800%), you can even see the tiny individual elements (the *pixels*) that make up a Paint picture. To try this out, click the **Magnifier** tool and click a magnification from the choices that appear at the bottom of the toolbox. Then click the area you want to magnify. Paint zooms in, as shown in the following figure.

The Magnifier tool in action.

Select a magnification option.

Select View, Zoom, Show Thumbnail to see this window.

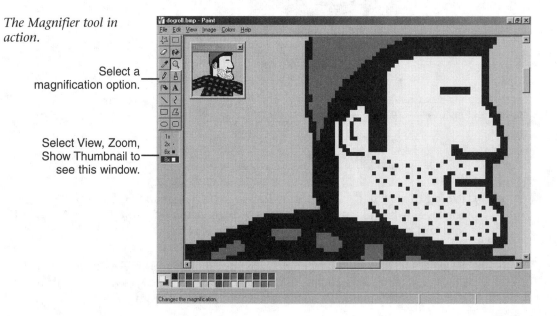

➤ **Select:** Use this tool to select a rectangular area of the drawing. (A selected chunk is called a *cutout* in Paint lingo.) You can then cut or copy the selected area. To use the Select tool, click the tool and move the pointer to the upper-left corner of the area you want to select. Drag the mouse until the box encloses the area you want to work with, and then release the mouse button.

➤ **Free-Form Select:** Use this tool to select any area that isn't rectangular. After clicking the tool, move the pointer into the drawing area and drag the mouse around the area you want to select. Release the button when you've completely outlined the area.

Pasting Cut or Copied Images

After you cut or copy your selected image (by using the **Edit** menu's **Cut** or **Copy** commands), you need to paste the image. When you select the **Edit, Paste** command, the image appears in the upper-left corner of the drawing. To position it, move the mouse pointer inside the image, and then drag the image to the location you want.

A Master Class in Paint

Now that you're familiar with all the Paint tools, let's check out a few more techniques that will enable you to take your Paint works of art to the next level.

Getting a Bigger Picture

Instead of using the Magnifier tool to see less of your drawing, you may prefer to see more of it. Here are a few Paint techniques for seeing the big (or, at least, bigger) picture:

➤ To expand the picture so that it takes up the entire screen, select the **View, View Bitmap** command (or press **Ctrl+F**). To return to Paint, click the mouse or press any key.

➤ You can create more elbow room by removing certain Paint features from the screen. Pull down the **View** menu and deactivate any or all of the following commands: **Tool Box**, **Color Box**, and **Status Bar**.

➤ If you'd prefer to keep the tool and color boxes onscreen, you can still create more room by dragging them out of their normal locations. This turns the boxes into "floating" toolbars that sit on top of your drawing.

Dragging-and-dropping a Cutout

If you need to move a cutout, or make one or more copies of a cutout, don't bother with the Cut, Copy, and Paste commands. You can move a cutout just by dragging it with your mouse and dropping it in the new location. To copy the cutout, hold down the **Ctrl** key while you drag it.

Creating Sweeps

This one's a real crowd-pleaser. After selecting the cutout, click the Transparent style. Now hold down the **Shift** key and drag the cutout around the drawing area. Whoa! As you drag the mouse, Paint leaves multiple copies of the cutout in its wake, as shown in the following figure.

Create sweeps by dragging cutouts while you hold down the Shift key.

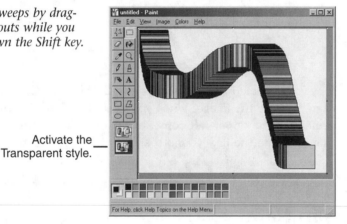

Activate the Transparent style.

The next few techniques show you some of the other special effects you can create in Paint. The next figure shows you examples of these effects.

Flipping a Cutout

You can flip a cutout either horizontally (so that left becomes right, and vice versa) or vertically (so that up becomes down, and vice versa). Select **Image, Flip/Rotate** (or press **Ctrl+R**) to display the Flip and Rotate dialog box. Activate either the **Flip horizontal** or **Flip vertical** option. You can also activate **Rotate by angle** and then choose one of the angle options.

Inverting a Cutout's Colors

Inverting colors means that black changes to white, white changes to black, and the other colors change to their complementary colors. To invert the colors in a cutout, select the **Image, Invert Colors** command (or tap **Ctrl+I**).

Stretching and Skewing a Cutout

If you need to scale a cutout to either a smaller or larger size, or tilt a cutout at an angle, the **Stretch/Skew** command (or pressing **Ctrl+W**) can do the job. The Stretch and Skew dialog box that appears has two groups:

➤ **Stretch:** Use the **Horizontal** and **Vertical** text boxes to specify a percentage value that you want to use to stretch the cutout. Use values greater than 100% to get a larger image; use values less than 100% to get a smaller image.

➤ **Skew:** Use the **Horizontal** and **Vertical** text boxes to enter the number of degrees by which you want the cutout tilted. You can enter values between –89 and 89.

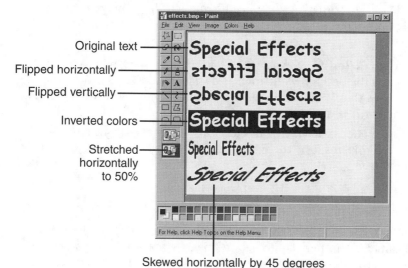

Original text

Flipped horizontally

Flipped vertically

Inverted colors

Stretched horizontally to 50%

Examples of Paint's cutout special effects.

Skewed horizontally by 45 degrees

Saving a Cutout to Its Own File

If you think you might need to use a cutout in other pictures, you can save it to its own file and then retrieve it when you need it. Select **Edit, Copy To**, enter a filename in the Copy To dialog box, and then click **Save**.

Pasting a File into Your Drawing

You can plop an entire file right into your drawing. To try this, select the **Edit, Paste From** command, highlight the file in the Paste From dialog box, and then click **Open**.

Setting the Image Attributes

Selecting the **Image, Attributes** command (or pressing **Ctrl+E**) displays the Attributes dialog box shown in the next figure. These controls govern the size of your picture and whether it displays colors. The numbers displayed in the **Width** and **Height** text boxes reflect the measurement units selected in the **Units** group.

Use the Attributes dialog box to change the size of a picture and toggle colors on and off.

Creating Custom Desktop Wallpaper

After you've finished your drawing, you may like it so much that you want to use it as your desktop wallpaper. Paint makes this easy by including two commands on its **File** menu:

➤ **Set As Wallpaper (Tiled):** If you select this command, Paint tells Windows 98 to use this image as the desktop wallpaper, and that Windows 98 should tile the image. (*Tiling* means that Windows 98 displays multiple copies of the image so that it covers the entire desktop.)

➤ **Set As Wallpaper (Centered):** If you select this command, Paint tells Windows 98 to use this image as the wallpaper, and that the image should be centered on the screen.

Capturing Screen Shots

The rest of this chapter shows you how to get images into your computer by using a scanner and digital camera. Another way to get an image without having to draw anything is to "capture" what's on your screen. You have two ways to go about this:

➤ To capture the entire screen, lock, stock, and taskbar, press your keyboard's **Print Screen** key.

➤ If you want to capture only whatever is in the active window, press **Alt+Print Screen**.

Either way, you can then toss the captured image into Paint by selecting **Edit, Paste**. If Paint complains that the image you're pasting is too large, click **Yes** to enlarge your drawing to fit the image.

Graphics Gadgetry: Working with Scanners and Digital Cameras

It used to be that the only way to get an image onto your computer was either to create it yourself or to grab a prefab pic from a clip art collection or photo library. If you lacked artistic flair, or if you couldn't find a suitable image, you were out of luck.

Now, however, getting images into digital form is easier than ever, thanks to two graphics gadgets that have become more affordable: image scanners and digital cameras.

> ➤ An image scanner is a lot like a photocopier, except that instead of processing the image onto a sheet of paper, you save it to a file on your hard disk.

> ➤ A digital camera is a lot like a regular camera, except that instead of film being exposed, the image is stored internally in the camera's memory. You can then connect the camera to your computer and send the images to your hard disk.

The big news is that Windows 98 understands both types of devices. In most cases, you can just install whatever software came with your scanner or camera, connect the cable, and then run the software to bring your images into Windows 98.

On the other hand, because Windows 98's Kodak Imaging program is conversant with many popular scanner and digital camera formats, you can use it as a one-stop digital imaging shop. This section shows you how to use Kodak Imaging to do just that.

Before continuing, make sure that your scanner or camera is properly installed and connected to your PC. Then select **Start, Programs, Accessories, Imaging**, and eventually you'll see the Imaging window shown in the following figure.

The Scan New button

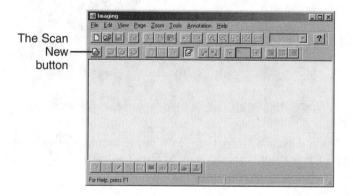

The Imaging window, ready for scanning action.

From Windows 98's point of view, there''s no difference between a scanner and a digital camera. Both are "scanners" that you use to acquire images from an external source, and whether you're using a scanner or digital camera, the basic steps you follow to lasso an image are the same:

1. If you're lucky enough to have more than one imaging device, run the **File, Select Scanner** command to display the Select Scanner dialog box.

2. Highlight the device you'd like to use, and then click **OK**. You're returned to the Imaging window.

3. Either select the **File, Scan New** command, or click the **Scan New** button in the toolbar (pointed out in the previous figure).

What happens next depends entirely on the device you're using. Basically, Windows 98 loads up whatever software the device uses to scan an image. For example, the following figure shows the window that appears for the Kodak DC120 digital camera. In most cases, you'll be able to perform at least the following functions:

➤ Take one or more pictures in the camera and send them to your computer.

➤ Delete one or more pictures from the camera.

➤ Take a new picture and send it to your computer.

➤ Access other camera functions, such as the focus, shutter speed, and flash.

This window shows up if you're using the Kodak DC120 digital camera.

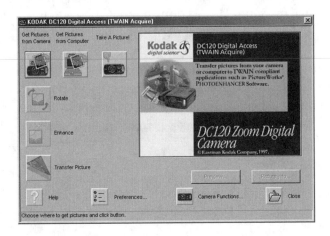

If you're using a scanner, you'll see a different window. For example, the one shown in the next figure is for an HP ScanJet scanner. Most scanner software lets you manipulate the image quality or select part of the image to scan.

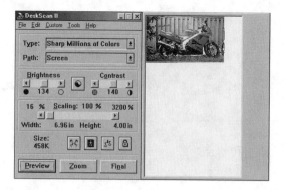

This window appears if you're using an HP ScanJet scanner.

No matter which way you obtain your image, it then appears in the Imaging window. At that point, you'd use Imaging's **File, Save** command to make a permanent copy of the image on your hard disk.

Rescanning the Image

After you've saved the image, you may decide that you want to rescan it. If so, don't select **File, Scan New** because that just creates a new file. An easier method is to select **Page, Rescan** (or click the Rescan Page toolbar button). This fires up the scanning software again so that you can get a new image to replace the current one.

Chapter 21

Bells and Whistles: Multimedia and Windows 98

In This Chapter

➤ Using a CD-ROM drive with Windows 98

➤ Playing and recording sounds

➤ Listening to audio CDs

➤ Playing animations and watching TV

➤ Windows 98's multitudinous multimedia marvels

The graphics gewgaws you gawked at in the previous chapter represent only a selection of Windows 98's visual treats. There are actually quite a few more goodies that fall into the "sights for sore eyes" category, and even a few that could be called "sounds for sore ears." In this chapter, you'll see that Windows 98 turns your lowly computer into a multimedia powerhouse capable of showing videos, playing audio CDs, making realistic burping noises, and even letting you watch *Gilligan's Island* reruns.

Windows 98 and CD-ROM Drives

These days, it's a rare computer that doesn't come with a CD-ROM drive jammed into its case or attached umbilically to a connector in the back. Happily, Windows 98 and CD-ROM drives get along just fine, thank you. Windows 98 should recognize your CD-ROM automatically, and display it as an extra disk drive when you open My Computer or Windows Explorer.

A CD-ROM drive doesn't act quite like a regular drive. For example, you can't move or copy files to a CD-ROM, and you can't delete files from a CD-ROM. That's what the *ROM* in CD-ROM is all about: it stands for *Read-Only Memory*, which, translated from its native geekspeak, means "you can only *read* the contents of a CD-ROM; you can't change them in any way." (Here, "reading" the contents means displaying text, viewing graphics, and running programs.)

Many CD-ROMs have setup programs that automatically install icons on the Start menu for easier access. Look for files named **Setup** or **Install** on the CD-ROM. Windows 98 also supports a CD-ROM feature called AutoPlay that promises to make CD-ROMs insanely easy to use. In a nutshell, a CD-ROM that supports AutoPlay does one or both of the following when you insert the disc:

➤ If you haven't yet installed whatever program comes on the disc, AutoPlay will automatically fire up the setup program so that you can perform the installation.

➤ If you've already installed the CD-ROM program, AutoPlay will launch that program without further ado.

Don't Forget the Disc!

After you've installed a CD–ROM program, you probably won't be able to run the program unless the original disc is in the CD–ROM drive. Most CD-based programs check to see whether their disc is present and, if it's not, issue a stern rebuke. It's also possible, however, that a missing disc can cause the program to go insane and lock up your computer! To avoid this problem, always make sure that the disc is in the CD-ROM drive each time you try to run the program. If the software's install program lets you install all the files on your hard drive, you could also choose that option.

Sound Advice: Working with Sounds in Windows 98

Take a stroll through any office these days and you're bound to hear all manner of boops, bips, and beeps emanating from cubicles and work areas. You might think that the bodysnatchers have replaced your colleagues with R2D2 clones; what you're actually hearing is evidence that today's modern Windows 98 user is truly wired for sound.

If you're sick of carrying on a one-way conversation with your computer (if the yelling, cursing, and threatening that most of us direct at our digital domestics can be considered conversation), you can get into the sound thing by getting a sound card. This is a circuit board that you (or a nearby, easily-cajoled-with-flattering-comments-about-his-pocket-protector computer guru) attach to your computer's innards. Popular examples include the Windows Sound System and the Sound Blaster. Many sound cards not only play sounds, but also let you record your own. (I'll show you later how to record sounds.) If you're shopping around for a sound card, make sure that the card you get is both MPC-compatible (MPC sort of stands for *Multimedia PC Marketing Council*; look for an MPC logo on the sound card's box) and Plug and Play-compatible. For the best sound, you should also spring for a pair of external computer speakers.

The next few sections, which assume that you have some sort of sound set up on your system, show you how to play sounds, adjust the volume, and record your own sounds.

Sounding Off: Playing Sounds

Sounds you play in Windows 98 come packaged as sound files (sometimes called *Wave* files, as in sound *wave*). Windows 98 comes with a small collection of sound files stored in your Windows folder (look inside the Media subfolder). And there's no shortage of sound libraries on the market that contain dozens of sound effects (I call them *CBS* collections: chirpin', burpin', and slurpin') and clips from old movies and cartoons (so that you can listen to Fred Flintstone say "Yabba dabba do" all day long).

Windows 98 gives you several ways to play sounds, but the two most common are by using the Sound Recorder and the ActiveMovie control. (Windows 2000 actually replaces the ActiveMovie control with a program called Media Player.) For starters, let's check out the Sound Recorder method. Here are the steps to follow:

1. Select **Start, Programs, Accessories, Entertainment, Sound Recorder**. As you wipe the sweat from your brow, the Sound Recorder window appears.
2. Select the **File, Open** command. Sound Recorder displays the Open dialog box.

3. Highlight the sound file you want to hear, and then click **Open**. (No sound files in sight? Try heading for your Windows folder and opening the Media subfolder to see the sound files that come with Windows 98.) Several Sound Recorder buttons come alive, as you can see in the following figure.

4. Click the **Play** button to play the sound from the beginning. For long files, you can drag the slider bar to any position in the sound file and then click Play. (The **Seek to Start** and **Seek to End** buttons move the sound to the beginning and end of the file, respectively.)

The Sound Recorder window, ready for action.

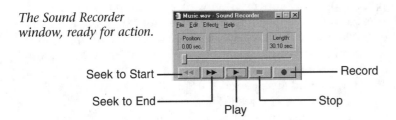

 For all other sound files, including MIDI (Musical Instrument Digital Interface) files and most of the sound files found on the Internet, you use Windows 98's ActiveMovie control. (Again, ActiveMovie is only available with the original version of Windows 98.)

Now I hear you thinking:

Whoa! If it's called "ActiveMovie," why the heck do I use it for sound files?

You *are* paying attention, aren't you? "ActiveMovie" is a bad name because this control is actually Windows 98's all-purpose media player. By that I mean that it plays everything from sound files to animations to digital movies. The "ActiveMedia control" would have been a better name.

To get the ActiveMovie control to play a sound file (I'll tackle digital movies a bit later), follow these steps:

1. Select **Start, Programs, Accessories, Entertainment, ActiveMovie Control**. ActiveMovie shows up for work and immediately displays the Open dialog box.

2. Use the dialog box to find the sound file you want to play and then click Open. The ActiveMovie window appears.

3. Click the **Run** button.

 If you have Windows 98 Second Edition, the stupidly-named ActiveMovie control has been sent down to the minors. In its place, you have the Media Player, which works like so:

1. Select **Start, Programs, Accessories, Entertainment, Windows Media Player**. The Windows Media Player window drops by for a visit, as shown in the following figure.

2. Select **File, Open** and use the **Open** dialog box to pick out a media file. (You'll probably want to click **Browse** to choose the file from a dialog box.) Click **OK** once you have the file.

3. Click the **Play** button.

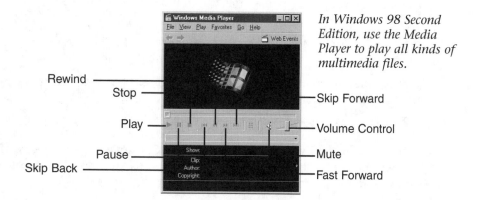

Rewind

Stop

Play

Pause

Skip Back

Skip Forward

Volume Control

Mute

Fast Forward

In Windows 98 Second Edition, use the Media Player to play all kinds of multimedia files.

Another way to go about this is to first use Windows Explorer or My Computer to find the sound file you want to play. (For example, you can use any of the MIDI files found in Windows 98's Media subfolder.) You now have two choices:

➤ To play the sound right away, either click the sound file (double-click if you have web integration turned off) or right-click the file and then click Play in the shortcut menu.

➤ To load the sound without starting it, right-click the file and then click **Open** in the shortcut menu. When the ActiveMovie window appears, click the **Run** button. (In Windows 98 Second Edition, look for the Media Player window and then click **Play**.)

Techno Talk

A Mini Look at MIDI

What's this MIDI stuff all about? Well, MIDI enables computers and musical instruments (especially synthesizers) to "talk" to each other. With MIDI, a musician can crank out a tune on his instrument, and the notes are transcribed automatically on the computer. You can edit the resulting MIDI file note-by-note, or you can alter the pitch and tempo of certain sections to get the jingle just so.

281

Keeping It Down to a Dull Roar: Adjusting the Volume

If your colleagues or family start complaining about the noise pollution drifting from your computer, you'll want to turn down the volume of your sound files to keep the peace. On the other hand, if you can hardly hear what Sound Recorder, ActiveMovie, or Media Player play, you may need to pump up the volume a bit.

For either situation, Windows 98 comes with a Volume Control program that you can use to adjust the decibel level of the sounds you play. First, use either of the following methods to display the Volume Control on the desktop:

➤ Limber up your clicking finger and then select **Start, Programs, Accessories, Entertainment, Volume Control**.

➤ Double-click the **Volume** icon in the taskbar.

Whichever method you choose, the Volume Control window appears. The setup of this window depends on the sound system you have installed. In most cases, though, you should see the following five sections:

➤ **Volume Control:** This section is the master volume control that affects the output of all the sounds you play. The rest of the controls affect only particular sounds, as you'll see.

➤ **Wave:** This section controls the output of normal sound files (Wave files) only.

➤ **MIDI:** This section controls the output of MIDI files only.

➤ **CD Audio:** This section controls the output of any music CDs you play (see "Playing Audio CDs in Your CD-ROM Drive," later in this chapter).

➤ **Line-In:** This section controls the output of any devices that are attached to your sound card, such as an external CD-ROM drive or a TV tuner card.

Each section has two sliders: **Balance** adjusts the balance between the left and right speakers, and **Volume** adjusts the volume level. Use your mouse to drag the slider bars to the settings you want (the higher the slider, the louder the sound).

Note, too, that you can add sections to the Volume Control window (or remove sections you don't use) by selecting the **Options, Properties** command. In the **Show the following volume controls** list, activate the check boxes for the sections you want to see, and then click **OK**.

When your settings are just right, select **Options, Exit** to shut down the volume control.

Rolling Your Own: How to Record Sounds

If you have a sound card capable of recording sounds (and you have a microphone attached to the sound card), you can have hours of mindless fun creating your own sound files. Preserving silly sounds for posterity is the most fun, of course, but you can also create serious messages and embed them in business documents.

To record a sound file, follow these steps:

1. Start Sound Recorder, as described earlier.

2. If Sound Recorder already has a sound file opened and you want to start a new file, select the **File, New** command. If you'd prefer to add sounds to an existing file, open it, and move to the position in the sound file where you want your recording to start.

3. Grab your microphone, clear your throat, get your script, and do whatever else you need to do to get ready for the recording.

4. Click the **Record** button.

5. Speak (yell, groan, belch, whatever) into the microphone. Sound Recorder shows you the length of the file as you record. Note that you have a maximum of about 60 seconds (depending on the settings you use) to do your thing.

6. When you're finished, click the **Stop** button.

7. Click the **Seek to Start** button and then click the **Play** button to hear how it sounds. If you're happy with your recording, select the **File, Save** command, enter a name for the file in the Save As dialog box, and click **Save**.

As if letting you record your own sounds weren't enough, Sound Recorder also comes with a host of cool options for creating some really wild effects. Here's a summary:

➤ **Mixing sound files:** You can mix two or more sound files so that they play at the same time. For example, you can combine one sound file that contains narration with another that has soothing music. To try this, open one of the sound files and move to where you want the second file to start. Select the **Edit, Mix with File** command, highlight the other sound file in the Mix With File dialog box, and then click **Open**.

➤ **Changing the volume:** If you recorded your sound file too loudly or too softly, pull down the **Effects** menu and select either **Increase Volume** (to make the sound louder by 25%) or **Decrease Volume** (to make the sound softer by 25%).

➤ **Altering the playback speed:** You can make your voice recordings sound like Alvin and the Chipmunks or Darth Vader by adjusting the speed of the playback. Pull down the **Effects** menu and choose either **Increase Speed** (to double the speed) or **Decrease Speed** (to halve the speed).

➤ **Adding an echo...echo...echo:** The **Effects, Add Echo** command creates a neat echo effect that makes your sound files sound as though they're being played in some cavernous location.

➤ **Reversing a sound:** Playing a sound file backward can produce some real mind-blowing effects. To check it out, select the **Effects, Reverse** command.

Playing Audio CDs in Your CD-ROM Drive

Another advantage of having a sound card lurking inside your system is that you can use it to play audio CDs through your CD-ROM drive. That's right, whether you're into opera or alternative, classical or country, rock or rap, your favorite tunes are now only a few mouse clicks away.

The Windows 98 program that makes this possible is CD Player. Before you look at it, take a second to pop an audio CD into your CD-ROM drive. After you do that, you can display the CD Player by using one of the following techniques:

➤ Most likely Windows 98 will crank up the CD Player automatically and start playing the disc. In this case, click the CD Player's taskbar button.

➤ If Windows 98 doesn't start CD Player automatically, select **Start, Programs, Accessories, Entertainment, CD Player**.

The CD Player window that appears is shown in the following figure. (If you don't see the toolbar in your window, activate the **View, Toolbar** command.)

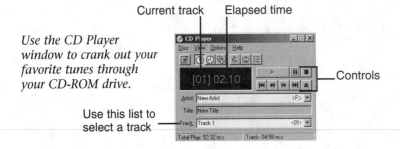

Use the CD Player window to crank out your favorite tunes through your CD-ROM drive.

The CD Player is set up to look more or less like a real CD player. The large black box shows the current track number in square brackets and (when the disc starts playing) the elapsed time for the track. Next to the box are the controls you use to operate the CD. The following figure shows the controls you have at your disposal. Note that if you want to play a specific track, you select it from the **Track** drop-down list.

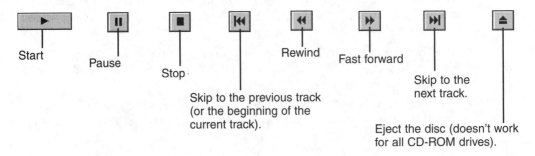

CD Player also gives you a few more playing options, some of which you normally find only on mid- to high-end CD players:

Click...	Or Select...	To Do This
🕐	**View, Track Time Remaining**	Show the time remaining for the current track
🕐	**View, Disc Time Remaining**	Show the time remaining for the entire disc
⇄	**Options, Random Order**	Play the tracks in random order
↻	**Options, Continuous Play**	Play the disc continuously (that is, start the disc over when the last track is finished)
⋮≣	**Options, Intro Play**	Hear just the first 10 seconds of each track

When you first slip in an audio CD, the CD Player displays **New Artist** in the Artist box and **New Title** in the Title box. Because it's unlikely that these are the actual names of the artist and disc, CD Player enables you to fill in the correct information. Not only that—you can also enter a title for each track on the CD, and you can create a *play list*. A play list is a list of the tracks you want to hear, in the order you want to hear them. Amazingly, CD Player "remembers" this info and loads it automatically the next time you plop that particular CD into your CD-ROM!

To try all this out, either select the **Disc, Edit Play List** command, or click the **Edit Play List** toolbar button. CD Player displays the Disc Settings dialog box.

In the **Artist** text box, fill in the name of the group or singer, and in the **Title** text box, enter the disc's title. To enter the track titles, follow these steps:

1. Select a track in the **Available Tracks** list.
2. In the **Track** text box, enter the title.
3. Click the **Set Name** button.
4. Repeat steps 1–3 for the other tracks.

The **Play List** box shows the current tracks in the disc's play list (which is every track, at first). To modify the play list, use the following techniques:

➤ To remove a track from the play list, select it in the **Play List** and click **Remove**.

➤ To add a track to the play list, select it in the **Available Tracks** list and click **Add**. (Yes, you can add your favorite tunes more than once.)

➤ To clear everything from the **Play List**, click **Clear All**.

➤ To change the order of the play list, use your mouse to drag the **Play List** tracks up or down.

➤ To revert to the original play list (all tracks, in disc order), click **Reset**.

When you're finished, click **OK** to put your play list into effect. The following figure shows an example of a completed dialog box.

A sample CD Player play list.

Big-Screen Windows: Playing Movies

As you might expect from the name, the ActiveMovie control I showed earlier does more than just play sounds. It can also handle most of digital video files you throw at it, including files in the Video for Windows, QuickTime, and MPEG formats. When you've got your popcorn popped, you can cue up a movie by finding a video file in Windows Explorer or My Computer and then opening the file.

Playing Movies with Media Player

If you have Windows 98 Second Edition, you use the Media Player program to watch digital movies. Use the same techniques that I outlined earlier for playing sound files.

No video files in sight? You'll find a few promotional videos for Microsoft products on the Windows 98 CD-ROM (look in the \cdsample\videos folder). The following figure shows ActiveMovie with cameras rolling.

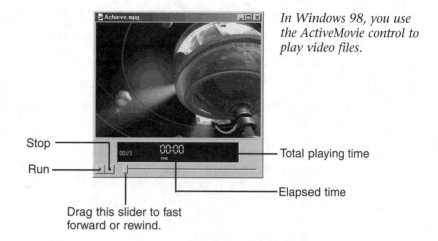

In Windows 98, you use the ActiveMovie control to play video files.

Stop

Run

Total playing time

Elapsed time

Drag this slider to fast forward or rewind.

As you saw earlier, the ActiveMovie control is simple to operate. Here's what to do:

➤ To launch a video clip, either click the **Run** button or press **Ctrl+R**.

➤ To pause a running movie, either click the **Pause** button or press **Ctrl+P**.

➤ To stop a running movie, either click the **Stop** button or press **Ctrl+S**.

➤ To fast forward or rewind move to a specific part of the video, drag the slider right or left.

Small-Screen Windows: Watching TV

 For years, television addicts have been known as couch potatoes. I guess it was inevitable that some clever wag would coin the phrase mouse potatoes to refer to folks who spend great gobs of time in front of their computer screens. Now some linguist will have to come up with a new phrase that describes people who do both at the same time. That's right: if you have the right equipment, Windows 98's WebTV for Windows program enables you to watch TV programs right on your computer. And you thought playing Solitaire was a time-waster!

Exactly what do you need for all this to happen? Quite a bit, unfortunately:

➤ Your computer should be a Pentium with a 120MHz or faster processor and something called a "PCI bus."

➤ At least 16 megabytes of memory.

➤ For the monitor, if you'll be doing nearby viewing, you'll need at least a 17-inch monitor capable of 800×600 resolution. For distant viewing, at least a 27-inch SVGA monitor capable of 640×480 resolution.

➤ The graphics adapter must be capable of "MPEG-2" compression and SVGA-level video. For TV signals, it must include a cable television tuner that support NTSC or PAL signals. (The ATI All-In-Wonder card is a good example that works flawlessly with Windows 98's TV trinkets.)

➤ If you'll be doing distant viewing, a wireless keyboard and mouse.

➤ Your sound card should be stereo-ready and Sound Blaster-compatible—a near certainty, so don't worry about it.

Note, too, that you must also have your computer set up for Internet access. Assuming that you have all this heavy-duty hardware, and that you've established a connection to the Internet, here are the steps to follow to configure WebTV for Windows:

SEE ALSO

➤ *Please surf to Chapter 15, "How to Get Connected to the Internet," to learn more about how to make Windows 98 and the Internet get along.*

1. Select **Start, Programs, Accessories, Entertainment, WebTV for Windows**, or click **Launch WebTV for Windows** in the taskbar's Quick Launch toolbar. WebTV takes a few seconds to get itself ready for action, and then it displays the Welcome screen.

2. Click **Next** to display the Get TV Listings screen.

3. To download the program listing for your area, click the **G-GUIDE** link. Internet Explorer shows up and takes you to the Get TV Listings Web site. (If at this point you see a Security Warning dialog box, click **Yes** to install some required software.)

4. The first time you do all this, you're sent to another page to specify your ZIP code. Enter your ZIP code or postal code. The Web page will then display a list of cable providers in your area.

5. Click the provider you want to use to receive program listings, then click **Save**. You're returned to the Get TV Listings page.

6. Click **Get Listings**. Internet Explorer downloads the data. The page shows you the progress of the download. Note that this may take quite some time (15 or 20 minutes) if you have a slowpoke connection.

7. When the page displays Success! to indicate a successful download, return to the WebTV screen.

7. Click **Next**. WebTV displays the Program Guide Tour screen, which takes you through the basic features of WebTV.

8. When the tour is complete, or anytime you just want to get on with it, click **Next**.

9. Click **Finish** in the final screen to get to the Program Guide.

When the WebTV setup is finished, and each time you launch the WebTV program, you'll see the Program Guide screen, which will look a lot like the one in the following figure. The bulk of the screen is taken up by the program listings, which show the available channels (numbers and call letters) on the left and the programs themselves arranged in a timeline. The area on the right side of the screen shows a preview of the currently selected channel as well as other data related to the program (such as a description and the program's rating, if it has one).

Click the program you want to preview.

Check out the TV signal and preview info here.

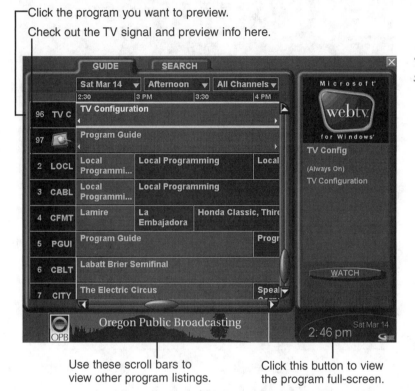

The Program Guide screen.

Use these scroll bars to view other program listings.

Click this button to view the program full-screen.

Here's a summary of the techniques you can use to work with the Program Guide:

➤ To preview a running program, use the vertical scroll bar to bring the channel into view, and then click the program.

➤ To get information about a program that isn't running, use both scroll bars to display the program, and then click it.

➤ If you'd like the TV Viewer to remind you to watch a future program, click the program and then click the **Remind** button. TV Viewer displays the Remind dialog box, which you use to set the reminder time and frequency.

➤ Click **SEARCH** at the top of the screen to use the Search feature (shown in the following figure), which enables you to view programs by category or to search for a word in the program's title.

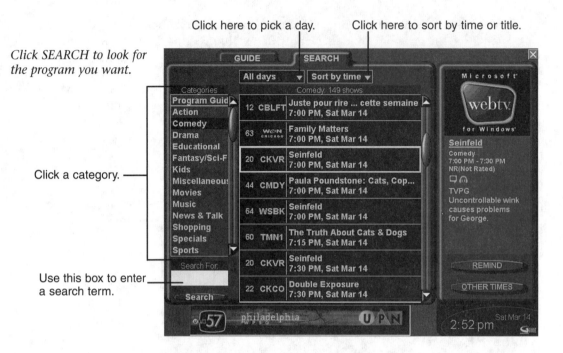

Click here to pick a day. Click here to sort by time or title.

Click SEARCH to look for the program you want.

Click a category. ——

Use this box to enter a search term.

➤ When at long last you're ready to settle down and watch a show, click the show in the program listings and then click the **WATCH** button. TV Viewer closes the Program Guide and displays the show full-screen for your viewing pleasure.

Getting Back to the Program Guide

When you're watching a program, you can return to the Program Guide by pressing **F10** to display the toolbar, and then clicking the **Guide** button.

Now that you know how to select a program, it's time to do some channel surfing. TV Viewer is designed to support remote control devices such as the Gateway 2000 Destination remote control.

If you don't have such a device, you can still control the TV Viewer from your keyboard. The following table lists the various keys and key combinations you can use.

Keystroke	Description
0–9	Used for entering channel numbers. If you enter a one- or two-digit number, you need to press **Enter**, as well. If you enter a three-digit number, TV Viewer changes the channel without your having to press Enter.
F6	Toggles TV Viewer between its normal full-screen mode and its windowed mode.
F10	Displays the TV Viewer toolbar.
Arrow keys	Used for scrolling up and down in the Program Guide.
⊞+V	Toggles mute on and off.
⊞+Ctrl+V	Turns up the volume.
⊞+Shift+V	Turns down the volume.
⊞+Ctrl+Shift+Z	Shows the Program Guide (grid view).
⊞+Ctrl+Alt+Z	Tunes the channel up.
⊞+Ctrl+Alt+Shift+Z	Tunes the channel down.
⊞+Ctrl+Alt+Shift+G	Recalls the last channel.

Chapter 22

Windows 98's Notebook Knickknacks

In This Chapter

➤ Using Briefcase to tote files around

➤ Using Direct Cable Connection to exchange files between machines

➤ Using power management to preserve notebook battery life

➤ Notebook hardware: PC Cards, docking stations, and infrared ports

➤ A complete look at all the Windows 98 notebook toys

If you have a notebook computer, then you know full well that these machines are fundamentally different from their desktop cousins, and that the difference goes well beyond mere luggability. There are batteries to monitor, weird "PC Card" wafers to slide in and out, docking stations to deal with, and infrared ports to furrow your brow over.

The Windows 98 programmers must have had to wrestle with notebooks a time or two themselves, because they've put together a passel of portable perks. This chapter fills you in on no less than six of these notebook niceties: the Briefcase, Direct Cable Connection, power management, PC Cards, docking stations, and infrared ports.

You *Can* Take It with You: Using My Briefcase

Sharing files between a desktop machine and a notebook is often fraught with difficulty because it's tough keeping everything synchronized. Sure, it's not hard to plop some files on a floppy disk, copy those files to your notebook, and then copy them back to the desktop down the road. But what if you modify only some of the documents when you work on the notebook? What if you create a *new* document on the notebook? What if the floppy disk you use contains other files? What if you make changes to the same document on both the desktop *and* the notebook?

These are thorny issues that until now required patience, careful planning, and often some knowledge of techno-esoterica (such as DOS batch files) to overcome. Now, however, these problems are a thing of the past because Windows 98 includes a feature that solves them all in one shot: My Briefcase.

My Briefcase is a special folder on your computer that you can use to hold the documents you transfer between your desktop and notebook computers. Instead of always copying individual documents back and forth, you usually just work with the My Briefcase folder. The real advantage of using My Briefcase, however, is that it automatically synchronizes the documents on both machines. If you work on a few documents on your notebook, for example, Windows 98 can figure out which ones are different and then let you update the desktop machine by running a simple command. There's no guesswork and no chance of copying a file to the wrong folder; no muss, no fuss.

Okay, let's put My Briefcase to work. The most straightforward way to deal with My Briefcase is to put it on a floppy disk and leave it there permanently. Your first chore is to move the My Briefcase folder from the Windows 98 desktop to the floppy disk. (If you want to create another My Briefcase folder later, you can do so by right-clicking the Windows 98 desktop and then clicking **New, Briefcase**.)

Now let's see what you have to do to get some files from your desktop to your notebook:

1. After you decide which documents you want to work with on your notebook, use Windows Explorer or My Computer to copy the documents into the My Briefcase folder on the floppy disk.

2. The first time you copy a file to My Briefcase, the Welcome to the Windows Briefcase dialog box appears. After you've read the brief overview of My Briefcase, select **Finish** to get rid of it.

3. Insert the disk into the notebook's floppy disk drive.

4. Using Windows Explorer or My Computer, display the notebook floppy drive and open the My Briefcase folder. You'll see a window similar to the one shown in the following figure.

5. In the My Briefcase window, select the files you want to work with and then copy them to whatever destination you like on the notebook's hard disk.

This column tells you where the "sync copies" (the original files) reside on the other computer.

This column tells you the current state of each copy compared to the original.

Make sure that you select Details view to see all this.

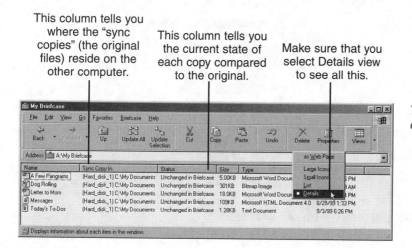

The My Briefcase folder on the floppy disk.

With the documents now safely stowed in the notebook's hard disk, you can go ahead and work on the files, using the appropriate programs on the notebook computer. To make sure that these files stay in sync with the files in My Briefcase, don't move or rename the files.

Now let's see how you get the files back to the desktop computer and update the original files with your changes:

1. If you created any new files, copy them to the My Briefcase folder on the floppy disk.

2. Open the floppy disk's My Briefcase folder. Notice that for those files you modified, the Status column says **Needs updating**.

3. To begin the update, you have two choices:

    ➤ If you modified every file, select the **Briefcase, Update All** command.

    ➤ If you modified only some of the files, select the files where the Status column says **Needs updating**, and then select the **Briefcase, Update Selection** command.

4. Windows 98 then displays the Update My Briefcase dialog box to show you which documents need updating (see the following figure). Click the **Update** button, and Windows 98 updates the floppy disk My Briefcase folder with the modified documents.

My Briefcase figures out which files you modified.

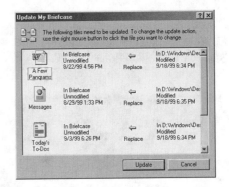

5. Slip the floppy disk into your desktop computer.

6. Open the floppy disk's My Briefcase folder. Again, by displaying **Needs updating** in the Status column, My Briefcase shows you which documents you modified.

7. Again, either run **Briefcase, Update All**, or select only the modified files and then run **Briefcase, Update Selection**. This time, Windows 98 compares the contents of the floppy disk My Briefcase with the original files on your desktop computer. If it finds any discrepancies, it displays the Update My Briefcase dialog box again.

8. Click **Update**, and Windows 98 perfectly synchronizes your desktop and notebook files.

From Laptop to Desktop and Back: Running Direct Cable Connection

In the "a chain is only as strong as its weakest link" department, the process of emigrating files from one computer to another via floppy disk suffers from not one, but two severe limitations: your basic floppy can hold only so much data, and floppy disk drives are notoriously slow.

You can bypass this "sneakernet" process and overcome both problems by running Windows 98's Direct Cable Connection program. As its name implies, Direct Cable Connection lets you sling a bit of cable between two computers and then transfer files along that connection. You can even send documents from one computer to a printer that's attached to the other computer! It takes a bit of effort to set up, but after that's done it works pretty well.

The first thing you need is a cable. Ask the friendly geek at your neighborhood computer store for either a *null-modem cable* or a *parallel LapLink cable* (the latter is also known as a *parallel InterLink cable*). Whichever cable he gives you, be sure to ask whether it connects to your computers' serial ports or their parallel ports.

296

To work with Direct Cable Connection, you configure one computer (usually the desktop machine) as the *host* and the other computer (usually the notebook) as the *guest*.

Let's start with the steps for configuring the host:

1. The host computer has to share its files and folders so that the guest computer can work with them.

SEE ALSO
> ➤ *I show you how to share files and folders in the "Playing Nicely with Others: Sharing Your Resources" section of Chapter 26, "Working with Network Connections and Email," p. 355. Please see that section now to set up sharing on the host computer.*

2. Select **Start, Programs, Accessories, Communications, Direct Cable Connection**. The first time you do this, the Direct Cable Connection Wizard loads.

3. Activate the **Host** option and then click **Next**.

4. The Direct Cable Connection Wizard checks the available ports on your system and displays a list of these ports, as shown in the following figure. Highlight the port you want to use and click **Next**.

Use this wizard dialog box to choose the port you want to use with Direct Cable Connection.

5. The next wizard dialog box asks whether you want the guest computer to use a password to access the host. If you do, activate the **Use password protection** check box, click the **Set Password** button, enter your password (twice) in the Direct Cable Connection Password dialog box, and click **OK**.

6. Click **Finish** to complete the host configuration. Then the wizard will wait for a connection from the guest.

7. Click **Close** (we'll get to the actual connection part in a second).

Configuring the guest computer is even easier than configuring the host:

1. Select **Start, Programs, Accessories, Communications, Direct Cable Connection** to get things off the ground.

2. In the first Direct Cable Connection Wizard dialog box, activate the **Guest** option and click **Next**.

3. Highlight the port you want to use and click **Next**.

4. Click **Finish**.

5. Click **Close**.

Okay, we're almost there. Now you need to tell the two computers to use the same "language" when they communicate. To do this, follow these steps on both computers:

1. Right-click the desktop's **Network Neighborhood** icon and then click **Properties**. (You could also open the Control Panel's **Network** icon.)

2. Click **Add** to display the Select Network Component Type dialog box.

3. Highlight **Protocol** and click **Add** to get to the Select Network Protocol dialog box.

4. In the **Manufacturers** list, highlight **Microsoft**; in the **Network Protocols** list, highlight **IPX/SPX-compatible Protocol** (see the following figure); then click **OK**.

Use this dialog box to select the language the two computers will use to yell at each other.

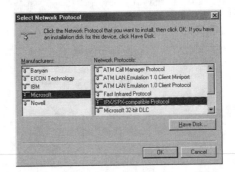

5. Follow the onscreen prompts for inserting your Windows 98 disc.

6. When you get back to the Network dialog box, click **OK**.

7. When Windows 98 asks whether you want to restart your computer, click **Yes**.

Whew! If you ask me, that's *way* too much work just to get a couple of lousy computers to share a file or two. Happily, you only have to run through all those steps once.

To get the connection between the two computers established, you need to do the following:

1. On the host computer, select **Start, Programs, Accessories, Communications, Direct Cable Connection**.

2. In the dialog box that appears, click the **Listen** button. Direct Cable Connection then waits for the guest computer to say hello.

3. Launch Direct Cable Connection on the guest computer.

4. In the dialog box that appears, click the **Connect** button.

Now the two machines exchange pleasantries along the cable. If the host computer is protected by a Direct Cable Connection password, you'll have to enter that password.

When the two machines finally see eye-to-eye, Direct Cable Connection opens a folder window on the guest computer that shows all the shared stuff on the host, as shown in the next figure. If the host is attached to a larger network, the guest computer can use this window (or the Network Neighborhood) to browse and work with the network's shared resources. Note, however, that neither the host machine nor the other network computers can see the guest.

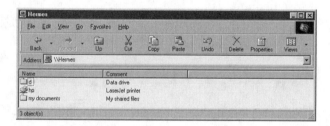

When the Direct Cable Connection session is established, the guest computer sees a folder containing the host's shared resources.

You can use Direct Cable Connection to transfer the files back and forth between the machines, using a single My Briefcase folder. Here's a rundown of the basic Briefcase procedure from a Direct Cable Connection point of view:

1. On the host machine, make sure that the folder containing the files you want to work with is either shared directly or resides in a shared folder.

2. On the guest computer, connect via Direct Cable Connection and access the shared folder.

3. Copy the files to the guest computer's **My Briefcase** folder.

4. Use the guest computer to work on the files from within the **My Briefcase** folder. You don't need to have the connection established at this point.

5. When you're finished, reestablish the connection, if necessary, and then open the **My Briefcase** folder on the guest computer.

6. Select **Briefcase, Update All**. This updates the host computer's files with the changed files in the guest computer's My Briefcase.

Other Treats for Notebook Users

The Briefcase and Direct Cable Connection are welcome additions to our notebook arsenals, but they're not the only Windows 98 weapons available for portables. The rest of this chapter gives you the skinny on four more hardware-related notebook niceties: power management, PC Cards, docking stations, and infrared ports.

Power Management Techniques for Preserving Batteries

A certain level of anxiety is always involved with running your notebook on its batteries, especially if no AC is in sight. You know that you have only a limited amount of time to get your work done (or play your games, or check your email, or whatever), and the pressure's on. To help change road worriers back into road warriors, most notebooks support some kind of *power management*. This means that the system conserves battery life by shutting down things like the display and hard drive after the computer has been idle for a specified interval.

When your notebook is running on batteries, Windows 98 displays a Power Meter icon in the taskbar's information area, as shown here.

When your notebook is running on batteries, Windows 98 displays a Power Meter icon in the taskbar.

Power Meter icon

When the notebook battery has a full complement of juice, the Power Meter icon is completely yellow. As you mess with your computer and deplete the battery power, the Power Meter's "level" decreases. For example, if the battery power is down to half, the Power Meter displays as half yellow, half gray. To see the current level, you have two options:

➤ Point your mouse at the Power Meter icon. Windows 98 displays a banner showing the number of hours remaining in the charge, and the percentage of battery life available.

➤ Double-click the Power Meter icon to display a dialog box with the battery life status.

The last thing you want to do is run out of power in the middle of a major memo. Windows 98 monitors the power level and sounds two battery alarms when things get tense:

➤ **Low:** This alarm is set off when the power level reaches 5%. (In Windows 98 Second Edition, this alarm is set to 10%.)

➤ **Critical:** This alarm is set off when the power level reaches 3%.

To control the power levels at which these alarms are sounded, open the Control Panel's Power Management icon and then select the **Alarms** tab, shown next.

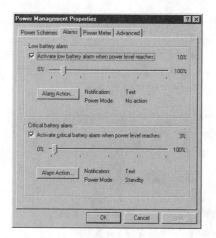

Use the Alarms tab to set options for the battery alarms.

In both the **Low battery alarm** and **Critical battery alarm** groups, you can perform the following actions:

➤ Use the check box to toggle the alarm on and off.

➤ Use the slider to set the power level at which the alarm is set off.

➤ Click the **Alarm Action** button to configure the alarm. When Windows 98 displays the Alarm Actions dialog box, you have the following options:

Sound alarm: Activate this check box to have Windows 98 beep your computer's speaker when the alarm is triggered.

Display message: Activate this check box to have Windows 98 display a warning message when the alarm is triggered.

When the alarm goes off, the computer will: Use this list to choose the action taken by Windows 98 when the alarm is triggered: **Standby** or **Shutdown**.

Force standby or shutdown even if a program stops responding: Activate this check box to tell Windows 98 to go ahead and implement the specified action even if a running program no longer responds to the system.

A good time to choose which power scheme to use is while the Power Management Properties dialog box is onscreen. The **Power Schemes** tab, shown in the next figure, lets you define the intervals after which Windows 98 puts the computer in standby mode (power consumption is reduced for all possible components), turns off the monitor, and turns off the hard disk. Notebook computers have options for both **Plugged in** and **Running on batteries** states. To work with these settings you have two choices:

➤ Use the **Power schemes** list to choose one of Windows 98's predefined power schemes (such as **Portable/Laptop**).

➤ Use the drop-down lists in the **Settings for *x* power scheme** group to select the intervals you want. To save these intervals as a power scheme, click **Save As**, enter a name for your scheme, and then click **OK**.

Use the Power Schemes tab to choose a power management scheme for your computer.

Adding On: Working with PC Card Devices

One of the problems that originally caused notebooks to be relegated to a lower status on the PC totem pole was their lack of expandability. Desktop systems had all kinds of internal "slots" and "drive bays" that intrepid hobbyists and power users could use to augment the capabilities of their systems. Notebook configurations, however, were generally set in stone; what you bought was what you got.

That all changed with the advent of the absurdly named *Personal Computer Memory Card International Association* (PCMCIA) and the standards it developed for notebook expansion boards. These standards let notebook manufacturers add to their machines small slots (called *sockets*) that can hold credit card–sized expansion modules for memory cards, hard disks, CD-ROMs, modems, and more.

An Easier Moniker

The "PCMCIA" tongue twister is now more or less obsolete. (Yes!) In its place, most notebook folks use the phrase "PC Card," and that's what I'll use throughout the rest of this section.

Before you use a PC Card device, you need to tell Windows 98 to set up your notebook's PC Card socket. This chore, which is performed by the PC Card Wizard, is usually done when Windows 98 is set up on your computer, and you may not have to bother. To find out, select **Start, Settings, Control Panel** and then open the **PC Card (PCMCIA)** icon. If you see the PC Card (PCMCIA) Properties dialog box, you can skip this phase. Otherwise, you'll see the Welcome to the PC Card (PCMCIA) Wizard dialog box.

Run through the Wizard's dialog boxes, answering the questions appropriately for your system. When you're finished, Windows 98 prompts you to shut down your computer. Click **Yes** and wait for the system to shut down. Then turn it back on to enable the PC Card socket.

One of the nice things about PC Cards is that you don't have to shut down your computer to swap them in and out of the slot. You can just leave Windows 98 running and shuffle the cards in and out at will. (In geek lingo, this is called *hot swapping*.)

If you've used and configured the PC Card before, Windows 98 beeps the speaker, and the card is available for use immediately. You'll see the PC Card (PCMCIA) Status icon appear in the taskbar's system tray, as shown in the following figure. If this is the first time you've inserted the card, Windows 98 gets right to work loading and configuring the appropriate software.

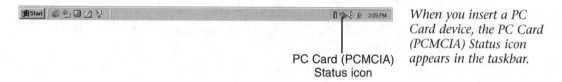

PC Card (PCMCIA)
Status icon

When you insert a PC Card device, the PC Card (PCMCIA) Status icon appears in the taskbar.

Although PC Cards are hot-swappable, you shouldn't just yank a device out of its slot willy-nilly. If you do, Windows 98 chastises you by displaying a warning dialog box. To avoid this, you should first tell Windows 98 to stop the device. You can stop PC Card devices by running through these steps:

1. Select **Start, Settings, Control Panel** and then open the **PC Card (PCM-CIA)** icon. (For faster service, you can also double-click the taskbar's PC Card (PCMCIA) Status icon.) Windows 98 displays the PC Card (PCMCIA) Properties dialog box, shown in the next figure.

2. Click the device you want to stop.

3. Click the **Stop** button. Windows 98 displays a dialog box to let you know that it's safe to remove the device.

4. Click **OK**.

You stop a PC Card device by using this dialog box.

Check This Out

A Faster Way to Stop PC Card Devices

Windows 98 offers an easier way to stop a PC Card device. Try clicking the **PC Card (PCMCIA) Status** icon in the taskbar. When you do, Windows 98 displays a menu of commands that stop each of the PC Card devices installed on your system. Click the command that corresponds to the device you want to stop. After a few seconds, Windows 98 displays a dialog box to let you know that it's safe to remove the device.

A Home for Your Notebook: Using a Docking Station

PC Cards are great way to pump up your notebook, but usually only one or two PC card sockets are available, and the number of devices you can have plugged in at any one time is limited. To solve this problem, many notebooks now come with separate *docking stations*. These are platforms into which you can slide your notebook and thus create a full-fledged desktop machine. The notebook provides the guts   the CPU, the memory, the hard drive   and the docking station provides everything else   drive bays; bus slots; ports for an external monitor, keyboard, mouse, printer, modem, and so on.

For newer notebooks, Windows 98 supports *hot docking*: inserting your notebook into, and removing it from, the docking station while Windows 98 is still running. Windows 98 examines the new hardware configuration and adjusts itself accordingly. Then Windows 98 establishes a new *hardware profile* (usually called Dock 1) for the docked computer. Windows 98 will then recognize whenever your machine is docked or undocked and configure the available devices accordingly.

Another advantage you get with the latest notebooks is the Eject PC command. You can find this command on the Start menu while your notebook is docked. Selecting the command tells Windows 98 to unload the drivers used in the undocked profile. When that's been done, Windows 98 either prompts you to undock your notebook or does it for you (if your docking station has an automatic undocking feature).

Air-to-Air Windows: Using Infrared Ports

Many of the latest notebook computers come with a built-in infrared (IR) port. This port acts like both a serial port and a parallel port, and you can use it to transfer files and send print jobs. (To send print jobs, you'll need a printer with an IR port.) You can also purchase infrared devices that attach to a serial port.

Windows 98 includes support for both Serial Infrared (SIR) devices and Fast Infrared (FIR) devices. To initialize this support, follow these steps:

1. Select **Start, Settings, Control Panel** and then open the **Add New Hardware** icon.

2. When the Add New Hardware Wizard appears, click **Next** and then click **Next** again.

3. When the wizard asks whether Windows 98 should search for new hardware, activate **No** and click **Next**.

4. In the list of hardware types that appears, highlight **Infrared devices** and click **Next**. Windows 98 brings the Add Infrared Device Wizard to the podium.

5. Click **Next**. The Wizard displays a list of infrared manufacturers and models.

6. Select the appropriate manufacturer and model and then click **OK**:

    ➤ **SIR device:** Highlight **Microsoft** in the **Manufacturers** list, and then select **Standard Infrared Serial (COM) Port** in the **Infrared Devices** list. After loading some files, the wizard will prompt you for something called a *transceiver type*. In most cases, you'll select **Generic Infrared Port** and then click **Next**.

    ➤ **FIR device:** Select one of the other devices listed. In the next wizard dialog box, make sure that the **Use defaults** option is activated, click **Next**, and skip down to step 8.

7. Now the wizard wonders about the port to which the SIR device is physically connected. Select the appropriate port and click **Next**.

8. The next dialog box, shown in the following figure, prompts you to specify simulated ports for the infrared serial and printer ports. You don't have to worry about this, so click **Next**. The wizard displays the last of its dialog boxes.

9. Click **Finish**.

Your IR port is now ready to go. Note that Windows 98 adds an infrared icon to the taskbar. The icon you see depends on whether the driver has another IR port in its sights. If no other port is in range, you see the icon shown in the next figure.

This is the infrared icon you see when no other IR device is within range.

The infrared icon when no device is in range.

If the port finds another IR device, the icon changes to the one shown here.

This is the infrared icon you see when another IR device is within range.

The infrared icon when another device is in range.

Get in the Infrared Zone

Infrared devices are a bit finicky. To ensure that they recognize each other, their ports must face each other directly, and they should be no closer than six inches and no farther than three feet to nine feet (depending on the device).

Windows 98 comes with a new utility for transferring files from one computer to another via their infrared ports. This utility is called Infrared Transfer, and you use it to transfer files by running either of the following methods:

➤ In My Computer or Windows Explorer, highlight the file or files you want to send and then select the **File, Send To, Infrared Recipient** command.

➤ Highlight the file or files you want to send, right-click the files, and then click **Send To, Infrared Recipient** in the shortcut menu.

Assuming that a good infrared connection exists between the two devices, Infrared Transfer will send the file or files immediately. Note that on the receiving computer, Windows 98 creates a new folder called **My Received Files** on the hard drive. The sent files are stored in this folder.

Part VII

Do-It-Yourself Windows 98: System Maintenance and Troubleshooting

From time to time, I find myself actually enjoying working in Windows 98. I'm comfortable with the look and feel, the applications are great, and I really do seem to squeeze more work into the day than I could with earlier versions of Windows. But then I get an "Out of memory" message, or the dreaded "This application has performed an illegal operation" error rears its ugly head, and my good mood is gone for the day.

Yes, Windows is nice, but it's so darned temperamental. Some days it seems you only have to cough a little too loudly and Windows gives up the ghost. When faced with such flakiness, one of the keys to remaining a productive (and, so, employed) member of society is to minimize the amount of time you spend hunting down and fixing problems. The three chapters here in Part 7 are designed to help you do just that. Chapter 23 begins by showing you some of Windows 98's preventative maintenance tools. Chapter 24 is the "Just in Case Department" where you learn how to make backup copies of your precious data. Finally, Chapter 25 faces facts and shows you how to recover from some of Windows 98's most common problems.

Tools for Keeping Your System in Tip-Top Shape

Like the proverbial death and taxes, computer problems seem to be one of those constants in life. But that doesn't mean you just have to sit back and wait for trouble. Believe me, a few minutes of protection now (what I like to call "ounce of prevention mode") can save you hours of grief down the road ("pound of cure mode"). And therein lies the good news: avoiding trouble really does take only a little extra work. Why, with just a few simple techniques and the easy-to-use system tools that come with Windows 98, you can set up some powerful preventative measures in no time at all. This chapter tells you everything you need to know.

Using ScanDisk to Avoid Hard Disk Hard Times

You've seen throughout this book that your hard disk acts as a sort of "safe house" for your documents. Open and unsaved files are accidents waiting for a place to happen, but after you save the files to your hard disk, you know that you can breathe easier. Your hard disk isn't infallible, however. Although most folk get years of good service from their faithful hard disk servants, these drives are subject to the general wear-and-tear that affects all electronic components.

To help prevent your hard disk from going south before its time, you should run Windows 98's ScanDisk program frequently. ScanDisk scours your hard disk for chinks in its armor and can even repair those chinks before they lead to further trouble.

Easier ScanDisk Scheduling

 ScanDisk is only useful if you run it regularly. Happily, you don't have to waste valuable brainpower trying to figure out when you last ran ScanDisk and when you should run it again. That's because Windows 98 offers an easier alternative: the Maintenance Wizard. This wizard lets you set up a maintenance schedule that runs ScanDisk automatically without any prodding from you. Check out "Using the Maintenance Wizard to Keep Your System Firing On All Cylinders," later in this chapter.

Here are the ScanDisk steps:

1. Select **Start, Programs, Accessories, System Tools, ScanDisk**. You'll see a ScanDisk window something like the one shown here.

Use the ScanDisk window to pick out the hard disk you want to check.

2. In the **Select the drive(s) you want to check for errors** list, click the disk drive you want to work with. (ScanDisk won't complain if you select multiple disks. To do so, hold down **Ctrl** and click each disk.)

3. Use the **Type of test** group to pick out the ScanDisk test you want to run. The one you choose depends on how much time you have to kill, how patient you are, and how paranoid you are about your hard disk having a nervous breakdown:

   ➤ **Standard:** This test runs various checks to ensure the integrity of your hard disk's files and folders. It should take less than a minute to perform this test. I recommend running this test every couple of days.

   ➤ **Thorough:** This test delves deeper and checks not only your hard disk's files and folders, but also the surface of the hard disk itself. Depending on the size of your hard disk, this test can take 15 minutes or more. You probably only need to run this test once a week.

4. Now you have to decide whether you want ScanDisk to automatically fix any errors it finds. This is handy if, for example, you want to perform the lengthy Thorough test and you'd like to head off to a three-martini lunch while it's running. To have ScanDisk fix any errors, activate the **Automatically fix errors** check box.

5. Click the **Start** button. ScanDisk begins nosing around in your hard disk's private parts and displays its progress at the bottom of the window.

6. If ScanDisk finds a problem (and you didn't tell it to fix errors automatically), a dialog box appears that gives you several options. In the example shown in the following figure, ScanDisk has found some "lost file fragments" and wants to know what to do with them. In this case, it's best to just chuck these fragments, so select the **Discard lost file fragment(s) and recover disk space** option and click **OK**. If you're really not sure what to do, you could try clicking the **More Info** button to display a dialog box with a few more facts. (Select **OK** when you're finished with this dialog box.) If that still doesn't help, just click **OK** and let ScanDisk figure things out for itself.

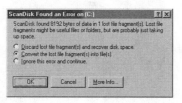

ScanDisk displays a dialog box like this one when it finds an error.

7. When ScanDisk's labors are complete, it displays the Results dialog box to let you know what happened. This dialog box is jam-packed with stats and numbers that are sure to warm the cockles of nerdy hearts everywhere. Nod your head knowingly and click **Close** to return to the ScanDisk window.

Automatic ScanDisk Scans

Way back in Chapter 2's "Shutting Down Windows for the Night" section, I told you that turning off your computer before exiting Windows 98 was a major no-no. If this does happen, however, Windows 98 is smart enough to recognize it and it will offer to run ScanDisk the next time you start your computer.

Spring Cleaning: Using Disk Cleanup to Delete Unneeded Files

If you find that your hard disk space is running low, one reason may be that it's littered with unnecessary files. This can happen if you turn off your computer before shutting down Windows 98, or if some sloppy program didn't clean up after itself. Here's how Windows 98 can help you tidy things up a bit:

1. Select **Start, Programs, Accessories, System Tools, Disk Cleanup**. A dialog box asks you which disk drive you want to clean up.

2. Use the **Drives** list to select the drive, and then click **OK**. This launches the Disk Cleanup program, which proceeds to look for files that can be safely chucked. When it's finished, you'll see a Disk Cleanup dialog box like the one shown here.

Need Head here please

Windows 98 offers another way to get Disk Cleanup on the job. In Windows Explorer or My Computer, right-click your hard disk and then click **Properties** in the shortcut menu. In the dialog box that appears, click the **Disk Cleanup** button.

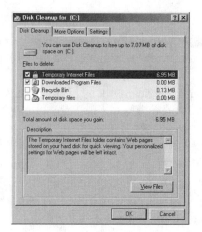

Use the Disk Cleanup utility to get rid of unnecessary files that are just taking up valuable hard disk space.

3. Activate the check boxes next to the types of files you want to expunge:

   ➤ **Temporary Internet Files:** These are files that your Web browser keeps handy for faster viewing. They can be safely deleted, but some Web pages may take a bit longer to load the next time you view them.

   ➤ **Downloaded Program Files:** These files, which get downloaded from the Internet for temporary use in certain Web pages, can be nuked.

   ➤ **Recycle Bin:** As you may remember, the Recycle Bin stores the files you "delete." If you're sure you don't need to restore any of these files, activate this check box.

SEE ALSO

➤ To get the goods on the Recycle Bin, head for Chapter 13, "Routine File Maintenance," and check out the "Deleting a File (and Undeleting It, Too)" section, p. 143.

   ➤ **Temporary files:** These are stray files that programs use to store data temporarily. Although most programs are civil enough to get rid of these files when they're no longer needed, some programs don't bother.

4. Click **OK**.

5. When Disk Cleanup asks whether you're sure, click **Yes**.

Using Disk Defragmenter to Put Your Hard Disk Affairs in Order

You can use Windows 98's Disk Defragmenter program to *defragment* the files on your hard disk. Defragmenting sounds pretty serious, but it's just Windows 98's way of tidying up a messy hard disk. It puts your files in order and does a few other neat-freak chores. (Don't worry though: Disk Defragmenter doesn't change the contents of the files, and they'll still appear in the same places when you look at them in Windows Explorer or My Computer.)

Before you use Disk Defragmenter, you need to do a little preparation:

➤ Use the Disk Cleanup utility described in the last section to delete from your hard disk any files that you don't need. Defragmenting junk files only slows down the whole process.

➤ Check for hard disk errors by running ScanDisk as outlined earlier in this chapter. You should probably run a Thorough test, just to be safe.

After you've completed these preliminary chores, you're ready to use Disk Defragmenter. Here's how it works:

1. Shut down all your running programs.

2. Select **Start, Programs, Accessories, System Tools, Disk Defragmenter**. Windows 98 displays the Select Drive dialog box, shown in the next figure.

3. Choose the disk drive that you want to work with and click **OK** to start the defragmentation. Disk Defragmenter starts pounding away at the chosen disk.

4. When Disk Defragmenter finally completes its labors (it may take 10–15 minutes, depending on the size of your disk, how cluttered it is, and how fast your computer is), your computer beeps, and a dialog box tells you that defragmentation is complete and asks whether you want to exit Disk Defragmenter. If you do, click **Yes**. Otherwise, click **No** to continue with Disk Defragmenter.

Use this dialog box to choose which disk drive to defragment.

How Often Should I Defragment?

How often you defragment your hard disk depends on how often you use your computer. If you use it every day, you should run Disk Defragmenter about once a week. If your computer doesn't get heavy use, you probably only need to run Disk Defragmenter once a month or so. As with ScanDisk, you can use the Maintenance Wizard to schedule regular Disk Defragmenter sessions.

Doubling Your Disk Space Pleasure with DriveSpace

It's great to see that our computers come with nice, fat hard disks these days. Because the programs we use are getting pretty hefty themselves, however, you may eventually find yourself bumping up against a storage ceiling. Disk Cleanup can help a bit, and that should be the first route you take to get more hard disk real estate. If you really want to get the most out of your current hard disk, however, you'll want to try out Windows 98's DriveSpace utility. This little marvel can effectively double the capacity of your hard disk by squeezing your files down to about half the size they are now. It's all perfectly safe and, aside from being a tad slower, your system will look and act the way it always has.

How DriveSpace Does Its Thing

Disk compression sounds like real pie-in-the-sky stuff, but it actually works. It's all based on an obscenely complex mathematical algorithm (called the Lempel-Ziv algorithm) that searches a file for redundant character strings and replaces them with small tokens. Let's look at a simple example. Consider the following phrase:

It was the best of times, it was the worst of times, it was the age of wisdom, it was the age of foolishness.

To compress this quotation, DriveSpace looks for repeated character strings. For example, "it was the" appears four times in this quotation, so DriveSpace would replace that phrase with a single token. The phrase "of times" appears twice, so that would get replaced by another token, and so on.

It sounds weird, but you usually end up with a file that's around half the size of the original. To decompress such data, all the program has to do is translate the tokens back to their original form.

As with Disk Defragmenter, you should do some preliminary chores before starting DriveSpace:

➤ Use Disk Cleanup to toss out any junk files that are hanging around.

➤ Run a Thorough ScanDisk test to weed out any drive errors.

➤ Back up your important documents, just in case some natural disaster occurs in the middle of the procedure.

SEE ALSO
➤ *For the basics of Backup, see Chapter 24, "Keeping Your Data Safe and Sound with Backup," p. 325.*

When you're all set, follow these steps to get started with DriveSpace:

1. Select **Start, Programs, Accessories, System Tools**. In the menu that appears, select the **DriveSpace** command, if it's there. If it's not there, select **Compression Agent**, instead, and then click **Yes** when you're asked whether you want to run DriveSpace 3 now.

2. In the DriveSpace 3 window that appears, use the **Drives on this computer** list to highlight the drive you want to compress.

3. Select the **Drive, Compress** command. DriveSpace examines the drive and displays the Compress a Drive dialog box that gives you an estimate of what the drive's new capacity will be. The dialog box you see depends on the size of your hard disk.

If you have a hard disk with a capacity less than 1 *gigabyte* (that's 1,000 megabytes, abbreviated as GB), then you'll see the dialog box shown in the following figure.

You'll see a dialog box like this one if your hard disk size is 1GB or less.

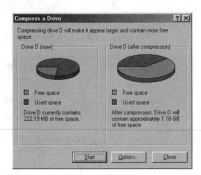

On the other hand, if the size of your hard disk is greater than 1 gigabyte, DriveSpace gets a little more complicated. When DriveSpace compresses your hard disk, it doesn't just shrink each file separately. Instead, it combines all your files into one monster file and compresses that. This file is a *compressed volume file* (or CVF, for short). If you open up, say, Windows Explorer, you won't see the CVF, however. Instead, you'll just see the normal contents of your hard drive.

If your hard disk is larger than 1GB, however, DriveSpace has to divide the disk into a compressed part (the CVF) and everything else (the uncompressed part). In Windows Explorer, the CVF appears as drive C, and the uncompressed part (the *host drive*) appears as drive H. (Actually, if the host drive has less than 2MB of free space, it won't appear in Windows Explorer at all.). In this case, you'll see a dialog box similar to the one in the next figure.

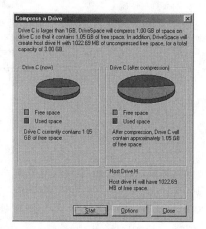

You'll see a dialog box like this one if your hard disk size is 1GB or more.

Either way, click the **Start** button in the Compress a Drive dialog box. Another dialog box appears, asking whether you're sure you want to compress the drive. (This dialog box also gives you the option of backing up your files.) If you're sure, click **Compress Now**. DriveSpace checks the drive for errors (yours should pass with flying colors because you've already run ScanDisk) and then starts compressing. When it's finished (it takes quite a while for larger hard disks), you're returned to the DriveSpace window.

The Windows 98 version of DriveSpace compresses files on-the-fly as you save them. DriveSpace uses three kinds of compression:

➤ **Standard compression:** This is the same compression method used with regular DriveSpace.

➤ **HiPack compression:** This option gives you a higher compression ratio (10 or 20 percent higher).

➤ **UltraPack compression:** This option gives you the highest compression ratio possible, and is available only through the Compression Agent (described a bit later in this section).

In your subsequent DriveSpace sessions, you may want to use a different compression type. To choose a compression method, select **Advanced, Settings** to display the Disk Compression Settings dialog box. These settings control the on-the-fly compression used by DriveSpace 3. You have the following options:

➤ **HiPack compression:** This option activates on-the-fly HiPack compression.

➤ **Standard compression:** This option activates on-the-fly standard compression.

➤ **No compression, unless drive is at least *x* % full:** This option turns off the on-the-fly compression. If the used space on the disk rises above the percentage entered in the text box, standard compression is activated.

➤ **No compression (fastest):** This option deactivates on-the-fly compression. This increases the performance of your system because DriveSpace will save files without using compression. If you elect to go this route, be sure to use Compression Agent (discussed next) to compress your files while you aren't using your computer.

After you've compressed a drive with DriveSpace 3, you can start using the Compression Agent to manage on-the-fly compression. Follow these steps to set up Compression Agent:

1. Select **Start, Programs, Accessories, System Tools, Compression Agent**. If you have multiple compressed drives, the Select Drive dialog box appears.

2. Select the compressed drive you want to recompress and click **OK**.

3. In the Compression Agent window, click Settings to display the Compression Agent Settings dialog box, shown in the next figure.

Use this dialog box to choose the compression method that you want Compression Agent to use.

4. Choose the files you want Compression Agent to compress, using UltraPack:

➤ **Do not UltraPack any files:** Choose this option to bypass UltraPack compression for optimum compression/decompression performance.

➤ **UltraPack all files:** Choose this option to achieve the maximum amount of compressed disk space.

➤ **UltraPack only files not used within the last *x* days:** Choose this option to have Compression Agent use UltraPack only on older files (which, presumably, you don't access very often).

5. If you didn't elect to use UltraPack compression on all your files, choose an option from the **Do you want to HiPack the rest of your files?** group:

➤ **Yes:** Choose this option to use HiPack compression on the non-UltraPack files.

➤ **No:** Choose this option to bypass compression on the non-UltraPack files.

6. Click **OK**. Compression Agent asks whether you want to use these settings when compression is invoked via the Task Scheduler.

7. This is a good idea, so click **Yes**.

8. Click **Start**. Compression Agent goes to work recompressing the drive. The Compression Agent window displays the progress of the operation.

9. When recompression is complete, a dialog box asks whether you want to recompress another drive. If you do, click **Yes** and repeat steps 3 through 8; otherwise, click **No** to return to the Compression Agent dialog box.

10. Click **Exit**.

Using the Maintenance Wizard to Keep Your System Firing on All Cylinders

You've seen quite a few handy tools so far. The crucial thing to keep in mind about all these programs is that they're only useful if you run them at regular intervals.

 Running them once a year or just whenever simply won't cut the system-maintenance mustard. Does that mean you have to plaster your monitor with sticky notes to remind yourself to run ScanDisk and friends? Fortunately, no. Windows 98 comes with a wizard that will do all the remembering for you. Not only that, but this wizard will even set things up so that all these system tools run automatically.

To get started, select **Start, Programs, Accessories, System Tools, Maintenance Wizard**. The wizard walks onto the screen and its first dialog box gives you a choice:

➤ **Express:** If you choose this option, the wizard will do all the scheduling for you. If you don't feel like messing around with this stuff, the Express route is the way to go.

➤ **Custom:** If you choose this option, you'll be able to set up custom schedules for the various maintenance tools, and even skip some tools you don't want (such as Disk Defragmenter).

Click **Next** when you've made your choice. The rest of this section takes you through the steps required for the Custom option. Here's how it works:

1. The wizard now displays the Select a Maintenance Schedule dialog box so that you can pick out when the maintenance programs should be scheduled to run. For example, if you leave your computer on all the time, select the **Nights** option. Click **Next** when you've made your choice.

2. Now the wizard may display the Start Windows More Quickly dialog box, which shows a list of the programs that load automatically each time you crank up Windows 98. For faster startups, deactivate the check boxes beside those programs that you don't need to launch automatically. When you're done, click **Next**.

3. The rest of the Maintenance Wizard's dialog boxes are related to the various system tools you saw in this chapter. For example, the Optimize Compressed Drive dialog box, shown in the next figure, is related to the Compression Agent utility. (You'll only see this dialog box if you have a compressed drive on your system.) In the rest of the Maintenance Wizard dialog boxes, you'll see the same two option buttons:

   ➤ **Yes:** Activate this option to schedule the task.

   ➤ **No:** Activate this option to bypass the task.

The rest of the Maintenance Wizard's dialog boxes help you schedule the system maintenance tools.

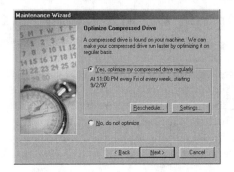

4. If you activate **Yes**, you can also work with the following buttons:

   ➤ **Reschedule:** This button displays the Reschedule dialog box, which you can use to specify a custom schedule for the task.

   ➤ **Settings:** This button displays a dialog box that contains settings related to the underlying program.

5. Here's a summary of the rest of the Maintenance Wizard dialog boxes that will come your way:

   ➤ **Speed Up Programs:** This dialog box is a front-end for Disk Defragmenter.

   ➤ **Scan Hard Disk for Errors:** This dialog box enables you to schedule a ScanDisk check. Note that because this is a *thorough* check, ScanDisk also checks disk surfaces. You may want to set an earlier start time or a less frequent schedule.

   ➤ **Delete Unnecessary Files:** This dialog box is a front-end for the Disk Cleanup program.

6. The last Maintenance Scheduler dialog box displays a summary of the options you chose. Click **Finish** to schedule the tasks.

The Scheduled Tasks Folder

The Maintenance Wizard only schedules the system tools to run at certain times. The actual dirty work of launching the programs at the specified times is the province of Windows 98's Scheduled Tasks folder. If you want to see the schedule, either open the Scheduled Tasks folder in My Computer or Windows Explorer, or select **Start, Programs, Accessories, System Tools, Scheduled Tasks**.

Is That All There Is? Windows 98's Other System Tools

While accessing the **Start, Programs, Accessories, System Tools** menu, you no doubt have noticed that it includes all kinds of scary-sounding programs that I didn't cover. The ones we looked at in this chapter are the most useful, but here's a quick look at some of the other tools, just so you know what's available:

➤ **Drive Converter (FAT32):** This utility converts your hard disk to a new format (called "FAT32"). This one's only for experts; I recommend leaving it alone.

➤ **System Information:** This program supplies you with a ton of data about your computer. The vast majority of the info is "geeks only" stuff, but it does give you semi-interesting tidbits such as the Windows 98 version, how much memory is on your system, and more.

➤ **Resource Meter:** This utility adds to the taskbar an icon that shows you the current level of system resources available to Windows 98.

SEE ALSO

➤ *I discuss system resources in a bit more detail in Chapter 25, "Troubleshooting Windows Woes." See the "Curing Memory Problems" section, p. 344.*

➤ **Scheduled Tasks:** This feature enables you to set up a program to run at a specific time. In fact, this is the feature that the Maintenance Wizard uses to schedule all those routine maintenance operations I showed you earlier.

➤ **System Monitor:** This program lets you monitor certain settings, such as the percentage of your computer's main processor that is being used at any one time.

Getting the Latest and Greatest from the Windows Update Web Site

When Microsoft releases a new version of Windows, the programmers take a day or two off and then get right back to work on the next version. (No flies on those folks!) In the past, whatever new goodies were being implemented for the new version were kept under wraps and unveiled only when everything else was ready for prime time a couple of years down the road. That all changed with the release of Windows 95. Microsoft started making bug fixes, updates, and new features available right away on its World Wide Web site. That was good news for the geeks who were willing to hunt down and install these new baubles, but the whole process was out of the league of the average user.

 With Windows 98, however, Microsoft brings these updates and enhancements down to earth. They've implemented a new feature called Windows Update, which uses a World Wide Web site as the starting point for all upgrades. From this site, a program examines your system and displays a list of the components for which newer versions are available. You can then select the items you need—and a couple of mouse clicks later the upgrades are downloaded and installed automatically! It's both mussless and fussless.

SEE ALSO

➤ *If you don't have an Internet connection up and running, refer to Chapter 15, "How to Get Connected to the Internet," p. 165.*

But assuming that you have an Internet connection up and running, you can get to the Windows Update site by following these steps:

1. Select **Start, Windows Update** to load Internet Explorer and display the Windows Update home page, shown in the following figure. You can also dial the following web address into your browser:

   http://windowsupdate.microsoft.com/

2. Click the **Product Updates** link.

3. Windows Update may ask if you want to install some software. This is a good idea, so click **Yes**.

4. Windows Update asks permission to scour your system to see which Windows 98 components are already installed on your system. Click **Yes**. After a while, you'll eventually see a list of all the available updates. The page you see will look something like the one shown here.

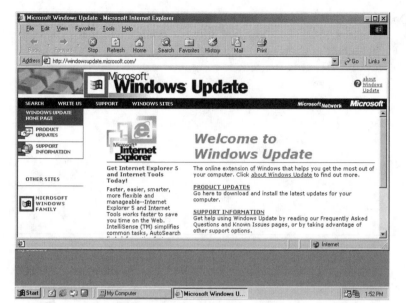

The Windows Update home page.

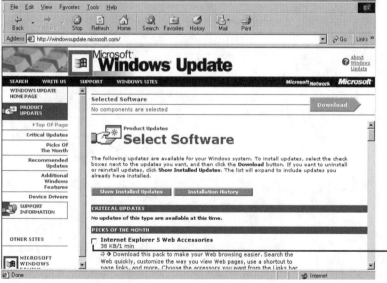

After the scan of your system is finished, this page shows you a list of the available updates.

Activate the check boxes beside the components you want to install.

5. To install an update, activate its check box.

6. When you're done, click **Download**. The next page gives you a list of the components you chose.

7. Click **Start Download**. (If you see a License Agreement at this point, studiously ignore the legalese and click **Yes**.) Windows Update downloads the component and then installs it automatically. Note that in some cases you may have to restart your computer after the upgrade is complete.

Keeping Your Data Safe and Sound with Backup

A few years ago, I turned on my computer in anticipation of another day's writing fun. I heard a couple of alarming beeps and then saw a **Hard disk configuration error** message on my screen. Yup. My hard disk had died a horrible death and there was nothing I could do about it. The worst part of it was that I had hundreds of documents on the disk that were now gone for good because I'd been too lazy to back up my files. It took me weeks to recover from that disaster, and I've been a rabid backer-upper up ever since.

I found out the hard way that there are two types of computer users: those who back up their documents and those who eventually wish they had. If you learn anything at all from this book, I hope it's this: Someday, sometime, somewhere, some sort of evil will befall your computer and all your data will be trashed. So be prepared by using the ever-so-easy Backup program that comes with Windows 98. This chapter shows you how it works.

Backing Up Is Easy to Do: Running the Backup Program

To get things going, select **Start, Programs, Accessories, System Tools, Backup**.

SEE ALSO

➤ *Don't see the Backup program anywhere? Unfortunately, it's not installed by default on some systems, and you'll need to put it on your computer by hand. To learn how, go to Chapter 11, "Installing and Removing Software and Hardware," and see the "Adding and Removing Windows 98 Components" section, p. 118.*

The first time you start Backup, it checks your system to see whether you have any "backup devices" installed. (What Windows 98 calls a backup device, the rest of us call a tape drive.) If you don't, Backup displays a dialog box asking whether you want to run the Add New Hardware Wizard to install a device. If you do have a backup device on your system, click **Yes** and use the wizard to specify the device. Otherwise, click **No** to continue.

Each time you start Backup, you'll see the Microsoft Backup dialog box shown in the following figure. You have these choices:

➤ **Create a new backup job:** If you activate this option and click **OK**, the program launches the Backup Wizard to take you step-by-step through the process of creating a backup job. I'll explain how this wizard works in a second.

➤ **Open an existing backup job:** If you've already defined a backup job, activate this option and click **OK**. In the Open Backup Job dialog box that appears, highlight the backup job you want to work with, and then click **Open**.

➤ **Restore backed up files:** If you've already run a backup job, activate this option to restore files from that backup job. (See "If Disaster Strikes: How to Restore Your Data," later in this chapter.)

If you don't want to run any of these choices right now, click **Close** to get to the Microsoft Backup window.

Backup presents you with this dialog box at startup.

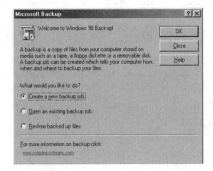

In Backup lingo, a *backup job* is a file that defines your backup. It includes three things:

➤ A list of the files you want to include in your backup

➤ The Backup options you selected, including the type of backup you want to use

➤ The destination drive and folder for the backed-up files

Windows 98's Backup program contains several wizards that take you through various backup-related operations. The Backup Wizard's role is to help you set up a new backup job. Here are the steps to follow:

1. You start the Backup Wizard using either of the following methods:

   ➤ In the startup Microsoft Backup dialog box, activate **Create a new backup job** and click **OK**.

   ➤ In the Microsoft Backup window, select **Tools, Backup Wizard**.

2. Either way, you'll see the first of the wizard's dialog boxes. You have two choices:

   ➤ **Back up My Computer:** Activate this option and click **Next** to perform a complete backup of your hard drives. If you choose this option, skip to step 4.

   ➤ **Back up selected files, folders, and drives:** Activate this option and click **Next** to choose the files you want to include in the backup job. This is the option I recommend in most cases because you can use it to back up just your precious documents.

3. If you decided to back up only selected files, you use the next wizard dialog box to choose those files. This dialog box is reminiscent of the Explorer window, with one important difference: In the Backup window, all the disk drives, folders, and files have a check box next to them. The basic idea, illustrated by the example in the following figure, is that you activate the appropriate check box for each drive, folder, and file you want to include in the backup. Click **Next** to move on.

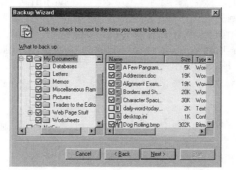

Use this wizard dialog box to choose the drives, folders, and files to include in the backup job.

4. The wizard next asks whether you want to back up **All selected files** or **New and changed files**. The latter means only those files that you've created or changed since the last time you did a backup. Make your choice and click **Next**.

5. Now the wizard wonders where you want the selected files backed up. Depending on your system, you'll see one or both of the following (click **Next** after you've made your choice):

   ➤ **File:** Select this option to back up your files to a single backup file. The wizard adds an extra text box so that you can specify the name and location of this backup file.

   ➤ **Backup device:** Select this option (the name of which varies depending on the backup device you have installed) to use your backup device as the destination.

6. Now the wizard presents the following options (click **Next** when you've made your choice):

   ➤ **Compare original and backup files to verify data was successfully backed up:** If you activate this check box, Backup checks each backed-up file against its original to make sure that the backup archived the file without any errors. Note that activating this option effectively doubles the backup time.

   ➤ **Compress the backup data to save space:** If you activate this check box, Backup compresses the backed-up files. The backed-up files will take up approximately half the space of the originals.

7. In the next wizard dialog box, use the text box to enter a name for your new backup job.

8. You're now ready to get the backup process under way. Click **Start** and Backup goes to work.

9. Backup may ask you for a unique name for the backup media. If so, enter a name and click **OK**.

10. During the backup process, you'll see the Backup Progress window. When the operation is complete, Backup displays a dialog box to let you know. Click **OK**, and then click **OK** in the Backup Progress window.

When Backup is finished, it drops you off at the Microsoft Backup window with the Backup tab displayed, as shown here. Note that you can use the various controls in this tab to define a backup job manually.

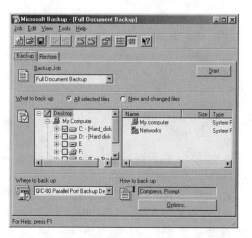

Instead of using the Backup Wizard, you can set up a backup job from the Backup tab.

Backup has various options you can work with, and the options you choose are stored with each backup job. To view the options, either click **Options** in the Backup tab or select the **Job, Options** command. Backup displays the Backup Job Options dialog box, shown in the next figure. The rest of this section looks at the options available in the General, Password, and Type tabs. (You can safely ignore the other tabs.)

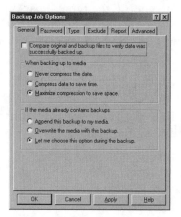

Use the Backup Job Options dialog box to customize some settings for your backup job.

In the **General** tab, use the **Compare original and backup files to verify data was successfully backed up** check box to toggle the verification process on or off.

The **When backing up to media** group contains the following three options:

➤ **Never compress the data:** Activate this option to turn off Backup's compression setting.

329

➤ **Compress data to save time:** This option compresses the data but doesn't use full compression, which speeds things up a bit.

➤ **Maximize compression to save space:** If the backup media is low on space, activate this option to use full compression on the backed up files. This reduces the size of the backup, but takes longer.

The **If the media already contains backups** group contains these option buttons:

➤ **Append this backup to my media:** This option adds your backup to the existing backups on the media.

➤ **Overwrite the media with this backup:** Activate this option to replace the old backup data with your new backup data.

➤ **Let me choose this option during the backup:** When this option is activated, Backup prompts you to append or overwrite the existing backup.

If you're backing up to a network drive or other public location, you can protect your backup from snoops by activating the **Protect this backup with a password** check box in the Password tab. Enter your password in both the **Password** and **Confirm password** text boxes.

You use the Type tab to choose the type of backup you want to run. For a full backup of every file in the backup job, activate the **All selected files** option. Otherwise, activate the **New and changed files only** option and then choose one of the following:

➤ **Differential backup type:** Backs up only those files that have changed since the last full backup.

➤ **Incremental backup type:** Backs up only those files that have changed since the last full or differential backup.

A Backup Strategy

Backing up is crucial but it's often a real hassle, either because it takes too much time to find all the files you want to back up or because you're backing up to a few dozen floppy disks. "Sorry, I'd like to do a backup, but I have to delouse my Rottweiler."

To minimize the hassle, take advantage of the three available types of backup. Your overall backup strategy might look something like this:

1. Do a full backup of all your documents once a month or so.

2. Do a differential backup of modified files once a week.

3. Do an incremental backup of modified files every day.

If Disaster Strikes: How to Restore Your Data

If some unforeseen disaster should occur, you'll need to restore your data from the backups. Happily, Backup has another wizard that takes you step-by-step through the process of restoring previously backed-up data. Here's the low-down on the Restore Wizard's workings:

1. Start this wizard using either of the following methods:

   ➤ In the startup Microsoft Backup dialog box, activate **Restore backed up files** and click **OK**.

   ➤ In the Microsoft Backup window, select **Tools, Restore Wizard**.

2. In the first wizard dialog box, select the device or file that contains the backup job and then click **Next**.

3. The wizard then displays a list of the backups found on the media. Activate the check boxes beside each backup job you want to restore, and then click **OK**.

4. Now the wizard creates a list of the drives, folders, and files in the chosen backup jobs. When it's finished, it displays a dialog box like the one shown in the next figure. Activate the check boxes beside the items you want to restore, and then click **Next**.

Use the Restore Wizard dialog box to choose the data you want to restore.

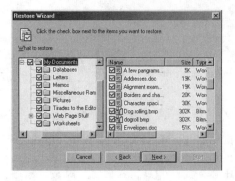

5. The wizard next asks where you want the files restored. You can select either **Original Location** or **Alternate Location**. If you choose the latter, a new text box appears so that you can specify the new location. Click **Next** when you're ready to proceed.

6. Now the wizard asks what it should do if a file with the same name already exists in the restore destination. Here are your choices:

   ➤ **Do not replace the file on my computer**: If you activate this option, Backup won't replace any files on the destination drive or folder with backed-up files that have the same name.

   ➤ **Replace the file on my computer only if the file is older**: If you activate this option, Backup only replaces files on the destination drive or folder with backed-up files of the same name that have a later date.

   ➤ **Always replace the file on my computer**: If you activate this option, Backup replaces any files on the destination drive or folder with backed-up files that have the same name.

7. Click **Start** to get the restore operation under way. Backup will prompt you to insert the media for the backup. Insert the media, if necessary, and then click **OK**.

8. The Restore Progress window appears during the restore operation. When Backup is finished, it displays a dialog box to let you know. Click **OK**, and then click **OK** in the Restore Progress window.

Backup Do's and Don'ts

Here are a few more hints and suggestions to make backing up easier and safer:

Do:

➤ Decide on a backup strategy and stick to it. Otherwise, you'll fall victim to one of computerdom's strictest laws: hard disks crash only when they contain priceless, irreplaceable data that isn't backed up.

➤ Put all your energy into backing up your documents because, unlike your programs, they are usually irreplaceable.

➤ Invest in a tape drive if you have a few dozen megabytes or more to back up. They're a little pricey, but they can hold hundreds of megabytes of data, and they do it all while you're doing lunch.

Don't:

➤ Scatter your documents around your hard disk. It's much easier to choose the files for the backup job if you store your data either in the My Documents folder or another folder you create yourself.

➤ Keep all your backup disks in one place. If a thief happens upon them, you'll be out of luck. Some folks even keep a copy in an offsite location, such as a safety deposit box.

➤ Use low-priced, no-name disks or tapes for your backups. Stick with high-quality media, and you'll sleep better at night.

➤ Be lazy or put it off. Back up your files now!

Chapter 25

Troubleshooting Windows Woes

In This Chapter

➤ Overcoming startup snarls

➤ Fixing Windows Explorer headaches

➤ Squashing memory complaints

➤ Dealing with mouse and printing problems

➤ Prescriptions for curing all kinds of Windows ills

There seems to be a bit of a backlash forming against the perceived unreliability of software. Rants of the "industry *x* would be out of business by now if it shipped products as problem-filled and incomplete as most computer programs" ilk seem to be popping up all over. Yes, it's true that software has a reputation for blowing up at the most inopportune times. It's also true, however, that this ain't no toaster we're dealing with. Windows 98 is a massive, complex hunk of technology that has to run on a slightly less than infinite variety of hardware combinations, and coexist with an equally wide array of other software programs. It shouldn't be too surprising, then, that problems will crop up from time to time.

SEE ALSO

➤ *As you saw back in Chapter 23, "Tools for Keeping Your System in Tip-Top Shape," p. 309, there are regular maintenance chores you can perform to fend off trouble. And, of course, you're running regular backups of your data anyway, right? No? Then head immediately to Chapter 24, "Keeping Your Data Safe and Sound with Backup," p. 325. Do not pass "Go," etc.*

However, if a problem does crop up, you'll need to know how to deal with it. This chapter gives you some troubleshooting basics and runs through a list of the most common Windows complaints.

Rescue 911: Using Windows 98's Troubleshooters

If the solutions presented later in this chapter don't get you out of whatever sticky Windows wicket you're in, you can always turn to the Windows 98 Troubleshooters. The Troubleshooters are an extension to the Windows 98 Help system that ask you a series of questions in an attempt to diagnose and solve your problem.

To run a Troubleshooter, follow these steps:

1. Select **Start, Help** to get to the Help system.

2. Open the **Troubleshooting** book and then open the **Windows 98 Troubleshooters** book to see the list of available topics.

3. Click the topic that corresponds to your problem. The Help system displays the Troubleshooter. For example, the following figure shows the Modem Troubleshooter. (Note that this is the Windows 98 Second Edition version of this troubleshooter.)

The Windows 98 Troubleshooters ask a series of questions to help get you out of a jam.

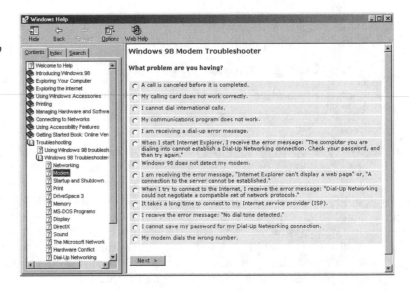

4. In the list of problems, activate the option button beside the one that most closely resembles your own problem, and then click **Next**.

5. From here, the Troubleshooter presents a series of questions and solutions for you to try. At each step, the Troubleshooter will ask whether the solution solved your problem. If not, you continue the process until, hopefully, all is right with your system again.

Some Windows Fires and How to Put Them Out

The rest of this chapter looks at a few of the ways that Windows 98 can go bad and offers nontechnical, relatively pain-free solutions.

Solving Startup Snags

Windows 98 startup problems can be frustrating, to say the least. When you have a deadline looming or an In basket full of paper, the last thing you need is for your operating system to refuse to operate. This section lays out several strategies for dealing with Windows 98 startup problems.

If Windows 98 won't load when you turn on your computer, there are several options you can try to see whether you can coax Windows 98 out of the starting blocks. For now, you need to restart your computer, using any of the following methods:

➤ Hold down both **Ctrl** and **Alt**, and then tap the **Delete** key.

➤ Press your computer's **Reset** button.

➤ Turn the obstinate beast off, wait a few seconds, and then turn it back on again.

While your computer gets itself back on its feet, hold down the **Ctrl** key. Eventually, instead of starting normally, Windows 98 presents you with a menu similar to the following:

```
Microsoft Windows 98 Startup Menu
=================================
1. Normal
2. Logged (\BOOTLOG.TXT)
3. Safe mode
4. Step-by-step confirmation
5. Command prompt only
6. Safe mode command prompt only
7. Previous version of MS-DOS

Enter a choice: 1
```

You select an option by pressing the number beside it and then pressing **Enter**. Here's a summary of what each of these options means:

➤ **Normal:** Starts Windows 98 in the usual way.

➤ **Logged (\BOOTLOG.TXT):** Starts Windows 98 and logs the progress of the startup in a text file called BOOTLOG.TXT in the main folder of your hard drive (C:\). If Windows 98 fails to start, BOOTLOG.TXT should tell you why. To check it out, restart your computer, hold down **Ctrl** to get the Startup menu again, and choose the **Safe mode command prompt only** option. At the **C:\>** prompt, type **edit bootlog.txt**. Keep your eyes peeled for a couple of lines that look something like this:

```
[000A94C1] Loading Device = C:\DOS\ATDOSHC.SYS

[000A94C1] LoadFailed = C:\DOS\ATDOSHC.SYS
```

This will tell you which file Windows 98 choked on. Other BOOTLOG.TXT keywords to look for are "Error" and "Fail." You'll need to report the error to Microsoft Technical Support.

➤ **Safe mode:** Starts Windows 98 with only a minimal configuration. Specifically, your mouse and keyboard will work, and your video display will be set to its lowest mode. Other goodies, such as your CD-ROM drive and networking, are checked at the door. Always try Safe mode first to see whether Windows will start with the minimal configuration. If it does, you can use Windows 98 to try to fix the problem. (I'll discuss that after I run through this list.)

➤ **Step-by-step confirmation:** Starts Windows 98 and displays a prompt such as the following at each phase of the startup:

```
Process the system registry {Enter=Y,Esc=N]?
```

Press **Enter** to perform the action, and watch your screen for error messages. If you see an error, make a note of where it occurred. You may be able to get Windows 98 to start by rebooting your computer, selecting the **Step-by-step confirmation** option again, and, when you get to the spot where the error happened last time, pressing **Esc** to bypass the process.

➤ **Command prompt only:** Displays the command prompt (**C:\>**) instead of the Windows 98 desktop. When you're at the command prompt, try to start Windows 98 by typing one of the following commands and pressing **Enter**:

```
win /d:f
win /d:s
win /d:v
win /d:x
```

If one of these commands starts Windows 98 properly, contact Microsoft Technical Support and tell them which command worked. They'll let you know what to do from there.

➤ **Safe mode command prompt only:** Starts Windows 98 in Safe mode and displays the command prompt instead of the desktop. Use this option if Windows 98 fails to start in Safe mode. Try starting Windows 98 using the commands outlined in the previous paragraph.

➤ **Previous version of MS-DOS:** Starts the version of MS-DOS that was previously installed on your computer. You'll only see this option if you installed Windows 98 in a directory separate from the one used by your previous version of Windows. This is the if-all-else-fails option.

As I mentioned earlier, you should always try to start Windows 98 in Safe mode first. If you manage to get it up and running, Windows 98 has a few tools you can use to investigate the problem. Those tools include the Help system Troubleshooters, the Control Panel, the Device Manager, and ScanDisk. The next few sections discuss each of these tools.

Help System Troubleshooters

As I mentioned earlier, Windows 98's Help system comes equipped with several Troubleshooters that lead you step-by-step through specific problem-solving procedures.

Control Panel

To use Control Panel to investigate a problem, select **Start, Settings, Control Panel**. The icons in Control Panel govern the settings for all kinds of devices on your system (such as your video display, your sound card, and your network adapter). Windows 98 may exhibit erratic behavior if these devices aren't set up correctly. Try selecting the icons for your equipment (most of which have been discussed elsewhere in this book) and checking to see whether the settings are correct.

Device Manager

The third tool available, Device Manager, gives you a forest-instead-of-the-trees look at all the devices installed on your system. A conflict between these devices can cause all kinds of bad things to happen, so the Device Manager examines your system for conflicts and lets you know whether there's a problem. You get to the Device Manager by opening Control Panel's **System** icon and then selecting the **Device Manager** tab in the System Properties dialog box. If there's a problem, Windows 98 displays a yellow exclamation mark over the icon of the device that's stepping on another's toes (see the following figure). Use the Help system's Hardware Conflict Troubleshooter to get things back in sync.

Device Manager uses icons to alert you to a hardware problem.

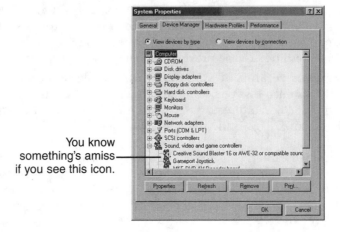

You know something's amiss if you see this icon.

ScanDisk

The final investigative tool is ScanDisk. If your hard disk has some files or folders that need fixing, or if some tiny chunk of your hard disk has gone to seed, it could cause all kinds of problems for Windows 98.

SEE ALSO

➤ *To make sure that your system is fit as a fiddle, run the ScanDisk accessory regularly (as described in Chapter 23, in the section titled "Using ScanDisk to Avoid Hard Disk Hard Times," p.309).*

If Windows 98 won't load even in Safe mode, you can run ScanDisk from the command prompt by following these steps:

1. Reboot your computer and hold down **Ctrl** to display the Startup menu.

2. Select the **Safe mode command prompt only** option.

3. When you get to the command prompt (the **C:\>** thingy), type **cd\windows\command** and press **Enter**.

4. Type **scandisk** and press **Enter** to start the ScanDisk program. If ScanDisk finds an error, make sure that you select **Yes** (or press **Y**) when it asks whether you want to fix the error.

5. When ScanDisk asks whether you want to run a surface scan, select **Yes**.

6. When ScanDisk has completed its labors, select **Exit** (or press **X**) to return to the command prompt.

7. Reboot your computer and see whether Windows 98 will start.

If Windows 98 won't load in Safe mode, à la mode, or in any other mode, your hard disk likely has a problem that has corrupted the files Windows uses to get itself out of bed in the morning. In this case, your only hope is to boot your computer, using your Windows 98 Startup disk.

SEE ALSO
➤ *To learn more about how to create a Startup disk, check out "Just In Case: Creating an Emergency Startup Disk," p. 159, in Chapter 14, "Storage Solutions: Working with Folders and Floppy Disks."*

Place the Startup disk in drive A: and reboot your computer. When you get to the **A:\>** prompt, type **scandisk c:** and press **Enter**. ScanDisk will check the integrity of your hard disk (I'm assuming here that you installed Windows 98 on drive C:), let you know what the problem is, and (hopefully) fix it for you. Make sure that you run the surface scan when ScanDisk asks.

Dealing with the Dastardly General Protection Fault

If you used Windows 3.1 regularly, you probably came across more than your share of General Protection Faults. These GPFs (as they were usually called) were particularly nasty errors that could ruin your data and cause your machine to lock up. Why did they occur? Well, applications, like people, have their own "personal space." For an application, this personal space is actually a chunk of your computer's memory. Basically, GPFs occur when one application invades the personal space of another.

Windows 98 improves this situation by making it harder for Windows 98 applications to bump into each other. Oh sure, GPFs still exist (Windows 98 now calls them "illegal operations"), but they should appear far less frequently.

When Windows 98 detects an illegal operation, all sorts of internal bells and alarms go off, and Windows 98 tries to minimize the damage wrought by the wayward program. When Windows has tidied things up as best it can, it displays a dialog box like the one shown in the following figure. Click the **Close** button to terminate the rogue program.

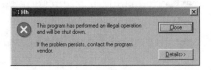

You'll see a dialog box like this when an application is caught trespassing.

If things are really ugly, however, the program may just freeze solid   and nothing you do or say will make it go again. If that happens, press **Ctrl+Alt+Delete** to display the Close Program dialog box. Then highlight the offending application (it should say **Not responding** beside its name) and click the **End Task** button.

Windows 98 does a reasonable job of preventing programs from running amok and locking up your entire machine. After you've shut down a delinquent application, you can often get right back to work. Because there's a chance that your system may be unstable, however, it's a good idea to exit the rest of your programs and reboot your computer.

Here are a few pointers that should prevent illegal operations (or GPFs, or whatever you want to call them) from occurring:

➤ **If you're running an application written for an earlier version of Windows 98, upgrade to a newer version.** Programs designed specifically for Windows 95 or Windows 98 offer the most protection from debilitating crashes. If possible, you should upgrade your existing Windows software to the Windows 95/98 versions.

➤ **Use ScanDisk to weed out disk errors.** Corrupted or damaged files on your hard disk are another common source of GPFs. To check for (and fix) these problems, use the Windows 98 ScanDisk accessory (as described in Chapter 23).

➤ **Keep an eye on your system resources.** You can bet your bottom dollar that a GPF is just around the corner if your system resources drop below the 20% mark. Keep an eye on them (as described later in this chapter) if you're working with large applications.

Overcoming Windows Explorer Exasperations

After you get the hang of Windows Explorer (which won't take long if you read the three chapters in Part 4), you'll probably find that it's one of the Windows 98 applications you use the most. But, of course, the more you use it, the more likely it is that some operation will go up in flames. This section takes you through some common Windows Explorer complaints.

Explorer Isn't Showing You the Correct Information

Sometimes what Windows Explorer *thinks* is in a folder or on a disk is not what's actually there. (Short attention span, I guess.) You can give Windows Explorer a poke in the ribs by selecting the **View, Refresh** command, or by pressing **F5**.

You Have Problems Trying to Copy, Move, Delete, or Rename a File on a Floppy Disk

As explained in Chapter 13, "Routine File Maintenance," Windows Explorer makes it easy to copy or move files to and from a floppy disk. you might run into problems however, if the following scenarios exist:

The disk is full: Windows Explorer, rightly so, won't allow you to copy or move a file to a disk unless there's sufficient space. If the disk is full, delete any unneeded files or use another disk.

The disk is write-protected: When a floppy disk is *write-protected*, you can't copy or move files to the disk or delete or rename files on the disk. For a 3 1/2-inch disk, write-protection is controlled by a small, movable tab on the back of the disk. If the tab is toward the edge of the disk, the disk is write-protected. To disable the write-protection, slide the tab away from the edge of the disk.

You Can't Copy a Disk

If Windows 98 won't let you copy a disk, try these possible solutions:

➤ Make sure that the disk is inserted properly. That is, make sure the disk is inserted all the way into the drive and that it's not upside down.

➤ Is the destination disk write-protected? Windows 98 won't copy files to a disk that's write-protected. Check the disk and disable the write-protection as described earlier.

➤ Are the two disks the same type? Windows 98's disk copying feature is designed to work only with two disks that have the same capacity and are of the same type. If you have two different types of disk drives, you can still copy a disk, but you have to use the same drive for both the source and destination.

You Can't Tell How Much Free Space Is Left on Your Hard Disk

With applications growing by leaps and bounds, it doesn't take long for a hard disk to run out of room. If you're not sure how much hard disk acreage you've got left, you can find out by using one of the following techniques:

➤ View the My Computer folder as a Web page (activate the **View, as Web Page** command), maximize the window, and then highlight the drive. Windows 98 displays a pie chart that shows you the used and free space on the drive (see the following figure).

➤ In Windows Explorer, highlight the drive and then either select the **File, Properties** command or click the **Properties** button in the toolbar. In this case, the pie chart appears inside a dialog box.

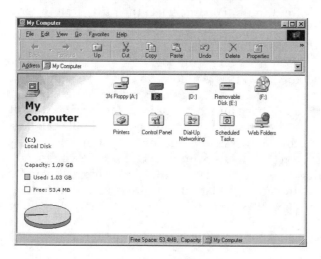

In Web page view, the My Computer folder tells you how much room remains on your hard disk.

Curing Memory Problems

Memory is to Windows 98 what money is to an investor. The more you have, the more things you can do, but if you run out, well, you're out of luck. This section presents a few solutions for those times when money, er, memory is scarce.

Close Down What You Don't Need

The most obvious (but the least convenient) solution is to close any running applications that you really don't need. The bigger the application, the more memory you'll save. I've performed careful, scientific experiments to try to determine the optimum Windows configuration. My data tells me unequivocally that the best way to prevent insufficient memory errors is to shut down all your programs and go read a good book.

Delete the Contents of the Clipboard

When you cut or copy a selection in a Windows 98 application, the program stores the data in an area of your computer's memory called the Clipboard. If you're working with only a few lines of text, this area remains fairly small. Cutting or copying a graphic image can increase the size of the Clipboard to several hundred kilobytes or more, however. If you've run out of memory, a chubby Clipboard may be the culprit. To trim the Clipboard and release most of this memory, try one of the following methods:

➤ If you have an application running, highlight a small section of text (a single character or word will do) and select **Edit, Copy**. This replaces the current Clipboard with a much smaller one.

➤ Select **Start, Programs, Accessories, System Tools, Clipboard Viewer**. When the Clipboard Viewer window appears, select the **Edit, Delete** command.

Release Some System Resources

System resources are small memory areas that Windows 98 uses to keep track of things like the position and size of open windows, dialog boxes, and your desktop configuration (wallpaper and such). You can have megabytes of free memory and still get **Insufficient Memory** errors if you run out of system resources! (Life can be so unfair.) How can you tell whether your system resources are getting low? In any Windows 98 folder window, select the **Help, About Windows 98** command. As you can see in the following figure, the About Windows dialog box tells you what percentage of the system resource area is still available. You should start to be concerned if this number drops below 30%, and problems may start cropping up when this number dives under the 20% mark.

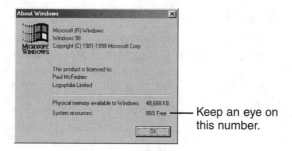

The About Windows dia-log box tells you what percentage of system resources is still available.

Keep an eye on this number.

Although Windows 98 has taken great leaps to improve the way it uses system resources, you may still run into problems with certain applications. If you do run into problems, try out these tips for preserving your system resources:

➤ When you're working with Windows 98 applications, don't leave open any unnecessary document windows.

➤ Turn off program features (such as status bars, rulers, and toolbars) that you don't use.

➤ Run DOS applications full-screen instead of in a window.

➤ Turn off the wallpaper on your desktop.

SEE ALSO

➤ *To learn about Windows wallpaper, see the "Renovating the Desktop: Working with the Desktop Properties" section of Chapter 10, "Customizing the Desktop and Taskbar," p. 104.*

Load Larger Applications First

Because of the way Windows 98 uses memory, you can often start more programs if you load your larger Windows 98 applications before your smaller ones.

Run the Help System's Memory Troubleshooter

The Memory Troubleshooter can help out with certain kinds of memory mishaps. In the Help window, open the **Troubleshooting** book, open the **Windows 98 Troubleshooters** book, and then select the **Memory** topic.

Shell Out the Bucks to Buy More Memory

The ultimate way to beat memory problems, of course, is simply to add more memory to your system. (Although, as you've seen, you still need to make sure that your system resources don't get too low.) Happily, memory prices have fallen over the past couple of years, and adding a megabyte or two shouldn't break your budget. If you do decide to take the plunge, contact your computer manufacturer to find out the best kind of memory to add to your system.

Fixing Mouse Mishaps

Using a mouse with Windows 98 is so easy that many people never learn how to work the program with the keyboard. This can present real problems, though, if your mouse decides to go wacko on you. (I once saw an otherwise-composed individual panic badly when his mouse quit on him during a Windows presentation; he didn't have a clue about Windows keyboard techniques.) The next few sections show you how to respond to various mouse problems.

Your Mouse Pointer Is Doing Weird Things

Some people would say that the mouse pointer *always* does weird things, but some of the weirdness may not be your fault. If you find that your mouse isn't responding or that the pointer is racing all over the screen, you can usually fix it by exiting and restarting Windows. If that doesn't work, try one of these easy solutions:

➤ **Make sure that the mouse is plugged in:** Yeah, I know, this seems pretty simple-minded, but the Number One Rule when troubleshooting any device is to first ask, "Is it plugged in?" You would be surprised how often the answer is a sheepish "No."

➤ **Try a mouse pad with a better surface feel:** A proper mouse pad is essential for consistent mouse movements. If the pad is too soft, the roller sinks in too deep, which can cause it to stick. If the pad is too hard or slick, however, the roller doesn't have anything to grab.

➤ **Have you cleaned the little guy lately?** If your mouse is behaving erratically, all you may need to do is clean its insides. A well-used mouse can take in quite a collection of dust, crumbs, and other alien substances that can play havoc on its delicate constitution. Your mouse documentation should tell you the proper cleaning procedure. If your mouse has a roller ball, you can also follow these steps:

1. Remove the cover on the bottom of the mouse.
2. Remove the roller ball.
3. Using a cotton swab dipped lightly in isopropyl alcohol or water, clean the rollers and other contact areas. (I also find a pair of tweezers or needlenose pliers comes in handy for pulling out the mini dust bunnies that accumulate inside the rollers.)
4. Wipe off any excess liquid, and then replace the ball and cover.

➤ **Try a different mouse driver:** Windows 98 supports several kinds of mice, each of which uses its own device driver. If you're using the wrong driver, the pointer may not move at all or it may do some crazy things. To remedy this, you need to change to the correct driver. To do so, you use the Add New Hardware Wizard.

SEE ALSO

➤ *Follow the steps that I outlined in Chapter 11, "Installing and Removing Software and Hardware," for using the Add New Hardware Wizard (see "Adding a New Hunk of Hardware," p. 124).*

When the wizard asks whether you want Windows to search for new hardware, activate the **No, I want to install other devices** option and click **Next**. In the list of hardware categories, select **Mouse** and then choose your mouse manufacturer and model.

Windows 98 Doesn't Always Respond to Your Double-Clicks

If Windows 98 ignores some of your double-clicks, you probably need to slow down the *double-click speed*. Here's how:

1. Select **Start, Settings, Control Panel** and then launch the **Mouse** icon. Windows 98 fires up the Mouse Properties dialog box.

2. Use the **Double-click speed** slider to adjust the speed. (Try moving the slider towards the **Slow** end.) Use the **Test area** to check that your double-clicks now work.

3. When you're done, click **OK**.

You Have Trouble Seeing the Mouse Pointer

If you use a laptop or if your eyesight isn't what it used to be, you might have trouble keeping track of the little mouse pointer. You may be able to improve things a bit by telling Windows 98 to display "trails" as you move the mouse.

The Mouse Pointer Moves Too Slowly or Too Quickly

The speed at which the pointer moves across the screen is governed by the *mouse tracking speed*. If this just doesn't feel right, you can change this setting to one that's more comfortable. To do this, open the Mouse Properties dialog box once again, display the **Motion** tab, and adjust the **Pointer speed** slider.

Repairing Printing Perplexities

As I explained back in Chapter 7, "Getting Hard Copy: Windows 98 Printing," printing is easy because your applications get to pass their printing bucks to Windows 98, which then handles all the dirty work. Unfortunately, this doesn't mean that printing is trouble-free. If you're having problems getting your printer to print, this section tells you what to do.

Windows 98 Reports an Error While Printing

If Windows 98 can't communicate with your printer for some reason, it displays the dialog box shown in the following figure.

*You'll see this dialog box
if Windows 98 and your
printer aren't on the
same wavelength.*

When this happens, try the following solutions:

Make sure that your printer is powered up and online. Before you start
any print jobs, verify that:

➤ Your printer is powered up.

➤ It's online (this means that it's ready to receive output). Most printers have
an Online button you can select.

➤ The cable connections are secure.

➤ There's paper in the printer.

➤ There's no paper jam.

Tell Windows 98 to be more patient: Depending on the print job, some
printers take an extra-long time to process the data Windows 98 sends them. If
they take *too* long, Windows 98 assumes that the printer is "offline," and you
get an error message. To fix this, follow these steps:

1. Select **Start, Settings, Printers**. Windows 98 displays the Printers window.

2. Highlight the printer you're using and select the **File, Properties** command (or right-click on the printer icon and select **Properties** from the
shortcut menu). Windows 98 displays the Properties dialog box for the
printer.

3. Select the **Details** tab.

4. Increase the number in the **Transmission retry** box, select **Apply**, and
then print your document again. Start with 120 seconds and, if you still
get an error, increase the value in increments of 60 seconds.

5. Click **OK** to return to the Printers window.

Part VIII
"No Tears" Windows 98 Networking

If you're running Windows 98 at work, chances are that your computer is connected to a whole whack of other machines in a company-wide network. This connection enables several machines to share things like printers and CD-ROM drives. It also lets you set up common folders that some or all of the folks on the network can use for storage. And, of course, no networked office would be complete without an email system so employees can exchange snarky notes about the boss. The capability to do all of these network tricks and more is build right in to Windows 98. The two chapters here in Part 8 let you in on this network know-how.

Chapter 26

Working with Network Connections and Email

In This Chapter

➤ Setting up your computer for networking

➤ Accessing folders and printers on other computers

➤ Sharing your folders and printers with others

➤ Exchanging email with network colleagues

➤ All the network know-how you need

In the wonderful world of Windows networking, a *workgroup* is a small group of computers connected by some kind of network cable. In most workgroups, the computers are related to each other somehow. For example, all the computers in a company's accounting department could form one workgroup, and the marketing department might have its own workgroup. Each workgroup has a name (Accounting, for example), and each computer in the workgroup has its own name (usually the name of the person using the computer, but it could just as easily be something silly).

The whole point of setting up a workgroup is so that the members of the group can share their resources. For example, if you have five computers in the group but only one printer (as I do), you can set things up so that each machine can print from that one printer, which is kinda neat. Similarly, you can share files, applications, and even CD-ROM drives. Does this mean that other people in the group can just play with your machine willy-nilly? Heck no, not if you don't want them to. *You* decide which resources on your computer are shared, and for extra safety, you can set up passwords to prevent undesirables and other coworkers from accessing sensitive areas. The first half of this chapter shows you how to do all this. The second half shows you how to exchange email messages with your colleagues.

A Drive Around the Network Neighborhood

Windows 98 calls your workgroup and network the "Network Neighborhood," which certainly sounds friendly enough. Here are a couple of different ways to see what's in your Network Neighborhood:

➤ Open the desktop's **Network Neighborhood** icon.

➤ Open Windows Explorer and select **Network Neighborhood** in the Folders list.

The following figure shows my Network Neighborhood folder. The Name column contains the following information:

➤ **Entire Network:** Open this folder to see all the workgroups that are part of the full network to which your computer is attached. (If you're just hooked up to your own workgroup, Entire Network shows only that workgroup.) Opening these workgroup folders displays the names of all the computers in each workgroup.

➤ **Some computer names:** The rest of the Name column displays the names of the computers in your workgroup (including your own). (If you don't see all the columns shown in the figure, activate the **View, Details** command.)

The Network Neighborhood: your computer's community.

These are the computers in my workgroup.

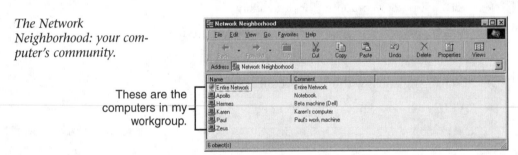

Because each Network Neighborhood computer is really just a folder, you can use the usual My Computer or Windows Explorer techniques to check out what's on the various machines. For each computer, you'll see those resources that the owner of the computer has chosen to share with the network. (I'll tell you how to share your resources later in this chapter.) For example, the next figure shows the window that appears when I open the folder for the computer named Hermes. Notice that this generous user is sharing all sorts of goodies: a printer, a CD-ROM drive, and a data folder. The other computers in the workgroup can access these resources as though the hardware and folders were part of their own systems.

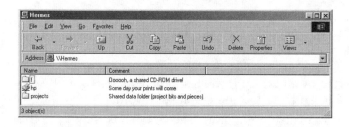

If you open the folder for a Network Neighborhood computer, Windows shows the computer's shared resources.

Actually, the level of access available for a shared resource depends on the *access rights* the sharer has granted the sharees. As you'll see later, you can prevent others from messing with your resources by giving them *read-only* access. If you run into, say, a shared folder that's read-only, you won't be able to change any of the folder's files. If you try, you'll see a curt error message telling you that **Network Access is denied**. Bummer.

It's also possible to tailor access to a shared resource by using passwords. For example, if you try to view a shared disk drive that has been password-protected, Windows 98 displays the Enter Network Password dialog box. You won't be able to access the drive until you enter the correct password in the **Password** text box. (Note, too, that unless you want to reenter the password every time you access this resource, you should leave the **Save this password in your password list** check box activated.)

Accessing Network Resources

As I've said, one way to play with the shared resources in your workgroup is to head into the Network Neighborhood and "open" the computers you see listed. Here are two other ways to work with these resources:

➤ You can "map" a network folder so that it appears to be a disk drive on your computer. For example, let's say that your system has two floppy disk drives (drives A and B) and a hard disk drive (drive C). If you map a network folder, it will appear as drive D on your computer. If you map another network folder, it will appear as drive E, and so on. This makes it easier not only to copy and move files to and from the network folder, but also to open files on the drive. It also makes the drive accessible from the MS-DOS prompt.

➤ You can install a network printer and use it (more or less) just like a printer attached directly to your computer. (Why "more or less"? Well, there are some things you won't be able to do, such as purging other people's print jobs.)

Mapping a Network Folder

Mapping a network folder is easier done than said. This is what you do:

1. Display the Network Neighborhood and open the computer that contains the folder you want to work with.

2. Try either of the following techniques:

353

➤ Highlight the network folder and select **File, Map Network Drive**.

➤ Right-click the network folder and click **Map Network Drive** in the shortcut menu.

3. If the drive is protected by a password, you'll see the Enter Network Password dialog box so that you can enter the appropriate password.

4. The Map Network Drive dialog box appears. The **Drive** box shows you the drive letter that Windows 98 will use to map the network folder. You can select a different letter, if you like.

5. If you'd like this folder to be mapped every time you log on to Windows 98, activate the **Reconnect at logon** check box.

6. When you're ready, click **OK** to map the drive. After a few seconds, the new drive appears in Windows Explorer's Folders list as part of the My Computer folder. (For those of you who have been paying attention: yes, the mapped drive also appears in the My Computer window.)

To disconnect a mapped drive, use either of the following techniques:

➤ Highlight the mapped drive in Windows Explorer and select the **Tools, Disconnect Network Drive** command. In the Disconnect Network Drive dialog box that appears, highlight the drive you want to disconnect, and then click **OK**. If Windows 98 asks whether you're sure you want to disconnect, select **Yes**.

➤ Right-click the network drive, and click **Disconnect** in the shortcut menu. Windows 98 disconnects the drive right away.

Using a Network Printer

One of the big advantages of setting up a workgroup in your workplace or home is that you can share expensive items—such as printers—among all your computers. You don't need to get a separate printer for each machine or put up with the hassle of swapping printer cables. Here are the steps to follow to install a network printer for use on your computer:

1. Display the Network Neighborhood, open the computer that has the shared printer, and then highlight the printer.

2. Select the **File, Install** command.

3. You may see a Connect to Printer dialog box mumbling something about the "server" not having "a suitable printer driver." If so, ignore the geekspeak and click **OK**.

4. If you were subjected to the Connect to Printer dialog box in step 3, you'll see a dialog box from the Add Printer Wizard. Use the **Manufacturers** and **Printers** lists to highlight the printer you want to install, and then click **OK**.

5. From here, you follow the same steps that I outlined for installing a printer in Chapter 7, "Getting Hard Copy: Windows 98 Printing."

SEE ALSO

➤ *The instructions for installing a printer can be found in the "Letting Windows Know You've Got a Printer" section, p. 73.*

Playing Nicely with Others: Sharing Your Resources

Networking is a two-way street. It's fine to play around with the resources on other people's machines, but only a real greedy-guts would refuse to share his own computer's resources. To avoid being shunned by your peers, you need to designate a resource or two that can be shared. Read on to learn how.

Sharing Folders and Disk Drives

If you have a CD-ROM drive or perhaps some data in a folder that the others in your workgroup are lusting after, you should put your coworkers out of their misery by sharing the drive or folder with them.

The first thing you need to decide is how you want to share your resources. For each drive or folder you share, Windows 98 gives you three choices (called *access rights*):

➤ **Read-Only:** At this level, someone else who accesses one of your shared drives or folders can only copy, open, and view files. They can't move files, modify them, rename them, delete them, or add new ones.

➤ **Full:** This anything-goes level gives others complete access to the files in the shared drive or folder. They can move, copy, open, view, modify, rename, and delete files, and they can even create new files.

➤ **Depends on Password:** This level enables you to assign separate passwords for read-only and full access.

Here are the steps to follow to share a disk drive, CD-ROM drive, or folder:

1. In Windows Explorer or My Computer, highlight the disk drive or folder that you want to share.

2. Select the **File, Properties** command, and then display the **Sharing** tab in the Properties dialog box that appears. Alternatively, you can right-click the drive or folder and click **Sharing** from the shortcut menu. The following figure shows the Sharing tab. (If your sharing tab looks different, read the instructions that follow these steps.)

No Sharing Tab?

If your Properties dialog box has no Sharing tab, your computer isn't set up to share your stuff. To remedy this, select **Start, Settings, Control Panel** to open the Control Panel folder. Open the **Network** icon to get the Network dialog box onscreen. Click the **File and Print Sharing** button, and then activate the **I want to be able to give others access to my files** check box. If you want to share your printer also, activate the **I want to be able to allow others to print to my printer(s)** check box. Click **OK** and then click **OK** again. When Windows 98 asks whether you want to restart, click **Yes**.

Use the Sharing tab to share a drive or folder with your workgroup pals.

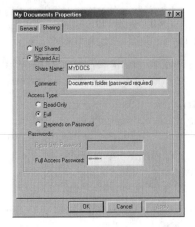

3. Activate the **Shared As** option button.

4. The **Share Name** text box shows either the letter of the disk drive or the name of the folder. Because this is what appears in the Network Neighborhood's Name column when other people access your computer, it's probably best that you leave the name as is. You should, however, enter a brief description of the resource in the **Comment** text box. (Something like "Hard disk" or "CD-ROM drive" or "Crucial workgroup files" is sufficient.)

5. Select the type of access you want for this resource: **Read-Only**, **Full**, or **Depends on Password**.

6. If you want others to enter a password to access the shared drive or folder, enter the appropriate password in either the **Read-Only Password** or the **Full Access Password** text box. If you selected **Depends on Password**, you need to enter a password in both text boxes. (If you do enter a password, don't forget to let the other people in your group know what it is!)

7. Click **OK**. If you entered a password, you're asked to confirm it. In this case, reenter the password and click **OK**. When you return to Windows Explorer or My Computer, you see a little hand under the folder's icon. This reminds you that you've shared the folder.

Depending on the way your network is set up, you may have to use a different technique to share your resources. Specifically, if you see the version of the Sharing tab shown in the next figure, your network is set up for "user-level" access to shared resources.

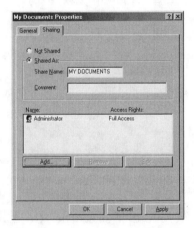

You'll see this Sharing tab if your network is set up with user-level access.

As before, you activate the **Shared As** option and enter a **Comment**. Next, you need to specify which users or groups of users are allowed to access your resource. Here's how it's done:

1. Click the **Add** button to display the Add Users dialog box, shown in the next figure. The Name list displays all the users and groups that are recognized as valid by your network.

Use the Add Users dialog box to specify which users and groups should be allowed access to the resource.

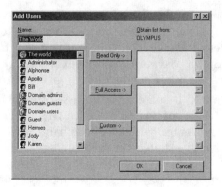

2. Highlight a user or group in the **Name** list.

3. Click **Read Only**, **Full Access**, or **Custom**.

4. Repeat steps 2 and 3 to add other users or groups to the lists.

5. When you're finished, click **OK**.

6. If you added any users or groups to the Custom list, you'll see the Change Access Rights dialog box. Use this dialog box to set up specific access rights for the users. When you're finished, click **OK**.

7. When you're back at the Sharing tab, click **OK**.

Sharing Printers

Sharing a printer among several computers in a workgroup is similar to sharing folders. First, you need to open the Printers folder, either by highlighting it in Windows Explorer's Folders list or by selecting **Start, Settings, Printers**.

Highlight the printer you want to share, and then select the **File, Sharing** command (or right-click the printer and click **Sharing** in the shortcut menu). Windows 98 displays the printer's Properties dialog box and selects the **Sharing** tab. Activate the **Share As** option, enter a **Comment**, and then enter an optional **Password**. Click **OK** to enable the share. (If you entered a password, the Password Confirmation dialog box appears. Reenter the password and click **OK**.)

Sharing an Internet Connection

Until recently, it has always been technically forbidding and financially prohibitive to set up an Internet connection that everyone in a workgroup could share. Fortunately, the kind programmers at Microsoft have put us all out of our misery by including a little something called Internet Connection Sharing in Windows 98 Second Edition.

Internet Connection Sharing works by designating one workgroup machine as the *gateway* (which sounds reasonable enough). You set up a working Internet connection on that machine, and then you can configure the other workgroup machines to use that connection for their own surfing needs.

So, assuming you've picked out a gateway and you can connect to the Internet successfully from that machine, your first chore is to get Internet Connection Sharing set up:

1. Select **Start, Settings, Control Panel** and then fire up the **Internet Options** icon. (You can also right-click the desktop's **Internet Explorer** icon and then click **Properties**.)
2. Display the **Connection** tab.
3. Click the **Sharing** button. The Internet Connection Sharing Wizard saunters in.
4. The initial dialog box is a waste of time, so click **Next**.
5. The next wizard dialog box wonders which adapter you use for the Internet connection. If you have a dial-up connection, this will be the `Dial-Up Adapter`. Click **Next** when you've made your choice.
6. Now the wizard would like to know which network adapter you use for your network connection. Select it from the list and then click **Next**. The wizard says something about creating a "Client Configuration Disk." This is the disk that you use to set up the other workgroup machines.
7. Click **Next**.
8. Plop in a floppy disk and then click **OK**.
9. When the disk is done like dinner, take it out and click **OK**.
10. In the last of the wizard's dialog boxes, click **Finish**.
11. When Windows 98 asks if you want to restart your computer, click **Yes**.

When you arrive safely back in Windows 98, crank up the Internet connection on the gateway machine.

Next on your to-do list is to set up each of the other workgroup computers to use Internet Connection Sharing. Here we go:

1. Insert the disk that you created a second ago.
2. Run Windows Explorer and display drive A.
3. Find the file named `icsclset.exe` and double-click it to shove the Browser Connection Setup Wizard onstage.
4. Click **Next** to avoid the introductory dialog box.
5. Click **Next**. The wizard mucks around with the computer's settings and then displays the last of its dialog boxes.
6. Click **Finish**.

Using Windows Messaging to Exchange Email Notes

In Appendix B, "Fast Fax Facts: Using Microsoft Fax," I show you how to use Windows Messaging's Microsoft Fax component to send and receive faxes from Windows 98. Windows Messaging has one other trick up its communications sleeve: it sends and receives Microsoft Mail messages over a network. The rest of this chapter shows you how to use the Microsoft Mail service to read and compose your digital network correspondence from the comfort of Windows 98.

For starters, you need to bear in mind that Windows Messaging isn't part of the regular Windows 98 package. What does this mean for would-be network emailers? There are two possibilities:

➤ If Windows 98 was installed over a version of Windows 95 that had Windows Messaging installed, then Windows Messaging will still be there and will work as advertised with Windows 98.

➤ If you have a new machine, or if you upgraded over Windows 3.1, Windows Messaging won't be on your system. use Windows Explorer to check out the Windows 98 CD and look for the folder **tools\oldwin95\message\us**. When you open this folder, you see a program called **wms**. Running this program will install Windows Messaging.

Assuming that you have Windows Messaging (or Microsoft Exchange, which is the old name for Windows Messaging), your first order of business is to install the Microsoft Mail service.

Just plow through these steps to add the Microsoft Mail service:

1. If Windows Messaging isn't already started, either launch the desktop's **Inbox** icon, or select **Start, Programs, Windows Messaging**.

2. Select **Tools, Services** to display the Services dialog box.

3. Click **Add**. Windows Messaging displays the Add Service to Profile dialog box.

4. Click **Microsoft Mail** and then click **OK**. The Microsoft Mail dialog box appears, as shown here.

5. Type the location of your Microsoft Mail postoffice in the **Enter the path to your postoffice** text box. (Again, if you're not sure of the path, either ask your network administrator or click the **Browse** button.)

6. In the **Logon** tab, enter the name of your Microsoft Mail mailbox and enter the password for that mailbox. If you want Windows 98 to log you on to that mailbox automatically, activate the **When logging on, automatically enter password** check box.

7. Click **OK**. Windows Messaging tells you that the service you just added won't work until you exit and restart the program.

Use this dialog box to set up the Microsoft Mail service.

8. Click **OK** and then click **OK** again to return to Windows Messaging.

9. Select **File, Exit and Log Off**.

Okay, now that all that malarkey is over with and Windows Messaging is pumped up and ready to roll, you can get right down to the nitty-gritty of reading and writing email messages. Your first chore is to wake Windows Messaging from its hard disk slumbers by either opening the desktop's **Inbox** icon, or by selecting **Start, Programs, Windows Messaging**. Enter your Microsoft Mail password, if prompted, and then click **OK** to log on.

The following figure points out a few interesting features in the Windows Messaging window that appears. (If you don't see the list of folders, activate the **View, Folders** command.)

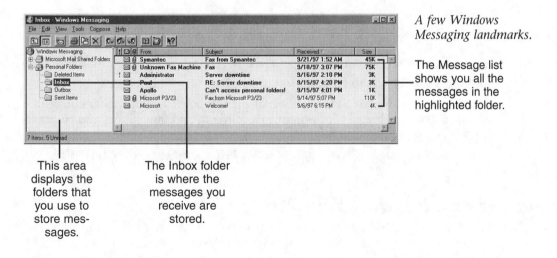

A few Windows Messaging landmarks.

The Message list shows you all the messages in the highlighted folder.

This area displays the folders that you use to store messages.

The Inbox folder is where the messages you receive are stored.

Shipping Out an Email Message

Here are the steps to follow to send a Microsoft Mail message:

1. Select **Compose, New Message** (or press **Ctrl+N**). The New Message window appears, as shown in the following figure.

Use the New Message window to compose your email missive.

...or click these buttons to select names from the address book.

Either type the recipients' names here...

Use this box to enter the message text.

2. Use the **To** box to specify the message recipient. You have the following choices:

   ➤ Type the mailbox name.

   ➤ If you want to type multiple names, use a semicolon (;) to separate each from the others.

   ➤ Click the **To** button to open the postoffice address box. Highlight a name and click **To**. Repeat as necessary and then click **OK**.

3. If you want to send a courtesy copy to a different recipient, use the **Cc** box.

4. Use the **Subject** box to enter a short description of your message.

5. Use the large blank box at the bottom of the window to enter the text of your message. Feel free to use the Formatting toolbar to add fancy fonts and colors to your message.

6. When your message is ready to ship, select **File, Send** (or press **Ctrl+Enter**).

Getting and Reading Your Mail

Email is, ideally, a give-and-take, thrust-and-parry deal. So not only will you be firing out messages to all and sundry, but you'll also receive a few notes. These messages are stored in your network post office mailbox until you go and get them. By default, Microsoft Mail checks your mailbox for new messages every 10 minutes, but you can check for mail anytime you like. All you have to do is run one of the following commands:

➤ If Microsoft Mail is the only Windows Messaging service installed, select **Tools, Deliver Now**.

➤ If you have multiple Windows Messaging services installed, select **Tools, Deliver Now Using, Microsoft Mail**.

Changing the Default Checking Intervals

If need be, you can force Windows Messaging to check for new messages after a different time interval. Select the **Tools, Services** command, highlight **Microsoft Mail** in the Services dialog box, and then click **Properties**. In the Microsoft Mail dialog box, select the **Delivery** tab, enter a new value in the **Check for new mail every *x* minute(s)** text box, and then click **OK**. When you're back in the Services dialog box, click **OK** to return to Windows Messaging.

Either way, Windows Messaging connects to the post office and then lugs back any messages that are waiting for you. The new messages then appear in the Windows Messaging Inbox folder. For each message, the Messages list shows you the name of the person who sent the message, the Subject line, the date and time it was sent, and the size.

Now that you have your stack of mail, you can read each message by highlighting it and selecting the **File, Open** command (or by just double-clicking on the message or pressing **Enter**).

A new window opens to display your message. After you've read the message, you can either close the window or use the following techniques to check out your other messages:

➤ To open the next message in the list, either select **View, Next** or click the **Next Message** toolbar button (**Ctrl+>** works, too).

➤ To open the previous message in the list, either select **View, Previous** or click the **Previous Message** toolbar button (you can also try **Ctrl+<**).

Further Email Fun

After you've read a message, there's a list of things you can do with it. The rest of this chapter tells you how.

Send a Reply

To send a rejoinder to the author of the message, either select **Compose, Reply to Sender**, or click the **Reply to Sender** toolbar button. (The keyboard shortcut is **Ctrl+R**.) Enter your reply in the window that appears, and then send the message as described earlier.

Send a Reply to All the Recipients

If the message was sent to several people, you can send a response to all the recipients by either selecting **Compose, Reply to All** or clicking the **Reply to All** toolbar button. (From the keyboard, press **Ctrl+Shift+R**.)

Forward the Message

If you would like someone else to eyeball the message, you can forward it to them by either selecting **Compose, Forward** or clicking the **Forward** button. (Keyboard mavens can press **Ctrl+F**.)

Print the Message

To get a hard copy of the message, either select **File, Print** or click the **Print** button (or press **Ctrl+P**).

Delete the Message

To get rid of the message, either select **File, Delete** or click the **Delete** button (or press **Ctrl+D**). In this case, Windows Messaging moves the messages to the Deleted Items folder. (If you change your mind, there's no problem moving the message back to the Inbox. Use the technique described next.)

Move It to Another Folder

You probably won't want to leave all your messages cluttering the Inbox folder. Any messages you want to keep should be stored in a separate folder. To move a message to another folder, select **File, Move** (or click the **Move Item** button), use the Move dialog box to highlight the destination folder, and then click **OK**. (If you want to create a new folder along the way, click the **New Folder** button in the Move dialog box.)

Chapter 27

Keeping In Touch: Mobile Computing with Dial-Up Networking

In This Chapter

➤ Setting up Windows 98 for Dial-Up Networking

➤ Creating a new Dial-Up Networking connection

➤ Connecting to the remote network

➤ Working with different dialing locations

➤ How to stay in the loop when you're out of town

There's an old saying that "Far folks fare well." No, I don't know what it means, either. However, folks who are far away from their company network can still fare well by using Windows 98's Dial-Up Networking program. This feature enables you to use a modem to establish a connection to your network lifeline when a physical connection just isn't physically possible (say, when you're working on the road or at home). This chapter shows you how to configure and use Dial-Up Networking. I'll also show you how to use different dialing locations and how to set up a remote Microsoft Mail session.

Setting Up a Dial-Up Networking Connection

Let's dive right into the deep end of Dial-Up Networking. To get the show on the road, you need to follow these steps:

1. Install and configure your modem if you haven't done so already.

SEE ALSO
➤ *For more about installing a modem, see the "Setting Up a Modem From Scratch" section, p. 166, in Chapter 15, "How to Get Connected to the Internet."*

2. Select **Start, Programs, Communications, Dial-Up Networking**. The Dial-Up Networking window appears.

3. Launch the **Make New Connection** icon. (The first time you start Dial-Up Networking, Windows launches this wizard for you automatically.) Windows 98 starts the Make New Connection Wizard so that you can specify the particulars of your Dial-Up Networking session. Windows 98 calls these particulars a *connection*, and each connection contains, among other things, a name, the modem to use, and the phone number to dial.

4. In the first wizard dialog box, shown in the following figure, you need to fill in two things and then click **Next**:

   ➤ **Type a name for the computer you are dialing:** Use this text box to enter a name for the new Dial-Up Networking connection.

   ➤ **Select a device:** If you've installed multiple modems, use this drop-down list to select the modem you want to use for this connection.

Use this dialog box to enter a connection name and choose the modem to use with Dial-Up Networking.

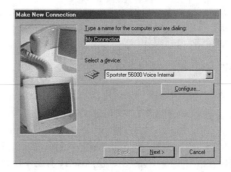

5. You use the next Make New Connection Wizard dialog box, shown in the following figure, to enter the area code, phone number, and country code for the computer you'll be connecting to. When you're finished, click **Next**.

6. That'll do it: your new connection is ready to roll. In the final dialog box, click **Finish** to shut down the wizard.

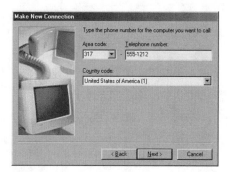

Use this dialog box to specify the phone number for your connection.

Remote Network Connecting and Disconnecting

Now you're ready to make the connection. Here are the steps to march through:

1. Make sure that your modem is hooked up properly and, if you have an external modem, that it's turned on.

2. If you haven't done so already, get the Dial-Up Networking window on board by selecting **Start, Programs, Accessories, Communications, Dial-Up Networking**.

3. As you can see in the following figure, the Dial-Up Networking window now includes a new icon that represents the connection you just made. Go ahead and launch that icon to get connected.

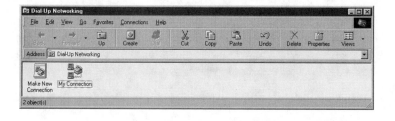

The connection you created appears as an icon in the Dial-Up Networking folder.

4. Windows 98 displays the Connect To dialog box in which you enter your **User name** and **Password** (see the next figure). If you activate the **Save password** check box, Dial-Up Networking will remember your password for future calls.

5. Click **Connect**. Dial-Up Networking dials the modem and then negotiates your logon with the remote system. (You may have to enter your network user name and password at this point.) When you're safely connected, the Connection Established dialog box shows up (see the next figure).

6. If you want to track the duration of your session, double-click the Dial-Up Networking icon in the taskbar (you can see the icon in this figure).

Use this dialog box to initiate the connection.

The Connection Established dialog box confirms your connection, and the "Connected to" dialog box tracks the length of your connection time.

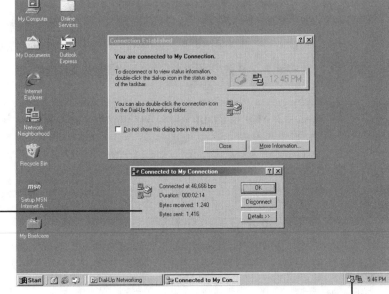

...to display this dialog box.

Double-click this icon...

7. When you're connected, your computer becomes a full member of the network. You can access network resources, browse the Network Neighborhood, and others on the network can see your computer, as well.

8. When you've finished your online work, you need to remember to disconnect to clear the line and avoid running up long distance charges (if applicable). To disconnect, you have two choices:

➤ Display the Connected to dialog box shown in the preceding figure, and then click the **Disconnect** button.

➤ Right-click the Dial-Up Networking icon in the taskbar, and then click **Disconnect**.

Digital Phone Jack Alert!

If you find yourself on the road with your notebook computer and want to connect to your office network, watch out for the digital phone systems used by many hotels. Most modems aren't compatible with digital systems, and you'll end up frying your modem if you attempt to connect over a digital line. Unfortunately, digital phone jacks look identical to regular analog jacks. You'll need to ask the hotel staff what kind of phone jacks they use.

Using Locations with Dial-Up Networking

You probably noticed that the Connect To dialog box has a **Dial Properties** button. This button enables you to specify different dialing locations, which tell Windows 98 whether you use a calling card, the number to dial to get an outside line, and more. Locations are particularly useful for Dial-Up Networking because notebook computer users often have to connect to their networks from different places:

➤ You may need to connect from home, where you have call waiting (which needs to be disabled).

➤ You may need to connect from a client's office where you have to dial 9 for an outside line.

➤ You may need to connect from out of town, and so have to dial the number as long distance and use your corporate calling card.

For such situations, you can change these and other location parameters by selecting the **Dial Properties** button in the Connect To dialog box. (If that button isn't available, select **Start, Settings, Control Panel**, open the **Modems** icon, and then click **Dialing Properties**.) The following figure shows the dialog box that appears.

Here's a rundown of the controls in this dialog box:

➤ **I am dialing from:** This list contains all the dialing locations you've defined. To set up another location, click **New**, enter a name in the Create New Location dialog box, and click **OK**. You then customize the rest of the dialog box fields to set up the dialing properties for the new location.

➤ **I am in this country/region:** Use this list to set the country from which you'll be dialing.

Use this dialog box to adjust the settings that Windows 98 uses to dial your modem.

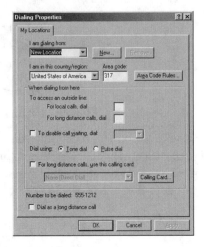

➤ **Area code:** Use this text box to set the area code from which you'll be dialing.

➤ **Area Code Rules:** This button enables you to set up 10-digit dialing and other area code customizations. Clicking this button displays the Area Code Rules dialog box (shown in the next figure), which has two groups:

When calling within my area code: In some cases, the phone company requires that you use the area code even if you're calling another number in the same area code. If the call isn't a long distance number, activate the **Always dial the area code (10-digit dialing)** check box. If some of the phone number prefixes in your area code are long distance calls (and thus require the country code), click **New** to add the prefixes to the list.

When calling to other area codes: In some larger cities, the phone company has run out of phone numbers in the main area code. To overcome this problem, the phone company usually splits off part of the existing customer base into a new area code and requires that calls between the two areas be prefaced with the appropriate area code. Because these aren't long-distance calls, however, no country code is required. In this case, click New to add the area codes for which Windows 98 shouldn't dial a 1.

➤ **To access an outside line:** Use the **For local calls, dial** text box to enter the code that must be dialed to get an outside line for local calls (such as 9). Use the **For long distance calls, dial** text box to enter the code that must be dialed to get an outside line for long distance calls (such as 8).

➤ **To disable call waiting, dial:** To deactivate call waiting before making the call, activate this check box and then either enter the appropriate code in the text box or select one of the existing codes from the list.

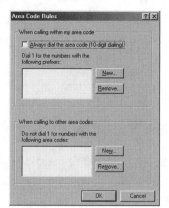

Use this dialog box to set up 10-digit dialing.

Disabling Call Waiting is a Must!

Because the extra beeps that call waiting uses to indicate an incoming call can wreak havoc on modem communications, you should always disable call waiting before initiating a data call. The sequences *70, 70#, or 1170 (which are the ones listed in the **To disable call waiting, dial** drop-down list) usually disable call waiting, but you should check with your local phone company to make sure. If you need to use a different sequence, type it in the list box.

➤ **Dial using:** Select **Tone dial** or **Pulse dial**, as appropriate for your telephone line.

➤ **For long distance calls, use this calling card:** These controls enable you to set up a calling card or long-distance carrier. This procedure is explained in detail next.

➤ **Dial as a long distance call:** Activate this check box to force Windows 98 to dial using the country code and area code.

Although most of your phone calls are likely to be free, at times this might not be the case, and you'll want to make some other arrangements for charging the call. Two situations, in particular, might crop up from time to time:

➤ You're dialing from a hotel and want to charge the call to your calling card.

➤ You need to make a long-distance connection, in which case you might want to first dial the number of a long-distance carrier.

Windows 98 can handle both situations. To specify either a calling card number or a long-distance carrier phone number, follow these steps:

1. Activate the **For long distance calls, use this calling card** check box in the Dialing Properties dialog box.

2. Click the Calling Card button to display the Calling Card dialog box.

3. Use the list box to choose the type of calling card or long-distance carrier you have (see the following figure).

Use the Calling Card dialog box to enter a calling card number or select a long-distance carrier.

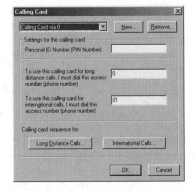

4. For a calling card, use the **Personal ID Number (PIN Number)** text box to enter your PIN.

5. Fill in the next two text boxes with the access numbers required by your calling card or carrier. The first text box is for long distance calls, and the second is for international calls.

6. To change the long distance dialing sequence for the calling card or carrier, click **Long Distance Calls** to display the Calling Card Sequence dialog box. In each step, select the appropriate **Dial** code and use the **then wait for** list to specify which signal Windows 98 must wait for before continuing. Click **OK** when you're finished.

7. To change the international call long distance dialing sequence, click **International Calls** and fill in the dialog box that appears.

8. Click **OK** to return to the Dialing Properties dialog box.

If your calling card or long-distance carrier doesn't appear in the list, follow these steps to add it:

1. In the Calling Card dialog box, click the **New** button to display the Create New Calling Card dialog box.

2. Enter a descriptive name for the calling card or carrier, and then click **OK**. Windows 98 tells you that you must now enter the dialing rules for the card or carrier.

3. Click **OK** to return to the Calling Card dialog box.

4. Follow steps 4 through 8 in the preceding series of steps to specify the dialing rules for your new card or carrier.

Accessing Microsoft Mail Remotely

In Chapter 26, "Working with Network Connections and Email," I showed you how to configure Microsoft Mail to send and retrieve messages over your network. For those times when you want to perform email chores while you're on the road, you can set up Microsoft Mail to use a remote Dial-Up Networking connection. This section shows you how it's done.

Before proceeding, you should create a new Windows Messaging profile for your remote Microsoft Mail sessions:

1. Select **Start, Settings, Control Panel** to display the Windows 98 Control Panel.

2. Open the **Mail** icon.

3. In the dialog box that appears, click the **Show Profiles** button.

4. In the Mail dialog box, make sure that **Windows Messaging Settings** is highlighted, and then click **Copy**. The Copy Profile dialog box, shown in the next figure, appears.

Use this dialog box to enter a name for your new profile.

5. Type a name for the remote Microsoft Mail profile (such as **Remote Microsoft Mail Profile** or something equally uncreative) and then click **OK**.

6. Click **Close** to return to the Control Panel.

7. Start Windows Messaging and then select **Tools, Options** to display the Options dialog box.

8. In the General tab, activate the **Prompt for a profile to be used** option, and then click **OK**.

373

With your new profile in place, restart Windows Messaging and, when the Choose Profile dialog box appears, select the remote Microsoft Mail profile you created and click **OK**.

You now need to configure a few properties for your remote connection:

1. Select **Tools, Services** to display the Services dialog box.

2. Click **Microsoft Mail** and then click **Properties**. Windows Messaging displays the Microsoft Mail dialog box.

3. In the **Connection** tab, activate the **Remote using a modem and Dial-Up Networking** option.

4. Select the **Dial-Up Networking** tab.

5. Select your Dial-Up Networking connection in the **Use the following Dial-Up Networking connection** drop-down list.

6. In the **Remote Configuration** tab, make sure that the **Use Remote Mail** check box is activated.

7. Click **OK**.

8. When Windows Messaging tells you that you have to log off to put the changes into effect, click **OK**.

9. Click **OK** to close the Services dialog box.

10. Select **File, Exit and Log Off**.

As you learned in the previous chapter, Windows Messaging checks your mailbox at regular intervals, grabs any and all messages that are waiting for you, and dumps them in your Inbox folder. This isn't the case when you're working remotely (that is, when you're using the Remote Mail feature). Instead, you have to connect to your network and then download your messages. Here's how it works:

1. Start Remote Mail by selecting **Tools, Remote Mail**.

2. The first item on the Remote Mail agenda is to download the headers of the waiting messages. (Message headers include information such as the author's name and email address, the Subject line of the message, the date and time the server received the message, and the size of the message.) To do this, select **Tools, Connect** to display the Connect to Server dialog box, shown in the following figure. You have five options:

    ➤ **Send mail:** Activate this check box to have Remote Mail send any messages that are waiting in your Outbox folder.

    ➤ **Receive marked items:** Later you'll see that after you get the message headers, you can mark the ones for which you want to retrieve the entire message. Activate this check box to tell Remote Mail to retrieve those marked messages.

    ➤ **Update view of mail headers:** Activate this check box to get the latest message headers.

➤ **Download address lists:** Activate this check box to download the latest address list from your Microsoft Mail post office.

➤ **Disconnect after actions are completed:** If you activate this check box, Remote Mail disconnects from the server after the download is completed.

Use this dialog box to tell Remote Mail what you want it to do when the connection is established.

3. When you've made your selections, click **OK**. After a few seconds (or minutes, depending on how many messages you have), the Remote Mail window displays the headers of the waiting messages, as shown in the next figure.

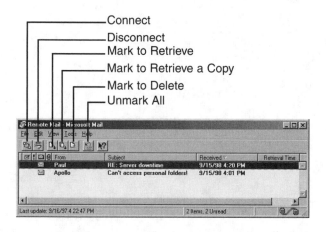

When you connect, Remote Mail grabs the message headers and displays them in the window.

4. Now you need to decide which messages you want to retrieve. Here are the techniques to use:

➤ To mark a message for retrieval, highlight it and select **Edit, Mark to Retrieve**, or click the **Mark to Retrieve** toolbar button.

➤ To retrieve only a copy of a message (the original stays on the server), highlight it and select **Edit, Mark to Retrieve a Copy**, or click the message and click the **Mark to Retrieve** button.

➤ To delete a message, highlight it and select **Edit, Mark to Delete**, or click the message and then click the **Mark to Delete** button.

➤ To start over, select **Edit, Unmark All** or click the **Unmark All** button.

5. When that's taken care of, you can transfer the marked messages by selecting **Tools, Connect**.

6. In the Connect to Server dialog box, make sure that the **Receive marked items** check box is activated.

7. Click **OK**.

8. When you're back in the Remote Mail window, select **Tools, Disconnect** (or click the **Disconnect** button) to sever the connection to the server.

9. Select **File, Close** to return to Windows Messaging.

Speak Like a Geek: The Complete Archive

accessory One of the miniapplications that comes free with Windows 98. Examples include WordPad, Paint, and Backup.

Active Desktop The newfangled Windows 98 *desktop*, which lets you replace the static desktop of Windows 95 with one that can hold Web pages and miniprograms (such as a clock, a stock ticker, or a weather map).

active window The window you're currently slaving away in. You can tell a window is active by looking at its title bar: if the bar shows white letters on a dark background, the window is active. (Inactive windows show light gray letters on a dark gray background.)

application Software that accomplishes a specific practical task. It's the same thing as a *program*.

application window A window that contains a running application, such as Windows Explorer or WordPad.

ASCII text file A file that uses only the American Standard Code for Information Interchange character set (techno-lingo for the characters you see on your keyboard).

backup job A Microsoft Backup file that includes a list of files to back up, the type of backup to use (*full*, *differential*, or *incremental*), and the backup destination.

boot Computer geeks won't tell you to start your computer, they'll tell you to *boot* it. However, this doesn't mean you should punt your monitor across the room. The term *booting* comes from the phrase "pulling oneself up by one's own bootstraps," which refers to the fact that your computer can load everything it needs to operate properly without any help from the likes of you and me.

bps   Bits per second. The rate at which a *modem* or other communications device spits data through a phone line or cable.

browser   A program that you use to *surf* sites on the World Wide Web. The browser that comes with Windows 98 is called Internet Explorer.

byte   Computerese for a single character of information. So, for example, the phrase *This phrase is 28 bytes long* is, yes, 28 bytes long (you count the spaces, too). See also *kilobyte, megabyte,* and *gigabyte.*

cascade menu   A menu that appears when you select certain pull-down menu commands.

CD-ROM drive   A special computer disk drive that's designed to handle CD-ROM discs, which resemble audio CDs. CD-ROMs have enormous capacity (about 500 times that of a typical *floppy disk*), so they're most often used to hold large applications, graphics libraries, and huge collections of junky shareware programs.

channel   A special World Wide Web site that features changing content that is sent automatically to your computer at predefined intervals. See *subscription.*

character formatting   Changing the look of text characters by altering their font, size, style, and more.

character spacing   The amount of space a font reserves for each character. In a *monospaced font*, every character gets the same amount of space regardless of its true width. In a *proportional font*, the space allotted to each letter varies according to the width of the letter.

check box   A square-shaped switch that toggles a dialog box option on or off. The option is toggled on when a check mark appears in the box.

classic view   The folder view used with Windows 95. That is, you click an icon to select it, and you double-click an icon to launch it. See also *Web view.*

click   To quickly press and release the left mouse button.

Clipboard   An area of memory that holds data temporarily during cut and paste operations.

command button   A rectangular doohickey (usually found in dialog boxes) that, when chosen, runs whatever command is spelled out on it.

commands   The options you see in a pull-down menu. You use these commands to tell the application what you want it to do next.

data files   The files used by you or your programs. See also *program files.*

delay   The amount of time it takes for a second character to appear when you press and hold down a key.

desktop A metaphor for the Windows 98 screen. Starting a Windows 98 application is similar to putting a folder full of papers (the application window) on your desk. To do some work, you pull some papers out of the folder (the document windows) and place them on the desktop.

device driver A small program that controls the way a device (such as a mouse) works with your system.

dialog boxes Ubiquitous windows that pop up on the screen to ask you for information or to seek confirmation of an action you requested (or sometimes just to say "Hi").

differential backup Backs up only files in the current *backup job* that have changed since the last *full backup*. See also *incremental backup*.

digital camera A special camera that saves pictures, using digital storage (such as a memory card) instead of film.

directory See *folder*.

diskette See *floppy disk*.

docking station A component that a notebook computer can attach to. The docking station provides ports for plugging in a regular monitor, keyboard, and mouse, as well as a number of expansion bays and other items that are usually too bulky to work with the notebook by itself.

document window A window opened in an application. Document windows hold whatever you're working on in the application.

double-click To quickly press and release the left mouse button *twice* in succession.

double-click speed The maximum amount of time Windows 98 allows between the mouse clicks of a double-click.

drag To press and hold down the left mouse button and then move the mouse.

drag-and-drop A technique you use to run commands or move things around; you use your mouse to *drag* files or icons to strategic screen areas and drop them there.

drop-down list box A list box that normally shows only a single item but, when selected, displays a list of options.

file An organized unit of information inside your computer. If you think of your hard disk as a house, files can be either servants (your applications) or things you use (data used by you or by a program).

floppy disk A portable storage medium that consists of a flexible disk protected by a plastic case. Floppy disks are available in a variety of sizes and capacities.

focus   The window that has the attention of the operating system (that is, Windows 98). See also *active window*.

folder   A storage location on your hard disk in which you keep related files together. If your hard disk is like a house, a folder is like a room in the house.

font   A character set of a specific typeface, type style, and type size.

formatting   The process of setting up a disk so that a drive can read its information and write information to it. Not to be confused with *character formatting*.

fragmented   When a single file is chopped up and stored in separate chunks scattered around a hard disk. You can fix this by running Windows 98's Disk Defragmenter program.

fritterware   Any software that causes you to fritter away time fiddling with its various bells and whistles.

full backup   Backs up all the files in the current *backup job*. See also *differential backup* and *incremental backup*.

gigabyte   1,024 *megabytes*. Those in-the-know usually abbreviate this as "GB" when writing, and as "gig" when speaking. See also *byte*, *kilobyte*, and *megabyte*.

hard disk   The main storage area inside your computer. In the computer house analogy, the hard disk is equivalent to the inside of the house.

hover   To place the mouse pointer over an object for a few seconds. In most Windows applications, for example, if you hover the mouse over a toolbar button, a small banner shows up that tells you the name of the button.

icons   The little pictures that Windows 98 uses to represent programs and files.

incremental backup   Backs up only files in the current *backup job* that have changed since the last *full backup* or the last *differential backup*.

infrared port   A communications port, usually found on notebook computers and some printers. Infrared ports enable two devices to communicate by using infrared light waves instead of cables.

insertion point cursor   The blinking vertical bar you see inside a text box or in a word processing application, such as WordPad. It indicates where the next character you type will appear.

Internet   A *network* of networks that extends around the world. By setting up an account with an Internet service provider, you can access this network.

Intranet   The implementation of *Internet* technologies for use within a corporate organization rather than for connection to the Internet as a whole.

IR   Short for infrared. See *infrared port*.

Jaz drive   A special disk drive that uses portable disks (about the size of *floppy disks*) that hold 1 *gigabyte* of data.

Kbps   One thousand bits per second (*bps*). Today's modern *modems* transmit data at either 28.8 Kbps or 56 Kbps.

kilobyte   1,024 *bytes*. To be hip, always abbreviate this to "K" or "KB." See also *megabyte* and *gigabyte*.

LAN   See *local area network*.

local area network   A *network* in which all the computers occupy a relatively small geographical area, such as a department, office, home, or building. All the connections between computers are made via network cables.

list box   A small window that displays a list of items such as filenames or directories.

maximize   To increase the size of a window to its largest extent. A maximized application window fills the entire screen (except for the taskbar). A maximized document window fills the entire application window.

Mbps   One million bits per second (*bps*).

megabyte   1,024 *kilobytes* or 1,048,576 *bytes*. The cognoscenti write this as "M" or "MB" and pronounce it "meg." See also *gigabyte*.

memory-resident program   A program that stays in memory after it is loaded and works "behind the scenes." The program normally responds only to a specific event (such as the deletion of a file) or key combination. Also called a *terminate-and-stay-resident* (TSR) program.

menu bar   The horizontal bar on the second line of an application window. The menu bar contains the application's pull-down menus.

minimize   To remove a program from the desktop without closing it. A button for the program remains on the taskbar.

modem   An electronic device that enables two computers to exchange data over phone lines.

multitasking   The capability to run several programs at the same time. Figuratively speaking, this simply means that Windows 98, unlike some people you may know, can walk and chew gum at the same time.

network   A collection of computers connected via special cables or other network media (such as *infrared ports*) to share files, folders, disks, peripherals, and applications. See also *local area network*.

newsgroup   An Internet discussion group devoted to a single topic. These discussions progress by "posting" messages to the group.

option buttons Dialog box options that appear as small circles in groups of two or more. Only one option from a group can be chosen.

point To place the mouse pointer so that it rests on a specific screen location.

port The connection into which you plug the cable from a device such as a mouse or printer.

program files The files that run your programs. See also *data files*.

pull-down menus Hidden menus that you open from an application's menu bar to access the commands and features of the application.

RAM Stands for random access memory. The memory in your computer that Windows 98 uses to run your programs.

repeat rate After the initial delay, the rate at which characters appear when you press and hold down a key.

right-click To click the right mouse button instead of the usual left button. In Windows 98, right-clicking something usually pops up a *shortcut menu*.

scalable font A font in which each character exists as an outline that can be scaled to different sizes. Windows 98 includes such scalable fonts as Arial, Courier New, and Times New Roman. To use scalable fonts, you must have a software program called a *type manager* to do the scaling. Windows 98 comes with its own type manager: TrueType.

scroll bar A bar that appears at the bottom or on the right side of a window when the window is too small to display all its contents.

shortcut A special file that points to a program or a document. Double-clicking the shortcut starts the program or loads the document.

shortcut menu A menu that contains a few commands related to an item (such as the *desktop* or the *taskbar*). You display the shortcut menu by *right-clicking* the object.

subscription A method of checking for new or changed data on a World Wide Web site or *channel*. The subscription sets up a schedule for checking a particular site to see whether it has changed in any way since the last time it was checked.

surf To travel from site to site on the World Wide Web.

system menu A menu, common to every Windows 98 window, that you use to manipulate various features of the window. You activate the Control menu by clicking on the Control-menu box in the upper-left corner of the window or by pressing Alt+Spacebar (for an application window).

system resources Two memory areas that Windows 98 uses to keep track of things like the position and size of open windows, dialog boxes, and your desktop configuration (wallpaper and so on).

taskbar   The horizontal strip across the bottom of the Windows 98 screen. Each running application is given its own taskbar button, and you switch to an application by clicking on its button.

text box   A screen area in which you type text information, such as a description or a filename.

text editor   A program that lets you edit files that contain only text. The Windows 98 text editor is called Notepad.

title bar   The area on the top line of a window that displays the window's title.

tracking speed   The speed at which the mouse pointer moves across the screen when you move the mouse on its pad.

TrueType   A font management program that comes with Windows 98.

type size   A measure of the height of a font. Type size is measured in *points*; there are 72 points in an inch.

type style   Character attributes, such as regular, bold, and italic. Other type styles (often called type *effects*) are underlining and strikethrough characters.

typeface   A distinctive graphic design of letters, numbers, and other symbols.

Web integration   The integration of World Wide Web techniques into the Windows 98 interface. See *Web view*.

Web view   The folder view used when *Web integration* is activated. With this view, you *hover* the mouse over an icon to select it, and you click an icon to launch it. See also *classic view*.

window   A rectangular screen area in which Windows 98 displays applications and documents.

word wrap   A word processor feature that automatically starts a new line when your typing reaches the end of the current line.

write-protection   Floppy disk safeguard that prevents you from changing any information on the disk. The 5 1/4-inch disks normally have a small notch on the side of the disk. If the notch is covered with tape, the disk is write-protected. Simply remove the tape to disable the write-protection. On a 3 1/2-inch disk, write-protection is controlled by a small movable tab on the back of the disk. If the tab is toward the edge of the disk, the disk is write-protected. To disable the write-protection, slide the tab away from the edge of the disk.

Zip drive   A special disk drive that uses portable disks (a little smaller than a *Jaz drive* disk) which hold 100 *megabytes* of data.

Fast Fax Facts: Using Microsoft Fax

Nowadays, faxing is just another humdrum part of the workaday world, and any business worth its salt has a fax machine on standby. Increasingly, however, dedicated fax machines are giving way to *fax modems* modems that have the capability to send and receive faxes in addition to their regular communications duties.

If you're looking to get into the fax fast lane, look no farther than the Microsoft Fax service. This appendix shows you how to install and configure Microsoft Fax, and how to use it to send and receive faxes.

Installing and Configuring Microsoft Fax

For starters, you can only use Microsoft Fax if it's installed on your computer. If you used Microsoft Fax with Windows 95, it will still work with Windows 98. If you have a new Windows 98 installation, however, you first need to make sure that one of the following programs is installed on your machine:

➤ Microsoft Exchange (this program shipped with the original version of Windows 95).

➤ Windows Messaging (this program replaced Microsoft Exchange in later versions of Window 95). If you don't have this program, you can install it from the Windows 98 CD-ROM. Insert the disc and display it in Windows Explorer or My Computer. Open the **tools\oldwin95\message\us** folder and launch the file named **wms** to install Windows Messaging on your system.

➤ Microsoft Outlook (not the Outlook Express program that comes with Windows 98).

With that step out of the way, you now need to install Microsoft Fax (assuming that it's not already on your system from your old version of Windows 95). Here are the steps to follow:

1. Insert the Windows 98 CD-ROM and display the disc in Windows Explorer or My Computer.

2. Open the **tools\oldwin95\message\us** folder again and launch the file named **awfax** to start the installation.

3. The license agreement appears. Read it and click **Yes**. Windows 98 then busies itself installing some stuff on your computer.

4. When the appropriate fax files have been installed, Windows 98 will ask if you want to restart your system. Click **Yes**.

Once your system restarts, you'll see a new desktop icon called Inbox. There are two methods you can use to start Windows Messaging:

➤ Open the desktop's **Inbox** icon.

➤ Select **Start**, **Programs**, **Windows Messaging**.

Windows Messaging gives you two ways to add Microsoft Fax to your profile and get it configured:

From the Inbox Setup Wizard: When you first start Windows Messaging, the Inbox Setup Wizard appears and displays a list of the information services it can install (see the following figure). Be sure to activate the **Microsoft Fax** check box and then click **Next**. The Inbox Setup Wizard then runs through a few dialog boxes that configure the basic faxing properties. You'll be asked to select the fax modem you want to use with Microsoft Fax, whether you want Microsoft Fax to answer incoming calls, and your name, country, and fax phone number (the fax number is required).

Make sure that you activate Microsoft Fax in the initial Inbox Setup Wizard dialog box.

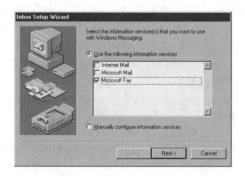

From within Windows Messaging: If Windows Messaging is already installed, it's no sweat adding the Microsoft Fax service from within Windows Messaging. What you need to do is select the **Tools, Services** command and then click **Add.** In the Add Service to Profile dialog box, shown in the next figure, highlight **Microsoft Fax**, click **OK**, and then click **Yes** in the dialog box that appears. You'll then see the Microsoft Fax Properties dialog box. All you need to do is fill in your fax number in the **User** tab and select your fax modem in the Modem tab.

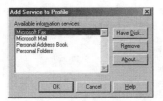

You can add the Microsoft Fax service if Windows Messaging is already installed.

Sending a Fax

Microsoft Fax offers the Compose New Fax Wizard that leads you step-by-step through the entire fax-creation process. Here's how it works:

1. To start the wizard, use either of the following techniques:

   ➤ Select **Start, Programs, Accessories, Fax, Compose New Fax**.

   ➤ In Windows Messaging, select **Compose, New Fax**.

2. The first wizard dialog box asks you which dialing location you want to use. You can click the **Dialing Properties** button to either select a different location or adjust the properties of the current location. Otherwise, click **Next**.

SEE ALSO

➤ *For more information about dialing locations, head for Chapter 29, "Keeping In Touch: Mobile Computing with Dial-Up Networking," and read the section titled "Using Locations with Dial-Up Networking," p. 369.*

3. In the next wizard dialog box, shown in the following figure, either enter a fax number or use the **Address Book** button to choose a fax recipient from your Personal Address Book. Then click **Next**.

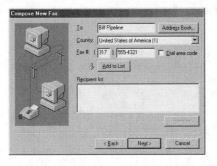

Use this wizard dialog box to enter the fax number of the recipient.

4. The next wizard dialog box asks whether you want a cover page. Either click **No**, or click **Yes** and highlight the cover page you want to use. You can also click the **Options** button to display some settings that relate to when you want the fax sent. Click **Next** to continue.

5. The wizard now prompts you to enter the **Subject** line and **Note** for the fax (see the following figure). If you're using a cover page, activating the **Start note on cover page** check box tells Microsoft Fax to begin your note on the cover page. If you deactivate this check box, the note begins on a fresh page. Click **Next** when you're finished.

Use this wizard dialog box to enter the subject line and note for the fax.

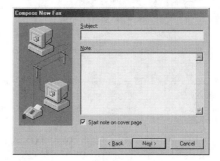

6. Your next chore is to specify any files you want to include with the fax transmission. If you want to have a file go along for the ride, click the **Add File** button, highlight the file in the Open a File to Attach dialog box that appears, and click **Open**. Click **Next** when you've added all the files you need.

7. In the last Wizard dialog box, click **Finish** to send your fax.

Receiving and Viewing an Incoming Fax

Shipping out faxes to all and sundry is, of course, only half the fax battle because you'll also receive faxes from time to time. This section explains how Microsoft Fax handles incoming faxes and shows you how to view those faxes when they're sitting in your Inbox.

First off, you have to decide how you want Microsoft Fax to handle incoming calls. To do this, follow these steps:

1. Select **Tools, Microsoft Fax Tools, Options** to display the Fax Modem Properties dialog box.

2. Select the **Modem** tab.

3. Highlight your fax modem and then click **Properties**. You'll then see the dialog box shown here.

Faxing from an Application

You can bypass Windows Messaging altogether and send a document directly from an application. You don't need applications with special features to do this, because when you install Microsoft Fax, it adds a new printer to Windows 98. *Printer?* Yeah. You see, this "printer" doesn't send a document to your real printer. Instead, it renders the document as a fax and then sends it to your modem.

To try this, open the document in your application and select the **File, Print** command. When the Print dialog box appears, use the **Name** drop-down list to select the Microsoft Fax printer driver. When you click **OK**, the Compose New Fax Wizard starts so that you can specify a recipient, a cover page, and other fax options.

Even better, if you have a particular document you want to fax, you don't have to open its application to fax it. Instead, just right-click the document, click **Send To** in the menu that appears, and then click **Fax Recipient**.

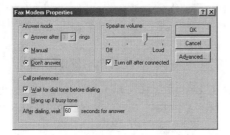

Use this dialog box to specify what you want Microsoft Fax to do when a call comes in.

4. The **Answer mode** group boasts three options that determine how Microsoft Fax deals with incoming calls:

    Answer after *x* rings: Tells Microsoft Fax to answer incoming calls automatically. This is the easiest way to handle incoming calls. In this mode, Microsoft Fax constantly checks your computer for calls. When it detects an incoming call, it waits for whatever number of rings you specified (which can be as few as 2 rings or as many as 10) and then leaps into action. Without any prodding from you, it answers the phone and immediately starts conversing with the remote fax machine. The Microsoft Fax Status window appears onscreen so that you can see the progress of the transfer.

Manual: Lets you answer incoming calls manually. When you work with Microsoft Fax in manual mode, you'll see the Receive Fax Now? dialog box whenever the program detects an incoming call. To have Microsoft Fax field the call, click **Yes**. If you know that it's a voice call, click **No** and answer the call yourself.

Handling Voice and Fax on the Same Line

Manual mode is ideal if you receive both voice calls and fax calls on the same phone line. Here's the basic procedure you'll need to follow for incoming calls:

1. When the phone rings, pick up the receiver.

2. If you hear a series of annoying tones, you know that a fax is on its way. In this case, click the **Yes** button in the Receive Fax Now? dialog box. If it's a voice call, click **No** instead.

3. After you click Yes, Microsoft Fax initializes the modem to handle the call. Wait until Microsoft Fax reports **Answering call** in the Microsoft Fax Status window, and then hang up the receiver. (If you hang up before this, you'll disconnect the call.)

Don't answer: Tells Microsoft Fax to ignore any incoming calls. If you know you have a fax coming in (if, say, you pick up the receiver and hear the tones from the remote fax machine), click the Microsoft Fax icon in the toolbar's information area. This opens the Microsoft Fax Status window. Now click the **Answer Now** button (or select the **Options, Answer Now** command).

Depending on the size of the fax transmission and the type of fax you're getting, Microsoft Fax takes anywhere from a few seconds to a few minutes to process the data. Eventually, though, your fax appears in the Windows Messaging Inbox.

Double-click the fax message to open it. (Depending on how the fax was sent, you may see a message window with a fax icon. In this case, double-click the fax icon.) Windows Messaging displays the image of the fax in the Imaging window, as shown in the following figure.

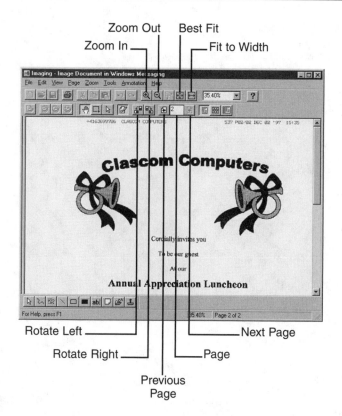

When you open a fax, Microsoft Fax uses the Imaging program to display the image.

Imaging is basically a graphics viewer with a few extra features that let you navigate multipage faxes. Here's a quick summary of the Imaging techniques you can use to examine your faxes:

Zooming the image: The **Zoom** menu contains commands (such as **Zoom In** and **Zoom Out**) that let you zoom into or out of the image. You can also choose specific magnifications: **25**%, **50**%, or **100**%. To fit the image to the window, select **Fit to Width**, **Fit to Height**, or **Best Fit**. Some of these commands are also available as toolbar buttons (see the previous figure).

Rotating the image: For faxes that come with the wrong orientation, the commands on the **Page, Rotate Page** menu let you turn the image so that you can read the fax. Select either **Right** or **Left** to rotate the image 90 degrees, or select **180°** to rotate the image 180 degrees.

Navigating multiple pages: Imaging has a few more tricks up its sleeve for moving between pages. On the **Page** menu, select **Next**, **Previous**, **First**, and **Last**. You can also select the **Go To** command to head for a specific page number.

Index

395

397

399

403

Q-R

A Little Knowledge Goes a Long Way ...

Check Out These Best-Selling COMPLETE IDIOT'S GUIDES®

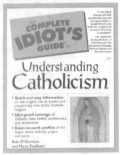

Understanding Catholicism

0-02-863639-2
$16.95

Learning Spanish on Your Own
SECOND EDITION

0-02-862743-1
$16.95

The Bible

0-02-862728-8
$16.95

Feng Shui

0-02-863105-6
$18.95

Playing the Guitar
SECOND EDITION

0-02-864244-9
$21.95 w/CD-ROM

Personal Finance in Your 20s & 30s

0-02-862415-7
$18.95

Creating a Web Page
Fourth Edition

0-7897-2256-9
$19.99 w/CD-ROM

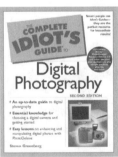

Digital Photography
SECOND EDITION

0-02-864235-X
$24.95 w/CD-ROM

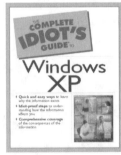

Windows XP

0-02-864232-5
$19.95

More than *400 titles* in *26 different categories*
Available at booksellers everywhere

ALPHA